Narrative Retellings

Advances in Stylistics

Series Editors: Dan McIntyre, University of Huddersfield, UK, and Louise Nuttall, University of Huddersfield, UK

Editorial Board

Jean Boase-Beier, University of East Anglia, UK
Beatrix Busse, University of Heidelberg, Germany
Szilvia Csábi, Independent Scholar
Yaxiao Cui, University of Nottingham, UK
Manuel Jobert, Jean Moulin University, Lyon 3, France
Lorenzo Mastopierro, University of Nottingham, UK
Eric Rundquist, Pontifica Universidad Católica de Chile, Chile
Odette Vassallo, University of Malta, Malta
Peter Verdonk, University of Amsterdam (Emeritus), The Netherlands
Chantelle Warner, University of Arizona, USA

Titles in the series include:

Chick Lit: The Stylistics of Cappuccino Fiction, Rocío Montoro
Corpus Stylistics in Principles and Practice, Yufang Ho
Crime Fiction Migration, Christiana Gregoriou
I.A. Richards and the Rise of Cognitive Stylistics, David West
Mind Style and Cognitive Grammar, Louise Nuttall
New Directions in Cognitive Grammar and Style, Marcello Giovanelli, Chloe Harrison and Louise Nuttall
Oppositions and Ideology in News Discourse, Matt Davies
Pedagogical Stylistics, Michael Burke, Szilvia Csábi, Lara Week and Judit Zerkowitz
Style in the Renaissance, Patricia Canning
Stylistic Manipulation of the Reader in Contemporary Fiction, Sandrine Sorlin
Sylvia Plath and the Language of Affective States, Zsófia Demjén
Telecinematic Stylistics, Christian Hoffmann and Monika Kirner-Ludwig
Text World Theory and Keats' Poetry, Marcello Giovanelli
The Stylistics of Poetry, Peter Verdonk
World Building, Joanna Gavins and Ernestine Lahey
World Building in Spanish and English Spoken Narratives, Jane Lugea

Narrative Retellings

Stylistic Approaches

Edited by
Marina Lambrou

BLOOMSBURY ACADEMIC
LONDON • NEW YORK • OXFORD • NEW DELHI • SYDNEY

BLOOMSBURY ACADEMIC
Bloomsbury Publishing Plc
50 Bedford Square, London, WC1B 3DP, UK
1385 Broadway, New York, NY 10018, USA
29 Earlsfort Terrace, Dublin 2, Ireland

BLOOMSBURY, BLOOMSBURY ACADEMIC and the Diana logo are
trademarks of Bloomsbury Publishing Plc

First published in Great Britain 2021
This paperback edition published in 2022

Copyright © Marina Lambrou and Contributors, 2021

Marina Lambrou has asserted her right under the Copyright, Designs and
Patents Act, 1988, to be identified as Editor of this work.

For legal purposes the Acknowledgements on p. xii constitute an
extension of this copyright page.

All rights reserved. No part of this publication may be reproduced or
transmitted in any form or by any means, electronic or mechanical, including
photocopying, recording, or any information storage or retrieval system,
without prior permission in writing from the publishers.

Bloomsbury Publishing Plc does not have any control over, or responsibility for,
any third-party websites referred to or in this book. All internet addresses given
in this book were correct at the time of going to press. The author and publisher
regret any inconvenience caused if addresses have changed or sites have
ceased to exist, but can accept no responsibility for any such changes.

A catalogue record for this book is available from the British Library.

Library of Congress Cataloging-in-Publication Data
Names: Lambrou, Marina, editor.
Title: Narrative retellings : stylistic approaches / edited by Marina Lambrou.
Description: London ; New York Bloomsbury Academic, 2020. | Series:
Advances in stylistics | Includes bibliographical references and index.
Identifiers: LCCN 2020032051 (print) | LCCN 2020032052 (ebook) | ISBN
9781350120020 (hardback) | ISBN 9781350195363 (paperback) | ISBN
9781350120037 (ebook) | ISBN 9781350120044 (epub)
Subjects: LCSH: Narration (Rhetoric) | Discourse analysis, Narrative. |
Literary style.
Classification: LCC PN212 .N3783 2020 (print) | LCC PN212 (ebook) |
DDC 808/.036–dc23
LC record available at https://lccn.loc.gov/2020032051
LC ebook record available at https://lccn.loc.gov/2020032052

ISBN:	HB:	978-1-3501-2002-0
	PB:	978-1-3501-9536-3
	ePDF:	978-1-3501-2003-7
	eBook:	978-1-3501-2004-4

Series: Advances in Stylistics

Typeset by Integra Software Services Pvt. Ltd.

To find out more about our authors and books visit www.bloomsbury.com
and sign up for our newsletters.

Contents

List of figures — vi
List of tables — vii
Notes on contributors — viii
Acknowledgements — xii

1 Introduction to narrative retellings: Stylistic approaches *Marina Lambrou* — 1

Part I Fictional retellings

2 Restorying: The creative act of retelling *Jeremy Scott* — 23
3 Adapting *Pride and Prejudice*: Stylistic choices as communicative acts *Anne Furlong* — 45
4 Narrative retelling in McGahern's 'Swallows': The intensifying power of repetition and return *Michael Toolan* — 61
5 Modern retellings of Jane Austen *Joe Bray* — 77
6 Rewriting misdirection: A stylistic approach to crime fiction writing *Christiana Gregoriou* — 93

Part II Factual retellings

7 Siegfried Sassoon, autofiction and style: Retelling the experience of war *Marcello Giovanelli* — 113
8 Retelling catastrophe through translation *Jean Boase-Beier* — 129
9 Retelling Hillsborough: A critical stylistic analysis of witness statements *Patricia Canning* — 143
10 'This is a sponsored post, but all opinions are my own': Advertising (re)tellings on social media *Helen Ringrow* — 163

Part III Pedagogical applications of retellings

11 Intervening in text-worlds: Retelling, Text World Theory and pedagogy *Ian Cushing* — 181
12 Retelling stories across languages and cultures: Literary imagination and symbolic competence *Chantelle Warner* — 199
13 Rereading as retelling: Re-evaluations of perspective in narrative fiction *Chloe Harrison and Louise Nuttall* — 217

Index — 235

Figures

6.1	'Make Robin more memorable' excerpt	100
6.2	'Add a scene where Robin, Sandra etc. go somewhere' excerpt	102
6.3	'Sandra suggests on first hearing that Robin should talk to [Banks]' excerpt	102
6.4	'Don't really create any suspicion in Bank's mind that Robin killed Alice' excerpt	103
6.5	'Graham not believable killer' excerpt	105
6.6	'In first scene with Andrea' excerpt	106
6.7	'To make Sharp guilty' excerpt	106
6.8	'Sharp with Wooller' excerpt	107
6.9	'Sharp's confession' excerpt	108
7.1	Construal relationships (adapted from Verhagen 2007)	121
10.1	A Problem-Solution pattern for cosmetics advertising discourse (Ringrow 2016:37)	169
11.1	World-switches in Charlotte's poem	193

Tables

4.1	An act/scene analysis of 'Swallows'	67
9.1	Types of negation in residents' statements	149
13.1	Experimental conditions and (re)reading tasks	222

Notes on contributors

Jean Boase-Beier is Professor Emerita of Literature and Translation at the University of East Anglia, UK. She is a translator and editor of poetry, most recently of *Poetry of the Holocaust: An Anthology* (Arc 2019). Her academic work focuses on style and translation, and Holocaust poetry. Recent academic publications include *Translating the Poetry of the Holocaust* (Bloomsbury 2015), the co-edited collections *Translating Holocaust Lives* (Bloomsbury 2015) and *The Palgrave Handbook of Literary Translation* (2018), and *Translation and Style* (Routledge 2020).

Joe Bray is Professor of Language and Literature and current Head of the School of English at the University of Sheffield. He is the author of, among others, *The Portrait in Fiction of the Romantic Period* (Routledge 2016) and *The Language of Jane Austen* (Palgrave 2018), and co-editor of *The Routledge Companion to Experimental Literature* (Routledge 2012). He is currently co-editing the *Edinburgh Companion to Jane Austen and the Arts* (Edinburgh University Press, forthcoming).

Patricia Canning is Assistant Professor in the Department of Humanities, Utrecht University, The Netherlands. She has worked with women prisoners, male ex-prisoners, forensic mental health patients, and people recovering from eating disorders and personality disorders, using stylistic approaches to understand and improve well-being and recovery. She is developing a research project *'No Ordinary Crowd': The Linguistics of Blame in the Evidence-Gathering Processes Following the Hillsborough Football Stadium Disaster*. She is currently writing two books: *From Literature to Life: Reading in Prison* (Palgrave) and *Discourse Analysis* (with Brian Walker, Routledge).

Ian Cushing is Lecturer in Education at Brunel University London, UK. His doctoral research explored the theorization, implementation and evaluation of a cognitive stylistic pedagogy for secondary school English teaching. His current research is investigating language education policies in UK schools, with a critical focus on how language ideologies come to be reproduced in classrooms. His work has appeared in journals such as *Language and Literature*, *Language in Society*, *English in Education* and *Metaphor and the Social World*.

Anne Furlong is Associate Professor in the English Department of the University of Prince Edward Island. She has published and presented on adaptation, theatre studies wit and humour, stylistics and canon formation from a relevance-theoretic perspective. Her current work applies relevance stylistics to adaptation and crime fiction, with particular emphasis on the role of the audience in developing non-spontaneous interpretation within the relevance theory framework.

Marcello Giovanelli is Senior Lecturer in English Language and Literature at Aston University, UK. He has particular research interests in applications of Text World Theory and Cognitive Grammar to literary discourse. Recent books include *Text World Theory and Keats' Poetry* (Bloomsbury 2013), *Cognitive Grammar in Stylistics: A Practical Guide* (with Chloe Harrison, Bloomsbury 2018) and *New Directions in Cognitive Grammar and Style* (with Chloe Harrison and Louise Nuttall, Bloomsbury 2020). He has published widely on cognitive stylistics, applied linguistics and the writing of Siegfried Sassoon in major international journals.

Christiana Gregoriou is Associate Professor in English Language at the University of Leeds, UK. She researches in (critical) stylistics and crime writing. Most notable are her three monographs: *Crime Fiction Migration: Crossing Languages, Cultures, Media* (Bloomsbury 2017); *Language, Ideology and Identity in Serial Killer Narratives* (Routledge 2011); and *Deviance in Contemporary Crime Fiction* (Palgrave 2007). She is a steering committee member of the Crime Studies Network, for which she generated several conferences and edited collection publications.

Chloe Harrison is Lecturer in English Language and Literature at Aston University, UK. Her research interests include cognitive stylistics (and specifically the application of Cognitive Grammar for literary-linguistic analysis), re-reading and contemporary fiction. She has a number of publications in these areas, including two recent books: *Cognitive Grammar in Contemporary Fiction* (Benjamins 2017) and *Cognitive Grammar in Stylistics: A Practical Guide* (with Marcello Giovanelli, Bloomsbury 2018). She is also Treasurer for the International Association of Literary Semantics.

Marina Lambrou is Associate Professor in English Language and Linguistics at Kingston University, UK, and Chair of the Poetics and Linguistics Association

(PALA). She has published widely on literary and non-literary stylistics, personal and trauma narratives, disnarration and the counterfactual, as well as on media stylistics. Her books include *Contemporary Stylistics* (co-editor with Peter Stockwell, Bloomsbury 2007), *Disnarration and the Unmentioned in Fact and Fiction* (Palgrave 2019), and she was also editor of the special issue on 'Narrative' for the journal *Language and Literature* (SAGE 2014).

Louise Nuttall is Senior Lecturer in English Language and Linguistics at the University of Huddersfield, UK. Her research centres on cognitive stylistics and reader response research with a focus on how minds are represented and responded to across text-types. She is the author of *Mind Style and Cognitive Grammar: Language and Worldview in Speculative Fiction* (2018) and co-editor of *Cognitive Grammar in Literature* (with Chloe Harrison, Peter Stockwell and Wenjuan Yuan, 2014).

Helen Ringrow is Senior Lecturer in Communication Studies and Applied Linguistics at the University of Portsmouth, UK. She is the author of *The Language of Cosmetics Advertising* (Palgrave 2016) and co-editor of *Contemporary Media Stylistics* (with Stephen Pihlaja, Bloomsbury 2020). Her current research explores the language of motherhood and the language of modest fashion in online religious communities.

Jeremy Scott is Senior Lecturer in English Language and Literature at the University of Kent, UK, and writes, teaches and researches on literature and language studies. As well as his own fiction, he has published on contemporary British and Irish writing, on literary-linguistic approaches to creative practice, on cognitive poetics and on narrative technique. A new short story, 'The Fetch', was published in *New Writing* journal (2020), and a second edition of his book *Creative Writing and Stylistics* will be forthcoming with Palgrave in 2021.

Michael Toolan is Professor of English Language at the University of Birmingham, UK, and the author of a number of books on stylistics and narrative analysis. His most recent monograph is *The Language of Inequality in the News: A Discourse Analytic Approach* (Cambridge University Press 2018).

Chantelle Warner is Associate Professor of German and Second Language Acquisition and Teaching at the University of Arizona, where she also co-directs the Center for Educational Resources in Culture, Language and Literacy

(CERCLL). Her research focuses on how language is involved in struggles for social and symbolic power and the educational potential of playful, literary language use and creative multilingualism. She has published on a variety of topics including play and gaming in foreign language education, aesthetic and experiential dimensions of language learning, and literary pragmatics and stylistics.

Acknowledgements

I would like to thank all the contributors who accepted my invitation to write a chapter for this volume – without you, this book would not exist. I would also like to thank Rocio Montoro for reading and commenting on my Introduction chapter, as while the editor edits the contributors' chapters, who edits the editor. I would like to thank Andrew Wardell and the Bloomsbury team for accepting my proposal to develop my ideas into a book to explore narratives beyond their first telling, and the series editors, Dan McIntyre and Louise Nuttall, for agreeing to the initial proposal.

I am grateful to have been granted permission by the Leeds University Crime Fiction archive (housed in the Brotherton Library) to reproduce images from Peter Robinson's notebooks for Christiana Gregoriou's chapter on crime fiction writing. Thanks also go to the teachers and students at Green Tree School and to Kevin Griffith for granting permission to reproduce his poem *Spinning*, in Ian Cushing's chapter. I would also like to thank the Barbara Levy Literary Agency for permission to reproduce in full, the poem *Lamentations* by Siegfried Sassoon in Marcello Giovanelli's chapter.

1

Introduction to narrative retellings: Stylistic approaches

Marina Lambrou

1.1 Introduction to narrative retellings

Narrative Retellings: Stylistic Approaches presents new work at the intersection of stylistics and narrative study to offer new insights into the diverse forms of fictional and factual narratives and the many ways that they are told and retold. The chapters in this volume take an empirical stylistic approach to consider what is understood by retelling through processes such as adaptation, translation and rereading for example, with explorations through specific cases studies, across a range of narrative genres, including classic and contemporary works of literature, factual experiences retold in a literary style, and personal narratives retold in witness reports.

Once told, it is inevitable that the narrative will be retold, reconstructed or reimagined into a new text where original elements, such as characters and plot, may or may not always be recognizable, influenced by factors such as the audience (reader, listener, etc.), the medium (and its affordances) and the rhetorical goal linked to its retelling. By understanding reworkings of narratives as process and product, it is possible to gain insights into the complexities involved in their reconfiguration. For example, the mechanisms for retellings (and in some cases, the inevitable evaluation of the retellings) are explored for a greater understanding of them, such as the responses to the cherished work of Austen and its modern adaptations, or the decisions made by an author revising a draft of their novel, or the stylistic choices taken when carefully translating the poetry of holocaust survivors, or reasons behind the conflicting testimonials following the 1989 Hillsborough disaster. Readers will be presented with discussions on a broad range of narratives and their retellings which focus on classic literary fiction; contemporary fiction (including crime fiction and a short story); the epic to fantasy fiction; personal traumatic experiences (as autobiography, autofiction and poetry); witness statements; advertorials; retelling through rereading; and pedagogical applications of retellings designed to facilitate the learning of language and literacy skills, cultural awareness, and a greater sensitivity to the text and its meaning through stylistic choices.

1.2 Narratives and storytelling

Before exploring the scope of this volume, it is useful to present an understanding of narratives – in terms of their form, function and presence in everyday discourse. Readers understand that storytelling is generally accepted as a universal activity practised across all cultures (Bruner 1990; Miller and Moore 1989) and it is through narrative that meaning is constructed and individuals are able to develop a sense of identity. Specifically, exchanging experiences through the narrative form is seen as social and transactional as through the act of storytelling, individuals represent and shape their lives in order for them to be shared. The cognitive psychologist Jerome Bruner (1990:7) goes as far as to argue that humans have a propensity or 'push' to construct experiences into the narrative form and that we 'cling to narrative models of reality and use them to shape our everyday experiences' (2003:7). This inclination to shape experiences into a version of reality through narrative is one way of making sense of our lives, albeit a subjective version, and is necessary for our cognitive functioning. In other words, it is through narrative that experiences can be memorized, recalled and retold as all individuals have the facility and ability to narrate experiences to be shared. Historically, personal experiences extended to shared narratives that called to question a nation's identity and values, often set up in opposition of the other, as commonly found in early heroic epics passed on as part of an oral storytelling tradition. It is no wonder that narratives emerged from the myths (or mythos) of early civilizations and in the narratives imitating reality (mimesis).

As a subject for research and study, narrative is at the intersection of numerous disciplines each with their own concerns but with some overlapping interests that bring new insights in their interdisciplinary explorations, for example, in areas such as linguistic choice and style at the micro-level; structure, plot and progression at the macro-level; memorization and recall at the cognitive level; and multimodal and paralinguistic at performance levels. Moreover, the growing and broadening interest in the narrative form supports the notion of a 'narrative turn' where narratological principles are usefully applied to other story forms as part of the interdisciplinary conversations that engage and unite researchers and critics alike. While these other forms are composed of their own distinct structural and stylistic rules, the emergence of a 'literary linguistic procedure' (Toolan 1992: xiv) enables each to be analysed systematically for original insights.

So what is a narrative? Narratives are conventionalized discourse structures; that is, they are comprised of minimal narrative units and paradigmatic structures which present 'a timebound linear form that can be heard, watched or read' (Keen 2003:16). The most prototypical narrative follows a linear or temporally ordered structure, though that is not to say that plots with anachronous, unconventional and metafictive plot strategies are not recognized as narratives too (see Dannenberg, 2008; Lambrou, 2019). Default temporal plot structures allow for creative manipulations (Sorlin 2020) and immersions into and out of the storyworld allowing for alternative forms of storytelling to emerge. Simply put, narratives by definition are

> a perceived sequence of non-randomly connected events, typically involving, as the experiencing agonist, humans or quasi-humans, or other sentient beings, from whose experience we humans can learn. (Toolan 2001: 8)

Narratives can also be distinguished by other familiar characteristics such as 'the presence of a story and a story-teller' (Scholes and Kellogg 1966: 4), which emphasizes the interactivity of the process and relationship between those involved. In other words, storytelling is a communicative act and this argues for a more dynamic model of narrative as a successful narrative depends not only on the constitutive elements and 'arrangement of the narrative but also on the context of the telling and to its "receiver"' (Prince 1982). Narratives, therefore, perform a rhetorical purpose as they are essentially about 'somebody telling somebody else on some occasion and for some purposes that something happened' (Phelan 2017: ix). Foregrounding the dynamic and dialogic nature of narratives and responses to them also offers a view that shifts away from a focus on form to consider 'the temporal dynamics that shape narratives in our reading of them, the play of desire in time that makes us turn pages and strive toward narrative ends' (Brooks 1984: xiii).

1.3 Narratives and their retellings

Why are stories told and retold so pervasively? Perhaps some stories are too good to not be shared and perhaps the propensity to form experiences into narrative also extends to their *re*-telling. Early studies on narratives and their retelling focused on memory and recall to establish what we now understand as schema theory, predominantly associated with the work of the psychologist Frederic Bartlett (1932). Schema theory was found to explain the cognitive structures and processes used in comprehension and memorization of information. In Bartlett's study, subjects were asked to read a Native American story containing details which differed from their own cultural backgrounds and then asked to recall the story. The memorized versions were found to differ from the original through a process of either 'flattening', where details were omitted; 'sharpening', where parts were elaborated and exaggerated; or 'rationalizing', where parts of the prose were filled in, as subjects tried to make sense of the recalled story. It was also argued these distortions resulted from an attempt to fulfil expectations of a coherent story by adhering to a story schema based on the subjects' prior knowledge of the narrative genre, dictated to some extent by the affective tone of the story. From these findings, Bartlett concluded that recall was a reconstructive process with schema providing the organizing principle.

Other experiments for recalling a story include Wallace Chafe's (1980) *Pear Story* project, which involved non-linguistic input via a silent film. In this experiment, the chosen subjects were speakers of diverse languages from around the world (including English, Japanese, Chinese, German, Greek, Haitian Creole, Mandarin and Mayan) who were asked to watch a silent film called the *Pear Story* and then recall it. The silent film deliberately contained universal themes, and the aim of the experiment was to compare how different individuals comprehend the same story through their discourse choices and, in this way, understand how cultural and linguistic differences affect narrative production.

Throughout our lifetime, individuals experience numerous personal experiences that culminate to 'express our sense of self: who we are and how we got that way' (Linde 1993:3). These 'life stories' are continuously being made and evolve as individuals navigate their way through a constantly revised life story, composed of numerous smaller episodes of stories documenting events in an individual's life. These life stories can be shared as the 'small stories' (Georgakopoulou 2007) that emerge in conversational narratives produced as talk-in-interaction, for example, and may be retold numerous times. Retelling experiences in conversational narratives is the subject of Polanyi's (1981:319) research which set out to investigate the idea of 'telling the same story twice' in an attempt to understand the existence of an 'underlying semantic structure' and 'script' – the elements of the story's macrostructure and its linguistic components – which are repeated in a second telling. Her findings showed that conversational narratives are socially situated and develop through local occasioning and recipient design, factors that shape the story in the same way that conversations develop generally (see Sacks et al., 1974). While the underlying structure in the retelling may replicate that of the original, it is likely that no two retellings are identical because of variables such as the audience, which requires tailoring the story, which in turn affects the rhetorical goal of the telling, its tellability, and the narrator's performance and stylistic choices.

1.4 Retellings in everyday discourse and contexts

Narrating and retelling stories play an important role in numerous contexts beyond their social and transactional purposes. For example, narrating traumatic experiences that break the continuity and normality of daily life can help individual's make some sense of these extraordinary events. Retelling as therapeutic practice is a well-established activity in psychotherapy where narrative storytelling provides a coping mechanism for dealing with trauma in all its forms (Tuval-Mashiach et al. 2004). The strategy of repetition where the practitioner picks out specific words or phrases uttered by the patient functions evaluatively as it foregrounds salient elements of the patient's experience and provides useful prompts for further exploration and insights into the patient's experience (Ferrara 1994). Trauma narratives that become part of a nation's oral history are characteristically compelling, such as the personal accounts of Holocaust survivors that convey unimaginable suffering. However, trying to find ways of narrativizing devastating experiences to make sense of them led one Holocaust survivor to ask questions of how to express what is indescribable:

> How do you describe a nightmare? Something which is shapeless, amorphous .... It is *not* a story. It has to be *made* a story. In order to convey it. And with all the frustration that implies. (Cited in Greenspan 2010: 199)

Perhaps it is 'because one can never immediately speak the present in the present' (Linde 1993: 105) as time and distance is necessary to allow for reflection to be able to express deep trauma. (See Giovanelli's chapter in this volume for a comparative analysis of the language of Siegfried Sassoon's experiences of war in his poetry and in the later reframing of his trauma in the novelized form.)

Shaping experiences into narratives enables survivors to tell their story and ensures unprecedented events and experiences are passed down and never forgotten. Through their translations, these experiences have been able to be shared widely and consequently have gained the status of a collective oral history. (See Jean Boase-Beier's Chapter in this volume.) (At the time of drafting this chapter, the world is experiencing the Coronavirus or Covid-19 pandemic which is seeing personal and collective narratives on grief and hope emerging daily on all media platforms as everyone navigates their lives through an unprecedented time.)

My own research into trauma narratives following the American 9/11 and London 7/7 terrorist attacks (Lambrou 2014a; 2014b) found that those who survived these terrible events felt the need to communicate their experiences to ensure that those who perished were remembered and the events never forgotten. As one survivor of 9/11, a father whose son Todd was killed in the same Twin Tower he managed to escape from, explained:

> I want to tell the story and I want to tell I think it primarily, honestly for my own healing but I also think it is important to tell the story because Todd's story in his life touches people that are alive, touches their lives, so in a way Todd lives. (Lambrou 2014b: 122)

In research that specifically looked at the phenomenon of retelling the same experience, I was particularly interested in how survivors of the London 7/7 terrorist attack make sense of extraordinary experiences through narrativization and, similar to Polanyi's (1981) enquiry, whether there is an underlying script or story structure that narrators map their stories onto. I asked: *To what extent does the second or retold story replicate the experience in the form of the linguistic structure of the first and which (prototypical) features of a personal narrative remain constant?* (Lambrou 2014a: 35). In one survivor's retold narrative, two and a half years after first narrating his experience of the attack, a number of differences embedded throughout the retelling at the structural, schematic and stylistic levels were found. One significant finding was that the second story fitted a prototypical narrative structure as described by Labov and Waletzky (1967) that filled in gaps as a result of what appeared to be local occasioning and recipient design. Another finding was that the retold story contained more factual details that were absent in the first narrative, which led me to conclude:

> The factual details reported on a daily basis were likely to have been absorbed and assimilated into Angelo's story to have become part of his personal narrative. In other words, Angelo's personal experience became informed by other news stories to become part of a much larger mediated narrative, a 'big story' (Georgakopoulou 2007) that had become part of the public's collective consciousness and repertoire of stories. (Lambrou 2014a: 44)

The elaborated second story is retold after a period of intense scrutiny by the media reporting on details that the subject could not have known at the time of experiencing the attack. These kinds of detailed and more organized repeated stories confirm earlier research on narrative retellings that illustrate the '"second-telling principle" to the effect that when a topic is verbalized a second time it is likely to be more complete and more coherent than the first time' (Chafe 1977:103).

In educational contexts, retelling is often used as a literacy strategy and as a comprehension and assessment tool. Research suggests that asking children to retell stories they have heard or read has several functions that include encouraging an increased focus on story structure and vocabulary, which supports the development of memory and recall. To help learners formulate story structure, theme, plot, and resolution, the argument is that teachers should guide children with prompts to support them as they develop their skills in narrating (Morrow 1985a; 1985b). Studies have also shown that retelling stories encourages greater productivity because it 'requires social engagement as the participants are involved in reading, writing, talking and listening' (Stoicovy 1997: 6). Children continue to construct the text after reading which fits in with the notion that reading a text involves several simultaneous processes of 'comprehending: the process of trying to make sense of a text; and comprehension, what the reader has understood the text to mean at any point in time' (Goodman 1982: 301).

In English language learning contexts, retelling as a pedagogical activity for the acquisition of story schemas can facilitate language development by organizing knowledge and language structures associated with specific genres (Cameron 1994; Kern 2000; Tompkin and McGee 1989). Creative teaching methods to encourage language learning include 'The Blogging Hobbit' project at a Swedish University where students were tasked with creating the 'voice' of a character from Tolkien's (1931) *The Hobbit* by filling in missing moments from the (original) story. Using collaborative, blog-based role-play to produce these missing episodes, students engaged in recreating their narratives, which resembled fan fiction stories. The creative activity was found to 'facilitate analysis of a literary text, learners' use of creative writing techniques, and language development, particularly at the level of lexis' (Sauro and Sundmark 2016: 414). It was also reported that some students tried to recreate the style of Tolkien's original character, which involved more complex cognitive processes in thinking about stylistic choices and characterization to maintain authenticity in retelling missing moments in their narratives. Creative and collaborative forms of retelling in a university undergraduate classroom is also the focus of O'Halloran's (2019: 134) activity on 'film poems' developed into an assessment. Students were required to reinterpret a poem as a film to create a 'film poem' where '[a] film poem is a cinematic creation which takes a written, often canonical, poem as its inspiration'. Using stylistic approaches as the basis for their analysis, students reimagined their interpretation by developing a screenplay that was made into a film using mobile devices. O'Halloran explains he helped students develop their interpretation of the poem's stylistic choices with '(a) a systematic description of particular stylistic dimension of literary work; and (b) rational justification for a (cinematic) interpretation because it is grounded in data from the literary work' (p.150). Other pedagogical applications for retelling in the classroom extend to intervention activities that can enhance the existing curriculum by teaching children elements of world-building in fictional texts and asking them to respond imaginatively through their own rewriting. (See Ian Cushing's and Chantelle Warner's Chapters in this volume on case studies that focus on pedagogical strategies for retelling.) Rereading as retelling where students are encouraged to experience the fictional world and understand how these might differ in a second reading also facilitates a greater engagement with the text as a creative learning experience. (See Chloe Harrison and Louise Nuttall's Chapter in this volume for their classroom-based research involving rereading a Margaret Attwood short story.) Activities such as these provide learners with a greater sensitivity to and engagement with the text as narratives are (re)imagined and (re)created.

1.5 Retellings as adaptation and translation

One of the most conventionalized forms of retelling is through the adaptation and translation of fictional and factual narratives across media formats and genres. Adaptations, according to Hutcheon (2006, xiv), are 'deliberate, announced, and extended revisitations of prior works' that are less like replications because of the creativity and variation involved in the adapting. Adaptations are, therefore, intertextual where '[a]ny text is constructed as a mosaic of quotations; any text is the transformation and absorption of another' (Kristeva 1980: 66). They are also 'palimpsestuous' (Hutcheon 2006: 6), so the adaptation cannot or should not be faithful to the original source as it is expected to differ. Hutcheon (2006) argues that adaptation is about *process* that involves interaction and negotiation as the adapted text is taken from one context and put into another and that questions about fidelity, replication and authenticity may be raised.

Transmedia storytelling across different media platforms (e.g. from novel, video game and comic to film) may be shaped less by the original source and more by the producer/film-maker's ideology as well as the affordances of the medium it is transposed onto, where affordances describe 'the opportunities made possible by a technology itself; in other words, what it allows or enables people to do' (Thurlow, Lengel and Tomic 2004: 250). The resulting intertextual relationship between the source and adapted text can vary on a scale from subtle to substantial differences and may require a greater effort to recognize their relationship (e.g. Shakespeare's *Romeo and Juliet* reimagined as the 1961 film *West Side Story*). Changes across formats in the adaptations may require different cognitive processing compared to the experience of reading and watching, as an understanding of multimodal and semiotic modes interacting with each other is needed (Gregoriou 2017). (Gregoriou uses the broader term of *migrating* because adaptations also cross languages and cultures as well as media formats.) In the film industry, adaptations are thought to 'account for up to 50 per cent of all Hollywood films and are consistently rated amongst the highest grossing at the box office' (Kuhn and Westwell 2012: 5), as demonstrated by the commercial success of the novels of J. R. R. Tolkien, J. K. Rowling and adaptations of superhero comics.

Translation as retellings may also involve interlingual (from one language to another) as well as intersemiotic (from one medium to another such as novel to film but also from novel to poem) changes, but as there are so many considerations, theorists claim it is unclear what translation is. Furthermore, Boase-Beier (2011:7) argues that stylistic choices are important for the process of translation so 'We might consider different varieties of a language, such as idiolects, registers, personal styles, or even different stages of acquisition as different languages for the purposes of translation'. Translation, then, attempts to preserve style as well as meaning, and this can be problematic in translating factual experiences such as trauma, for example, where the priority is to replicate the sense of the source text as faithfully as possible, issues which Jean Boase-Beier discusses in her analysis of translating Holocaust poetry in her Chapter.

Literary adaptations of classic works, such as the retellings of Homeric epics, can also offer challenges as well as opportunities for authors to make significant changes while ensuring that the source text is recognizable for an intertextual comparison. Pat Barker's (2019) *Silence of the Girls*, a retelling of *The Iliad*, Madeline Miller's (2019) *Circe*, a rewriting of *The Odyssey*, and Natalie Haynes's rewriting of the Trojan War, *A Thousand Ships*, are all rewritten from the perspectives of women protagonists to offer retellings of familiar narratives with a twist. Appropriations can overshadow the source text to become the dominant narrative, as seen in Shakespeare's canon, for example. It is well established that Shakespeare drew many of his plots and characters from classical works including those by Plutarch (the source for *Julius Caesar, Antony and Cleopatra, Coriolanus* and *Timon of Athens*) and Ovid (the source for *Titus Andronicus* and *Midsummer Night's Dream*). In some cases, Shakespeare merged two of the primary sources together to create his version of *The Merchant of Venice* and also changed parts of the plot as in Cinthio's version of *Othello*, which originally had Iago murder Desdemona. As Mullen (2018) explains, 'Shakespeare inhabited a literary culture in which imitation of earlier models was applauded' but adds that Shakespeare differed from his contemporaries because 'he is not showing off his literary knowledge but adapting narrative patterns and fragments of dialogue lodged in his memory' (p. 15). (See also Jeremy Scott's and Anne Furlong's Chapters in this volume on their explorations of translations and adaptations.)

As well as myths, another story genre that has been retold, adapted and translated is the fairy tale, literary appropriations of oral folk tales adapted by storytellers such as Perrault, the Brothers Grimm and Hans Christian Andersen. Fairy tales provide revisionist retellings of plots that reflect the moral, ethical and ideological codes that align with the time of their new telling/adaptation. We see the moral code shift in Perrault's (1697) *Little Red Riding Hood* to the Brothers Grimm's (1812) *Little Red Cap* from being a tale about sexuality and dangers of the wood to a narrative about disciplining children for disobeying instructions (i.e. *Little Red Cap* did not do as she was told and went straight to her grandmother's house). Transmedia adaptations of fairy tales to film see different reimaginings of the original story (animation, comedy, musicals, etc.), none more so than the treatment of 'Disneyfication' that presents fairy tales without many of the disturbing qualities of the original story so as to be suitable for a younger audience while still retaining aspects of the original plot and characters.

1.6 The scope of this volume: Structure and chapters

Narrative Retellings: Stylistic Approaches presents the first book-length treatment of a wide range of narrative genres and their retellings explored through stylistic approaches. The contributors for this volume were invited to contribute with new (i.e. never before published) writing in their specific areas of expertise on an aspect of narrative and asked to interpret *retelling* broadly with the following terms given as helpful prompts. Retelling can be interpreted as:

adaptation, translation, recounting, reimagining, reconfiguring, recreating, restorying, revising, remembering, manipulating, rereading, rewriting, reframing, reinterpreting, editing, disnarrating, transferring, migrating, repeating, experimenting, transposing, and transforming.

The next task was to decide how to structure the book into sections with chapters that reflected the different themes and genres of the narratives analysed and discussed across the volume. What at first appeared to be a straightforward exercise presented some difficulties because of the different options i.e. whether by genre (e.g. classic, contemporary fiction, autobiographical, fictional/non-literary), by narrative theme (e.g. personal, trauma narratives) or by the process of retelling (e.g. adaptation, translation, rewriting and rereading). However, as many of the chapters crossed over into several categories, the volume was structured into three broad headings or *parts* to reflect the coherent relationship between the chapters in those sections: Part One – Fictional retellings, Part Two – Factual retellings and Part Three – Pedagogical applications of retellings.

Part One, Fictional retellings, presents a collection of chapters focusing on a range of literary forms beginning with a chapter by Jeremy Scott who proposes a new way of thinking about creative retelling as *re*-storying. Scott argues that in the process of adaptation the source text or 'pre-text' can be *re-energized* as the adapted text will be greatly influenced by the adaptor's perspective, giving the retelling a new creative impetus, a discussion that Furlong also makes in the following Chapter 3 where adaptation is described as a 'communicative act'. Scott offers three distinct definitions of restorying (*recycling, recontextualizing* and *reinterpretation*) and applies these notions to works by J. R. R. Tolkien, who famously recast Old English epics for his plots, Simon Armitage's (2007) translation of *Sir Gawain and the Green Knight* and A. S. Byatt, for a compelling discussion of a new way of looking at adaptation.

Anne Furlong in her chapter proposes that retelling through adaptation is more than aesthetic decision-making as the adaptor's stylistic choices fulfil a specific communicative purpose. She argues that adaptation – which necessitates the selection, reshaping and retelling of narrative elements – is neither incidental nor ornamental as it is a communicative act that performs a communicative function to fulfil the adaptor's aims. Furlong's discussion highlights the complex relationship between the source text, its adaptation, reception and interpretation, maintaining that the adaptor's stylistic choices 'are crucial to communicating their attitude toward the source and to shaping the audience's experience'. To illustrate the role of the adaptor's choices in the selection, reshaping and retelling of narrative elements, Furlong explores a range of diverse adaptations of Austen's ([1813] 1938) novel *Pride and Prejudice* that include a murder mystery (James 2011a, *Death Comes to Pemberly*); a horror-comedy (Austen and Grahame-Smith 2009, *Pride and Prejudice and Zombies*); media and transmedia adaptions (including the 2014 video game *Stride and Prejudice*); and even a card game (Game Salute's *Marrying Mr Darcy*).

Repetition as a strategy for retelling within the same narrative is the focus of Michael Toolan's chapter, which analyses McGahern's (1992) short story, 'Swallows'. The story is shaped around a brief encounter and conversations between a Surveyor and a police Sergeant, which prompts the police Sergeant to reflect on his unfulfilled life, with hints of what might have been, enacted through multiple kinds of repeating and retelling. Toolan describes how the numerous repetitions link not only the experiences of the two characters but also the paragraph structure across the story and claims that because the story lacks a foregrounded near-final passage (Toolan 2016), usually induced through specific stylistic devices to create High Emotional Involvement (HEI), the final part of the story is unlikely to conform to a reader's requirement of a satisfactory ending. Instead, 'Swallows' resorts to strategies of retelling as an alternative means of achieving story completion.

Retellings of Jane Austen's novels are also the focus of Joe Bray's chapter, which takes a critical view of *The Austen Project*, a series of new books commissioned by HarperCollins in 2011. He explains the project's aim was for six contemporary authors to retell Austen's 'most cherished novels' in novelistic form although only four new modern retellings were written: *Sense & Sensibility* (2013) by Joanna Trollope, *Northanger Abbey* (2014) by Val McDermid, *Emma* (2014) by Alexander McCall Smith and *Eligible* (2016) by Curtis Sittenfeld (a retelling of *Pride and Prejudice*). The mixed reviews by critics and readers alike, who describe the work as a 'pale imitation' of the original, prompt Bray to consider 'the worth of *any* kind of retelling'. To explore these differences, Bray provides a comparative analysis of passages from Austen's novels with its modern retellings and discusses the complex issue of whether stylistic analysis can be entirely separated from assessments of value as stylisticians have largely shied away from value judgements, possibly because of the objective analytical methods underlying stylistic approaches to texts. As part of his persuasive argument, Bray looks to Wittgenstein's (1921) notion of 'language games' to argue that making judgements is unavoidable, if we are to understand the negative reception of Austen's modern retellings.

Retelling through rewriting is the focus of Christiana Gregoriou's chapter which examines the crime fiction rewriting process through a stylistic analysis. She focuses on the handwritten notebooks and annotated early novel drafts of

Peter Robinson's novel (2004 [1987]) *Gallows View* and compares them with the published edition. Gregoriou argues that crime fiction is the art of 'misdirection', a genre-typical set of techniques that deliberately misleads the reader away from the precise nature of the circumstances surrounding the crime that is achieved by 'foregrounding and burying' (Emmott and Alexander 2014: 343). She examines in detail the stylistic means through which Robinson creates reader misdirection in the novel while simultaneously responding to the challenge of the 'fair play' rule (Sayers 1947: 225) where there is sufficient detail to ensure certain characters are seen as suspicious but not enough to reveal the criminal too early on in the plot. By analysing the author's original notes from *Gallows View*, readers are given insights into the nature of misdirection in crime fiction writing and the careful crafting required to develop a compelling crime narrative that balances misdirection and 'playing fair'.

Part Two, Factual retellings, focuses on factual experiences, predominantly based on personal narratives narrated through poetry, autofiction, witness statements and advertorials. The section opens with Marcello Giovanelli's chapter on the First World War solider and poet Siegfried Sassoon's retelling of his 1917 poem *Lamentations* (Sassoon 1918) in his second Sherston novel, *Memoirs of an Infantry Officer* (Sassoon 1930). One of six prose autobiographical novels, *Memoirs of an Infantry Officer*, draws on Sassoon's own war diaries, letters and poems detailing his experiences at the Front to reconstruct his war experience as autofiction, a genre that conflates and places the author and main protagonist-as-narrator and merges factual detail with elements of fiction. Using Langacker's (1987) cognitive grammar notion of a construal relationship, Giovanelli presents a comparative, stylistic analysis of Sassoon's language across the two genres to explore the reframing of traumatic events. He suggests that the novelized autofictive retelling offers a more complex treatment of those wartime events, influenced by self-reflexivity and the distance created by time.

Jean Boase-Beier's chapter explores issues associated with translation as retelling, specifically the poems written by Holocaust survivors. In her examination of the process, she asks whether there is a specific 'Holocaust poetics' (Boase-Beier 2015) that characterizes this form of retelling. She highlights other conflicting concerns such as what happens when a translator undertakes this task and whether it is even at all possible for someone else's trauma to be retold faithfully. Boase-Beier explains that a translator's retelling can be seen as an act of *prosopopoeia* because it gives a voice to those who were silenced. Translation enables these experiences to be told and shared, but speaking for others also raises further ethical questions (see Gubar 2003). Using narratological and stylistic approaches to discuss the challenges and ethics of translating Holocaust poetry, Boase-Beier gives readers insights into the important linguistic choices and constraints of this important and sensitive undertaking.

The theme of trauma and its discourse is also central to Patricia Canning's chapter, which provides a close examination of eyewitness statements following the 1989 Hillsborough Football Stadium Disaster that resulted in the deaths of ninety-six football fans. Taking Labov and Waletzky's (1967) model of narrative and using a critical stylistic approach, Canning's analysis of witnesses' retellings (from the investigative process) shows evidence of institutional linguistic representation influencing the witness accounts. Canning argues this problem is exacerbated by the asymmetric, interactional interviewing process led by the interviewing officer responsible for the construction of the narrative, citing as an example the interviewing officer's strategy of raising negative appraisals of the behaviour of Liverpool fans that never happened. As Canning argues, introducing an idea into the discourse even if it did not happen, foregrounds the subject and makes it noticeable (Mukařovsky 1964 [1932]; Lambrou 2019). Canning's chapter considers the way narrative retellings in forensic contexts 'can (inadvertently or otherwise) reify a witness's own story by controlling or promoting topics, through (undocumented) questioning or probing' and calls for greater transparency and witness control in collecting and producing witness narratives.

Retelling in Helen Ringrow's chapter shifts in mood and media format to focus on the advertorials of UK bloggers on social media, specifically on data from two popular UK-based influencers. Ringrow explains that 'influencers' or 'microcelebrities' are paid to promote specific products to followers of their accounts after being given an original product brief which they then *re*-tell in an advertorial, often by creating a personalized narrative on how the product suits their lifestyle and beauty care needs. Ringrow applies Hoey's (1983) 'Problem-Solution' pattern to understand how the product is constructed and endorsed through disclosure language, such as highlighting beauty issues (e.g. dry hair) followed by a solution on how to deal with the problem. Ringrow offers further insights into the retelling process of beauty advertorials and how they are personalized for very specific goals through Multimodal Critical Discourse Analysis by comparing the original briefing notes with the final finished advertisements.

Part Three, Pedagogical applications of retellings, explores pedagogical practices and applications of narrative retellings in educational contexts and presents case studies of the different activities where learning can be facilitated creatively through rereadings and retellings of existing narratives. Ian Cushing's chapter discusses a secondary school project among Year 8 learners (12- to 13-year- olds) with Kevin Griffith's (2006) poem *Spinning* as the literary text for a creative activity using textual intervention (Pope 1995) and Text World Theory (Gavins 2007; Werth 1999). Cushing describes how he worked with teachers over an eighteen-month period to train them 'in key aspects of the theory, the pedagogical principles [...] and its metalanguage during regular visits to the school' resulting in the design of new lessons to facilitate learning that broke from the curriculum. Pupils engaged in new concepts using stylistic approaches to analyse the poem and developed textually sensitive literary responses by creating their own poems through reimagining and rewriting. Cushing argues for the place of cognitive stylistics as a critical-creative pedagogy in the English curriculum deepen learners' understanding of literary language to then be able to respond to texts.

Retelling as a classroom activity with second language learners of German is also the subject of Chantelle Warner's chapter which describes a writing assignment in a US-based classroom inspired by autobiographical works of authors framed as 'foreign' (Johann Wolfgang von Goethe, the Turkish-born German author Feridun Zaimoğlu and Elias Canetti). With the autobiographical works providing the original hypotexts, students were asked to reimagine their own autobiographical narrative and construct personal meanings in their retellings that showed a willingness to explore possibilities of difference. Warner emphasizes the importance of understanding stylistic elements, including deixis and world building, as well as lexical and grammatical awareness to provide an aesthetic dimension to the writing, and presents the written work of two students as case studies for this discussion. She also argues that with an understanding of stylistic metalanguage, retelling can be a means of developing 'symbolic competence' (Kramsch 2006) and intercultural communicative competence to enable language learners to 'interact across cultural boundaries' (Byram 1997: 7).

Rereading as retelling is the focus of Chloe Harrison and Louise Nuttall's chapter, carried out with undergraduate English students of stylistics across three UK universities. Their research explores readers' responses to a short story in a study that provides insights into how prior knowledge and close reading affect understanding of the text. Students were asked to read Margaret Atwood's short story (2014) 'The Freeze-Dried Groom', chosen because it generates different experiences of the fictional world on a first and second reading. Harrison and Nuttall explain that students-as-readers were put into three groups with differing experimental conditions to investigate whether closer reading and attention affected responses to the text. Using knowledge of schema domains to understand the story, students were also asked to produce a paragraph on 'what happens next' and complete a questionnaire. A qualitative analysis of the responses found that second more attentive rereadings tended to specify the external narrator in more detail alongside that of the main character-focalizer, leading Harrison and Nuttall to suggest that rereading facilitates a re-evaluation of perspective with a recognition of alternative points of view and voices within the narrative.

Narrative Retellings: Stylistic Approaches exemplifies the broadening interest in narrative study through stylistic approaches in new and exciting research by experts in the field. The volume presents many of the diverse narrative forms that pervade our lives and explores their retellings, whether as product or process, as adaptation, translation, restorying, recreation or repetition, across fictional and factual modes and genres of storytelling. It is hoped that the interdisciplinary perspectives offered here will introduce readers to a range of methodologies and frameworks for an understanding of how stylistic analysis offers new ways of approaching spoken and written narrative discourses and new insights into why we tell and retell narratives.

References

Armitage, S. (trans.) (2007), *Sir Gawain and the Green Knight*, London: Faber and Faber.
Atwood, M. (2014), 'The Freeze-Dried Groom', in *Stone Mattress: Nine Wicked Tales*, 135–65, London: Virago, Bloomsbury.
Austen, J. (1938 [1813]), *Pride and Prejudice*, Harmondsworth, UK: Penguin.
Austen, J., and Grahame-Smith, S. (2009), *Pride and Prejudice and Zombies*, Philadelphia: Quirk Books.
Bartlett, F. C. (1932), *Remembering*, Cambridge: Cambridge University Press.
Barker, P. (2019), *Silence of the Girls*, London: Penguin.
Boase-Beier, J. (2011), *A Critical Introduction to Translation Studies*, London: Continuum.
Boase-Beier, J. (2015), *Translating the Poetry of the Holocaust: Translation, Style and the Reader*, London: Bloomsbury.
Brooks, P. (1984), *Reading for the Plot: Design and Intention in Narrative*, New York: Knopf.
Bruner, J. (1990), *Acts of Meaning*, Cambridge, MA: Harvard University Press.
Bruner J. (1991), 'The Narrative Construction of Reality', *Critical Inquiry*, 18: 1–21.
Bruner, J. (2003), *Making Stories: Law, Literature and Life*, London: Harvard University Press.
Byram, M. (1997), *Teaching and Assessing Intercultural Communicative Competence*, Clevedon: Multilingual Matters.
Cameron, L. (1994), 'Organizing the World: Children's Concepts and Categories, and Implications for the Teaching of English', *ELT Journal*, 48 (1): 28–39.

Chafe, W. (1977), 'Caddo Texts', in D. R. P Parks (ed.), *Caddoan Texts* (International Journal of American Linguistics Native American Text Series 2, No.1, 27–43, Chicago, IL: University of Chicago Press.

Chafe, W. (ed.) (1980), *The Pear Stories: Cognitive, Cultural, and Linguistic Aspects of Narrative Production*, Norwood, NJ: Ablex.

Dannenberg, H. P. (2008), *Coincidence and Counterfactuality: Plotting Time and Space in Narrative Fiction*, Lincoln and London: University of Nebraska Press.

Emmott, C., and Alexander, M. (2014), 'Foregrounding, Burying, and Plot Construction', in P. Stockwell and S. Whiteley (eds), *The Handbook of Stylistics*, 329–43, Cambridge: Cambridge University Press.

Ferrara, K. (1994), *Therapeutic Ways with Words*, Oxford: Oxford University Press.

Fludernik, M. (1996), *Towards a 'Natural' Narratology*, London: Routledge.

Gavins, J. (2007), *Text World Theory: An Introduction*, Edinburgh: Edinburgh University Press.

Georgakopoulou, A. (2007), *Small Stories, Interaction and Identities*, Amsterdam: John Benjamin.

Goodman, Y. (1982), 'Retellings of Literature and the Comprehension Process', *Theory into Practice*, 21 (4): 301–7.

Gregoriou, C. (2017), *Crime Fiction Migration, Crossing Languages, Cultures and Media*, London: Bloomsbury.

Greenspan, H. (2010), *On Listening to Holocaust Survivors: Recounting and Life History, beyond Testimony*, 2nd edition, St Paul, MN: Paragon House.

Griffith, K. (2006), 'Spinning', *Mid-American Review*, 26 (2): 17.

Grimm, J., and Grimm, Wilhelm (1812), 'Little Red Cap' [Rotkäppchen], in *Kinder- und Hausmärchen [Children's and Household Tales (Grimms' Fairy Tales)]*, trans. D. L. Ashliman, 1st edition, Vol. 1, No. 26. Berlin.

Gubar, S. (2003), *Poetry after Auschwitz: Remembering What One Never Knew*, Bloomington: Indiana University Press.

Haynes, N. (2019), *A Thousand Ships*, London: Mantle.

Hoey, M. (1983), *On the Surface of Discourse*, London: Allen and Unwin.

Hutcheon, L. (2006), *A Theory of Adaptation*, New York: Routledge.

Hymes, D. (1996) *Ethnography, Linguistics, Narrative Inequality: Toward an Understanding of Voice*, London: Taylor and Francis.

James, P. D. (2011a), *Death Comes to Pemberley*, New York: Random House Limited.

Keen, S. (2003), *Narrative Form*, London: Palgrave.

Kern R. (2000). *Literacy and Language Teaching*, Oxford: Oxford University Press.

Kirby, J. T. (1991), 'Mimesis and Diegesis: Foundations of Aesthetic Theory in Plato and Aristotle', *Helios*, 18, 113–28.

Kramsch, C. (2006), 'From Communicative Competence to Symbolic Competence, *Modern Language Journal*, 90 (2): 249–52.

Kristeva, J. (1980), *Desire in Language: A Semiotic Approach*, New York: Columbia University Press.

Kuhn, A., and Westwell, G. (2012), *A Dictionary of Film Studies*. Oxford: Oxford University Press.

Labov, W. (1972), *Language in the Inner City*, Philadelphia: University of Pennsylvania.

Labov, W., and Waletzky, J. (1967), 'Narrative Analysis: Oral Versions of Personal Experience', in J. Holm (ed.) *Essays on the Verbal and Visual Arts*, 12–44, Seattle, WA: University of Washington Press.

Lambrou, M. (2014a), 'Narrative, Text and Time: Telling the Same Story Twice in the Oral Narrative Reporting of 7/7', *Language and Literature*, 23 (1): 32–48.

Lambrou, M. (2014b), 'Narratives of Trauma Re-lived: The Ethnographer's Paradox and Other Tales', in B. Thomas and J. Round (eds), *Real Lives, Celebrity Stories: Narratives of Ordinary and Extraordinary People across Media*, 113–28, London: Continuum.

Lambrou, M. (2019), *Disnarration and the Unmentioned in Fact and Fiction*, London: Palgrave.

Langacker, R. (1987), *Foundations of Cognitive Grammar: Volume 1 Theoretical Prerequisites*, Stanford, CA: Stanford University Press.

Linde, C. (1993), *Life Stories*, Oxford: Oxford University Press.

McCall Smith, A. (2014) *Emma: A Modern Retelling*, London: The Borough Press.

McDermid, V. (2014), *Northanger Abbey*, London: The Borough Press.

McGahern, J. (1992), 'Swallows', in *Collected Stories*, 200–10, London: Faber.

Miller, M. (2019), *Circe*, London: Bloomsbury.

Miller, P. and Moore, B. B. (1989), 'Narrative Conjunctions of Caregiver and Child: A comparative Perspective on Socialization through Stories', *Ethos: Journal of the Society for Psychological Anthropology*, 17 (4): 428–49.

Morrow, L. M. (1985a), 'Reading and Retelling Stories: Strategies for Emergent Readers', *The Reading Teacher*, 38: 870–5.

Morrow, L. M. (1985b), 'Retelling Stories: A Strategy for Improving Children's Comprehension, Concept of Story Structure and Oral Language Complexity, *Elementary School Journal*, 85: 647–61.

Mukařovsky, J. (1964 [1932]), 'Standard Language and Poetic Language', in P. Garvin (ed.), *A Prague School Reader on Aesthetics, Literary Structure and Style*, 17–30, Washington, DC: Georgetown University Press.

Mullen, J. (2018), 'From Greek Myth to Renaissance Hairdos: This Rich Account Reveals the Dizzying Range of Shakespeare's Sources', *The Guardian Review*, 7 April 2018, p. 5.

O'Halloran, K. (2019), 'Filming a Poem with a Mobile Phone and an Intensive Multiplicity: A Creative Pedagogy Using Stylistic Analysis', *Language and Literature*, 28 (2): 133–58.

Perrault, C. (1697), 'Le Petit Chaperon Rouge' ['Little Red Riding Hood'], in *Histoires ou contes du temps passé, avec des moralités: Contes de ma mère l'Oye*, Paris.

Phelan, J. (2017), *Somebody Telling Somebody Else: A Rhetorical Poetics of Narrative*, Columbus: The Ohio State University Press.

Polanyi, L. (1981), 'Telling the Same Story Twice', *Text*, 1 (4): 315–36.

Pope, R. (1995), *Textual Intervention: Creative and Critical Strategies for Literary Studies*, Oxon: Routledge.

Prince, G. (1982) *Narratology: The Form and Functioning of Narrative*, Berlin: Mouton.
Prince, G. (1999), 'Revisiting Narrativity', in W. Grünzweig and A. Solbach (eds), *Grenzenüberschreitungen: Narratologie im Kontext/Transcending Boundaries: Narratology in Context*, 43–51, Tübingen: Gunter Narr Verlag.
Robinson, P. (2004) [1987]), *Gallows View*, London: Macmillan.
Sacks, H., Schegloff, A., and Jefferson, G. (1974), 'A Simplest Systematics for the Organization of Turn-Taking for Conversation', *Language*, 50 (4): 696–735.
Sassoon, S. (1918), *Counter-Attack and Other Poems*, London: Heinemann.
Sassoon, S. (1930), *Memoirs of an Infantry Officer*, London: Faber and Faber.
Sauro, S., and Sundmark, B. (2016), 'Report from Middle-Earth: Fan Fiction Tasks in the EFL Classroom', *ELT Journal*, 70 (4): 414–23.
Sayers, D. L. (1947), *Unpopular Opinions*, New York: Harcourt, Brace.
Scholes, R., & Kellogg, R. (1966), *The Nature of Narrative*, New York: Oxford University Press.
Sittenfeld, C. (2016), *Eligible*, London: The Borough Press.
Sorlin, S. (ed.) (2020), *Stylistic Manipulation of the Reader in Contemporary Fiction*, Bloomsbury: London.
Stoicovy, C. E. (1997), 'Retelling as a Culturally Responsive Strategy for Micronesian Students: Eduard's Story', *Micronesian Educator*, 8: 3–20.
Stoicovy, C. E. (2004), 'Using Retelling to Scaffold English Language for Pacific Island Students', *The Reading Matrix*, 4 (1): 1–10.
Stride and Prejudice (2014), [Videogame], Dev. C. Fisher. USA: No Crusts Interactive, LLC.
Svanoe, E. (2013), *Marrying Mr Darcy:* The Pride and Prejudice Card Game.
Thurlow, C., Lengel, L., and Tomic, A. (2004), *Computer Mediated Communication*, London: Sage.
Tolkien, J. R. R. (1937), *The Hobbit, or There and Back Again*, London: George Allen and Unwin.
Tomkin, G. E., and McGee, L. M. (1989), 'Teaching Repetition as a Story Structure', in I. Muth and K. Denise (eds), *Children's Comprehension of Text*, 59–78, Newark, DE: International Reading Association.
Toolan, M. (1992), *Language, Text and Context: Essays in Stylistics*, London: Routledge.
Toolan, M. (2016), *Making Sense of Narrative Text: Situation, Repetition, and Picturing in the Reading of Short Stories*, London & New York: Routledge.
Toolan, M. J. (2001), *Narrative, a Critical Linguistic Introduction*, 2nd edition, London: Routledge.
Trollope, J. (2013), *Sense & Sensibility*, London: HarperCollins.
Tuval-Mashiach, R., Freedman, S., Bargai, N., Boker, R., Hadar, H., and Arieh Y. Shalev, A. Y. (2004), 'Coping with Trauma: Narrative and Cognitive Perspectives', *Psychiatry*, 67 (3): 280–93.
Werth, P. (1999), *Text Worlds: Representing Conceptual Space in Discourse*, London: Longman.
Wittgenstein, L. (1921), *Tractatus Logico-Philosophicus*, New York: Harcourt.

Part One

Fictional retellings

2

Restorying: The creative act of retelling

Jeremy Scott

2.1 Introduction

The telling of stories is an ancient practice. Stories, myths, tales, *narratives* are the threads that we use to weave the fabric of cultures, societies and identities. It follows, then, that our understanding of the world around us is, to a large extent, based upon processes of *storying*: using narrative structures to interface with and make sense of a highly complex environment. However, stories are, inescapably, interdependent, self-referential and dialogic. They are reconfigured, recycled, *retold*. The telling and the creation of stories are both complementary facets of the same process. This chapter sets out to explore aspects of this relationship in more detail and in a new way by proposing the term *restorying* – a form of retelling – as a mode of capturing this interdependence from the perspective of the writer. The term should also be read as including the sense of its half-homophone, *restore*. Restorying involves a restoration of other texts (or *pre-texts*): a rejuvenation, a re-energizing, even a resurrection.

This cultural phenomenon (the all-pervading nature of restorying is by no means confined to literary discourse) has been widely explored by narratologists and stylisticians: by structuralist narratology under the influence of Saussurean linguistics (Barthes 1957; Genette [1987] 1997; Prince 1974; Todorov and Weinstein 1969: 9), through close linguistic analysis (Shen 2005; Toolan 2001), in terms of Fludernik's conception of natural narratology (1996), via psychoanalytical theory (Brooks 1984), feminist theory (Lanser 1986), postcolonial literary theory (Prince 2005), as personal oral narratives of, for example, trauma or illness (Lambrou 2014, Schauer et al. 2011), political/ideological approaches (Bal 2004), cognitive poetics and reader response (Mason 2019) and even through the lens of evolutionary biology (e.g. Boyd 2009; Dawkins 1976). As Mason (2019: 1–2) argues, the precise nature of the influence of a pre-text upon another is difficult to define in any principled manner at the level of discourse, and the many different types of relationship between texts (and, indeed, discourses) are branded conventionally as *intertextuality*, viewed by Saussure (1974), Kristeva (1980, 2010); Bakhtin (1981, 1984); Genette ([1987] 1997) and Riffaterre (1987, 1990) as a defining characteristic of literary discourse. One of the most well-known accounts of the ubiquity of intertextuality comes from Kristeva: 'Any text is constructed as a mosaic of quotations; any text is the transformation and absorption of another' (1980: 66).

Kristeva's debt to Bakhtin, especially his notions of dialogism and heteroglossia as proposed in *The Dialogic Imagination* (1981), is well known (Mason 2019: 4–5; Moi 1986: 34). Like Bakhtin, Kristeva (along with other contemporary critics such as Althusser and Foucault) sees intertextuality as often ideologically motivated and connected to conceptions of identity (personal, regional, national, linguistic), class or gender. The 'literary word', Kristeva writes, is 'an intersection of textual surfaces rather than a point (a fixed meaning), … a dialogue among several writings' (1980: 65). She continues: '[E]ach word (text) is an intersection of other words (texts) where at least one other word (text) can be read' (1980: 66). She maintains that texts should be understood not as hermetically sealed systems but as relational, since they are created in response to pre-texts and discourses and are shaped by the repetition and adaptation of other textual structures (Alfaro 1996: 268).

If Kristeva is right, and all texts rely intrinsically on their differences from and relations to other texts, then intertextuality is an essential facet of literary texts. However, this hypothesis is essentially non-falsifiable. Mason (2019) instead proposes splitting the phenomenon into two components: *narrative interrelation* – the process by which a reader makes a link between one narrative and another as a mental process – and *intertextual reference*: the articulated product of these narrative interrelations, available for direct analysis (2019: 21). Thus, intertextuality resides, as it were, in the eye of any beholder, and is a cognitive process common to all readers, not just literary critics.

The term *restorying* as defined in this chapter aims to capture narrative interrelation from the other end of the telescope: from the perspective of the *writer* and creative practice. Three definitions of types of restorying are advanced here with a view to outlining and exemplifying a new model with scope for further extension and development.

Type 1: Restorying as recycling

This is the most oblique of the three forms and can be viewed as a process of recycling in the sense of a transformation by a writer of a mixture of source materials, of 're-using'. Concrete elements of the narrative structure of the pre-text(s) will not, for the most part, be retained,[1] but aspects of style and content (themes, character types, settings, genre features and so on) will be present. This is a matter of broad influence (e.g. in terms of creative ethic, ideology or aesthetic philosophy) and may be unconscious or conscious.

Type 2: Restorying as recontextualizing

This type involves a conscious and deliberate relocation of the original pre-text(s) to a new context, involving fundamental changes in mediation (discourse) and thus storyworld. The pre-text(s) are more readily identifiable than in Type 1, either in terms of genre or archetypal narrative tropes. Typically, Type 2 restorying comes about through the use of, in Stanzel's (1986) terms, a new narrative situation (stylistically, and in time, space, cultural context and so on) and will fundamentally alter the original pre-text(s), giving new creative impetus. Crucially, it will entail, on the part of the reader, a refreshing of existing genre schema.

Type 3: Restorying as reinterpretation

Here, the act of restorying involves a single pre-text. The order, structure and progression of that pre-text's narrative remain unchanged (indeed, fidelity to the pre-text is deemed essential), but there are concrete changes in style/linguistic choice to render the original accessible to a different audience, and these changes can be measured and defined through analysis. In formalist terms, the plot (or fabula) remains the same, but the pre-text's discourse is transmuted.

2.2 Type 1: Recycling

As a way of discussing the legendarium[2] of writer and linguist J. R. R. Tolkien, the concept of Type 1 restorying provides many useful insights, especially when the wide series of its pre-texts are taken into account. Both *The Hobbit, or There and Back Again* (1937) and *The Lord of Rings* trilogy (1968) make extensive use of a process of 'quotation' which, as per Type 1, is both conscious and unconscious. Indeed, literary fantasy as a genre is particularly reliant on readers' existing conceptions of pre-texts to the extent that such knowledge could be categorized as a *genre schema*: the reader expects and anticipates that the narrative (or fabula) will proceed and develop in a specific fashion and that characters will accord to certain archetypes (hero, adversary, helper, sender and so on). Tolkien's work, arguably, is the progenitor of the genre as currently recognized (Mendlesohn 2013).

The sources it recycles are numerous. Alongside the Anglo-Saxon epic poetry exemplified by *Beowulf*, early English texts such as *Gawain and the Green Knight*, English folk tales, Arthurian romance, the Norse/Eddic Sagas and Germanic fairy tales, one of the most central pre-texts of Tolkien's legendarium, and arguably the least known outside of the Nordic region, is *The Kalevala*, the national epic of Finland.

Published in its final form in 1849, *The Kalevala* is based on the collecting of Finnish folk oral poetry, some of which dates back to the first millennium. Its 'assembly' (for it is not 'written' in the conventional sense and herein lies a large part of its appeal) and interest was the work of Elias Lönnrot, who travelled the country collecting narrative poems, which originally were often sung. The epic begins with the story of the creation of the world from broken eggs and ends with a mysterious reinterpretation of the virgin birth. At various points in between, the tales arising from the establishing of a northern nation and its coming to terms with its environment are detailed in fascinating poetic form, which ranges from the epic to the lyrical. As several scholars have already argued (Bardowell 2009; Flieger 2002; West 2004), *The Kalevala* was fundamental in establishing Tolkien's *poesis* or creative practice; Tolkien himself used the term *poesis* to describe this interrelationship of creation/making and of speaking/poetry (Bardowell 2009: 91).

Previous scholarly discussion of its influence has focused on parallels in terms of elements of narrative, themes and motifs. Whittingham (2007) discusses the influences from the Torah, the New Testament and the Eddic Sagas on Tolkien's creation myth and considers how narrative elements of Finnish folklore found their way into Tolkien's work (2007: 34–42). Other scholars, however, have tended to focus solely on the Christian roots of Tolkien's work, citing evidence of the author's faith (Gough 1999; Kocher 1985). Indeed, Gough goes so far as to state categorically that the sources of the principle narrative arcs that make up *The Silmarillion* owe no debt to the Nordic cultures (1999: 8). West (2004), however, sees a fundamental relationship, arguing that the poems of The Kalevala profoundly influenced Tolkien's creative philosophy.

To build on West's perspectives and align them with the concerns of this chapter and volume, Tolkien's work can be read as a conscious Type I restorying of the Finnish epic. Thus, the interrelationship should not be seen in terms of specific narrative form[3] but in terms of the author's creative ethic (poesis) and, in places, style. To focus first on the latter: reading *The Kalevala* as a young man sparked off a life-long interest in Finnish language and culture (West 2004: 285).

Tolkien felt the collection of poems, myths, spells and hero-tales contained an utterly unique voice that did not fit neatly within broader European mythology and linguistics. In a letter to W. H. Auden, Tolkien writes:

> I was immensely attracted by something in the air of *The Kalevala*, even in Kirby's poor translation. [Finnish grammar] was like discovering a complete wine cellar filled with bottles of an amazing wine of a kind and flavour never tasted before. It quite intoxicated me. (Carpenter 1981b: 214)

In a subsequent essay on *The Kalevala*, Tolkien even writes of the change of 'mind-set' that will engulf the reader on a first encounter with this strange and unfamiliar world, an explicit reference to a process of schema refreshment:

> You feel like Columbus on a new Continent .... When you first step onto the new land you can if you like immediately begin comparing it with the one you have come from. Mountains, rivers, grass and so on are probably common features to both. The plants and animals may seem familiar enough ... but it is more likely to be the often almost indefinable sense of newness and strangeness that will either perturb or delight you. ... This is how it was for me when I first read the *Kalevala* – that is, I crossed the gulf between the Indo-European-speaking peoples of Europe into this smaller realm of those who cling in queer corners to the forgotten tongues and memories of an elder day. (Tolkien 2010: 246)

Tolkien's subsequent research at Oxford led to the study of many ancient languages, including Old English, Old Norse, Latin, Welsh, Anglo-Saxon and Icelandic. He felt strongly that the language of a culture and the narratives (stories and mythologies) that emerged from and within it were intimately intertwined. The stories of these cultures, it seemed to him, existed in a symbiotic relationship with their languages that was difficult for him to properly define given the theoretical paradigms of the time: 'It was just as the 1914 war burst on me that I made the discovery that "legends" depend on the language to which they belong; but a living language depends equally on the "legends" which it conveys by tradition' (Carpenter 1981a: 231).

The realization of this essential interdependence led Tolkien to try and learn Finnish in order to properly access the mysteries of *The Kalevala*; however, the notorious complexity of the language was a stumbling block. However, the attempt bore other fruits. As Carpenter writes:

> He never learned Finnish well enough to do more than work through part of the original Kalevala, but the effect on his language inventing was fundamental and remarkable. He ... began to create a private language that was heavily influenced by Finnish. (1981a: 66–7)

In creating the myths of Middle-Earth, Tolkien thus felt that he needed an 'authentic' language if his own work was to match the richness and evocativeness of its pre-texts, and so, he set about inventing one: the two forms, one 'high' (Quenya), one the 'lower' language of peoples in exile (Sindarin), of Elvish. The development of these *artlangs* was fundamentally influenced by Finnish. Quenya, like Finnish, does not use a definite article, has an '-at' ending for plural nouns and, like the Finnish of *The Kalevala*, is highly musical and suitable for song (Goering 2014).

Tolkien's writing is replete with songs and poems, often in a traditional ballad form. The Finnish epic is written within a strictly formal system, known as 'The Kalevala Meter', which is drawn from the manner in which the original poems were sung by folk performers, sometimes unaccompanied, but at other times accompanied by a traditional Finnish stringed instrument, the *kantele*. The opening of Poem 3, 'The Singing Match', runs as follows in the original (stresses are my own in strict trochaic tetrameter):

Vaka **van**ha **Väi**nä**möi**nen
elele**vi ai**ko**jan**sa
noilla **Väi**nö**län a**hoilla,
Kale**va**lan **kan**ka**hil**la.
Laule**le**vi **vir**siänsä,
laule**le**vi, **tai**te**le**vi.

Steady old Väinämöinen
is living his times
in those glades of Väinö-land
on the Kalevala heaths
is singing his tales
singing, practising his craft.
(Lönnrot 2008: 22)

In *The Lord of the Rings*, when Aragorn sings the 'Song of Beren and Lúthien' to distract the four hobbits from their night-time terror at the camp on Weathertop, he explains:

'That is a song,' [Aragon] said, 'in a mode that is called *ann-thennath* among the Elves, but is hard to render in the Common Speech, and this is but a rough echo of it.' (Tolkien 1968: 210)

The parallels with the 'losses' incurred by translating *The Kalevala* into English are clear – again, the language is integral to the effect – as is the influence of the tetrameter form. Note too Tolkien's description of the way in which Aragorn performs the ballad, with clear echoes of the 'singing' of the original *Kalevala* verses as collected by Lönnrot: 'He was silent for some time, and then he began not to speak but to chant softly' (208). Tolkien, 'fictionalising' the processes of translation, reverses the trochaic metering of *The Kalevala* to the iambic, more natural for the alternate stress patterning of English (standing in for the Common Tongue in his legendarium), but similar alliteration, full rhyme and assonance are in evidence:

> The leaves were long, the grass was green,
> The hemlock-umbels tall and fair,
> And in the glade a light was seen
> Of stars in shadow shimmering.
> Tinúviel was dancing there
> To music of a pipe unseen,
> And light of stars was in her hair,
> And in her raiment glimmering.
> (208)

It is not simply in terms of language and style that the Finnish epic informed Tolkien's writing; these influences are oblique, but discoverable through close analysis. More fundamentally, there is an ideology and creative ethic (poesis) underpinning Tolkien's work which is drawn directly from *The Kalevala*. He had great admiration for Lönnrot himself and envisaged his own creative project progressing along similar lines, especially in terms of Lönnrot's goal of creating a national epic worthy of giving mythic voice to, or of 'storying', a newly emerging independent Finland:

> Tolkien envisaged himself doing exactly [what Lönnrot did], contracting a world of magic and mystery, creating a heroic age that, although it might never have existed, would give England a storial sense of its own mythic ... identity. (Flieger 2005: 29)

He remarked, 'I would that we had more of it left – something of the sort that belonged to the English' (Carpenter 2000: 67). This is restorying, then, in its most broad and fundamental sense: lending narrative coherence and mythic grounding to a national culture, just as *The Kalevala* did for the newly independent Finland. It is an attempt at, as Schniewind puts it, '[t]he expression of unobservable realities in observable form' (quoted in Leach 1969).

Addressing only the oblique surface parallels between Tolkien's work and *The Kavevala*, then, does not do justice to the influence it had on him. The pre-text informs his entire creative ethic. To draw on a metaphor advanced in his essay 'On Fairy Stories' (1964), Type 1 restorying functions rather in the manner of the material in a compost heap (hence the use of the term 'recycling' to define it).

A story is 'nourished' (Bardowell 2009: 105) by its many pre-texts, while being in and of itself a new and original creation. Tolkien's writing is derived from many sources (particularly *The Kalevala*), but no one could rightly accuse it of being derivative. The telling of stories begets the making of new ones.

2.3 Type 2: Recontextualizing

Type 2 restoryings will typically maintain many of the pre-texts' key stylistic elements (characters, essential plot dynamics, structure and so on). However, the storyworlds engendered by Type 2 restoryings will differ significantly from those of the pre-text(s). Indeed, as the use of the plural parenthesis implies, many of the pre-texts that are restoried in this category tend to be archetypes of one kind or another: myths, legends, fairy and folk tales. It is in the different nature of the entailed storyworld that a principal difference between Type 1 and Type 2 restorying resides: Tolkien's work restories *The Kalevala* by evoking fantastical worlds and tales that are similar in conception and construction to those of the pre-text; a reader's genre schema (in this case, pertaining to myth, folktale and, later, fantasy) is reinforced. In Type 2 restorying, the writer deliberately disrupts or confounds this schema in some way: through setting, through types of mediation, through the progression of the narrative itself and so on.

In short, even though the fundamental elements or tropes of narrative structure may remain consistent across Type 2 restoryings (the hero still marries the princess, the witch still ensnares the traveller), the storyworld cued up in the mind of the reader will be different from the pre-texts, due to alterations in setting, style or in terms of the manner in which the narratives are resolved.

The concept of 'story' in this sense can be usefully defined in terms of its cognitive reception and recognition by readers (as opposed to more proscriptive structuralist approaches). As with genre schema, narrative schemas (Mason 2014) form the basis of our understanding of the concept of 'story' itself. In other words, they lie at the heart of the patterns readers look for in discourse, relatable in some ways to our tendency to find faces or images in clouds; we are 'hard-wired' to look for the shape of a story as a structuring principle. It could be argued, further, that narrative schemas themselves were born in myth and folktale and our early apprehension of these (Lambrou 2019). Thus, it is to contemporary Type 2 restoryings of folktale (rather than Tolkien's Type 1 restorying of *The Kalevala*) that this chapter will turn to for its second case study.

Propp's (1968) structuralist systematization of the familiar narrative elements and structures of folktales into a set of detailed 'functions' is still a useful way of appreciating how narrative schemas are constructed: a significant action or event defined according to its place in the plot (such as 'a forbidding edict is passed upon the hero' or 'the hero makes an effort to attain knowledge needed to fulfil their quest' and so on). In Propp's system, the morphology of the folktale is a mediating syntax for the storyworld; in the Saussurean structuralist manner, the arrangement of these narrative functions and the functions themselves are 'signifiers', while the storyworlds constructed by readers in response are 'signifieds'. This analogy helps to make clear why the concept of storyworlds in Herman's (2009: 72–3) sense of the term is an illustration of the fundamental inter-connectedness of, to use formalist terms, discourse and fabula. Type 2 restoryings maintain key elements of the functions of the narrative but fundamentally change the manner in which these are mediated. Indeed, it is in this particular adaptability of *folktales*' structures and the ways in which their conventions can be worked against that Type 2 restoryings find their power and resonance. They are archetypal narrative structures, recognizable without much particular knowledge of the original or pre-text, and often speak to perceived elemental and universal truths about the human experience.

A. S. Byatt's short story collections *The Djinn in the Nightingale's Eye* (1995) and *Elementals* (1998) are both tributes to the resonance of Type 2 restoryings. As Byatt (2004) herself has written, 'Anyone who has looked at the 345 variants of the Cinderella stories collected by the redoubtable Marian Roalfe Cox in 1893 will know how the mosaic pieces slip, slide and recombine.'

In essence, Byatt's (2004) restoryings of folktales are attempts to mark, celebrate and explore their universal significance through the imposition of *difference*, through a 'working against' the familiar genre and narrative schema; it is a recontextualization of a familiar genre in an attempt to reuse, and yet manipulate, transform and *restore*. She also accedes to the concept of a narrative grammar and seems to be in agreement with one of the central premises of this chapter: that *all* creative writers are engaged with varying forms of restorying:

> Writers have always used the forms of the fairy tale – if my idea that they form, or until recently formed, the narrative grammar of our minds is correct, then writers must have done. The happy endings of fairy tales underpin the comedies of Shakespeare – we have the comfortable sense that tribulations will result in safety and reconciliation.

Byatt's short stories also cast a wry glance at the power of these archetypes, hinting to some extent at how difficult it is for writers to ever escape the 'tyranny' of plot. 'I am in a pattern I know, and I suspect I have no power to break it,' the heroine of 'The Story of the Eldest Princess' wonders aloud. Consider the opening of the story:

> Once upon a time, in a kingdom between the sea and the mountains, between the forest and the desert, there lived a King and Queen with three daughters. Their eldest daughter was pale and quiet, the second daughter was brown and active, and the third was one of those Sabbath daughters who are bonny and bright and good and gay, of whom everything and nothing was expected. (1995: 41)

Many familiar elements of the folktale or fairy story are in evidence here: the formulaic opening four words; a king and queen; a trio of daughters, whose characteristics vary greatly (shy and reclusive, bold and brash, morally suspect), a kingdom of sea, mountains, desert and forest, and even an allusion to the register and alliterative patterns of nursery rhymes ('bonny and bright and good and gay'). In addition, an element of the uncanny or magical soon raises its head. The blue sky has vanished, replaced by a green one. The three daughters, like Tolkien's hobbits, embark upon a long magical quest – in this case, to find a silver bird, whose magical qualities should return things back to normal. The folktale functions identified by Propp inform the shape of the narrative; however, its development is given a contemporary twist by the way in which the daughters refuse to play out their designated (by folktale morphology) roles in full. The eldest two princesses refuse to fulfil their quest, leaving the youngest 'without a story'. Each of the archetypal females rebels against what the machinery of the narrative expects and compels them to do. It turns out that they *do* have the power to break the pattern. The ideological overtones of this device are inescapable: it is possible for imposed roles, including those entailed by gender, to be refused. And so the third princess manages to escape and begin a story of her own:

> The thread glittered and twisted, and the Princess began to roll it nearly in, and took a few steps along it, and gathered it, and rolled it into a ball, and followed it, out of the orchard, across the meadow, and into the woods, and … but that is another story. (70)

Similarly, Byatt's (1998) story 'Cold' is in every respect a fairy tale, featuring, once again, many of the Proppian functions; it also contains other familiar folktale features: the earth cools due to a magical curse, there are palaces of ice, and mysterious visitors come and go in the dead of night. There are also cycles of events in threes: three bearers of gifts, three northmen, three envoys. However, once again the form is subverted in a way that has inescapable metafictional effects. To reiterate, these restoryings centre upon subversions of folktale archetypes that are both schema disrupting and refreshing: 'a schema change that is the equivalent of tuning ... or the notion in literature not so much of defamiliarisation as refamilarisation' (Stockwell 2002: 79). As Tiffin (2006: 47) points out, this subversion of narrative schema also has an ideological function: the images of ice and glass are metaphors for the idea of narrative as fixed and immutable *artefact*. The modes of representation that folktales have in common are both entrapping and empowering and, thus for Byatt, through their subversion, allow a feminist exploration of the processes of creative writing by refusing the 'tyranny' of plot. This signature use of 'embedded narrative', of Type 2 restorying, highlights important ideological aspects inherent in the interactions between reality and its fictional representation.

Byatt has said of this particular story that it is 'a metaphor for the writer in myself', the story of an Ice Princess 'whose existence is predicated on not making contact' (Gooderson 2005). Princess Fiammarosa becomes encased within an icy second skin, a metaphor for her own self-imposed isolation:

> She had been so much loved, as a little child, and all that heaping of anxious love had simply made her feel ill and exhausted. There was more life in coldness. In solitude. Inside a crackling skin of protective ice that was also a sensuous delight. (1998: 133)

This isolation leads to bursts of creativity, expressed once again through the conceptual metaphor STORIES ARE THREADS: 'tapestries, with silver threads and ice-blue threads ... unlike anything seen before in that land' (134–5). When Fiammarosa marries Prince Sasan, she does so because his glass clothing reminds her of frozen water; she moves to his hot desert kingdom and melts (literally and metaphorically), and he builds for her a glass palace on a snowy mountaintop in which her layer of ice re-forms. She begins studying and writing again, and thus the story ends with a moment of metaphorical flourish rather than a more traditional 'happily ever after'; it is through contact, not isolation, that creativity and well-being can thrive.

The ideological nature of these Type 2 restoryings, then, arises through a return to and recontextualization of mythic archetypes systemized – an appeal to the essential narrativizing instincts of humankind and to its taste for the fantastic and magical. As Angela Carter and Salman Rushdie have both separately claimed, there is more energy in old tales than in recent social realism.

2.4 Type 3: Reinterpretation

If Type 2 addresses the reworking of familiar narrative structures and tropes, then Type 3 restorying implies a concrete retelling and fidelity to the form of a single pre-text; the two renderings of the story are far closer than in Type 1, where the traces of a pre-text on the newer text at the level of discourse are sporadic. The focus in Type 3 restorying, rather, is on discourse: the events that take place within the storyworld remain the same, the order (Genette 1983) is the same, and there is a sense of 'duty' or obligation to adhere as closely as possible to the original language, treating it as the work of the original writer, while rendering it accessible to new readers and audiences. Alterations from the original are at the level of discourse: lexical choice, register and mode, phonological patterning, syntax and, in the broadest sense of the term, style. These alterations and the choices which underpin them are particularly acute when the original text is a poem. A concrete example of Type 3 restorying, then, is translation of a text from an older variety of a language to a modern one[4] where, as discussed in Section 2.2, these linguistic choices carry even greater weight due to the importance of phonological patterning in poetic effect. As Attridge (2004: 146) puts it, a crucial effect of poetic discourse, indeed to some extent a defining characteristic, is that 'the series of linguistic sounds *and* their referents receive simultaneous, if separate, enhancements'. Of course, linguistic structures do not in and of themselves embody 'real world' attributes but serve as gateways to understanding and interpreting literary texts vis-à-vis their relationship to that 'real world'.

Type 3 restorying that is translated from older varieties of a modern language involves significant compromises. As a case in point, this section will examine excerpts from different translations of *Sir Gawain and the Green Knight* by Simon Armitage, Bernard O'Donoghue and J. R. R. Tolkien. The poem, whose author is, famously, unknown and referred to simply as '[t]he Gawain-Poet', is one of the best known of the Arthurian stories and an archetypal quest narrative. In it, Sir Gawain, a knight of King Arthur's Round Table, accepts a challenge from a mysterious Green Knight who arrives unannounced one day at Camelot, daring any of those present to set about him with an axe if, in return, he will accept a return blow in exactly one year and one day. Sir Gawain accepts this challenge and duly severs the Green Knight's head with a single blow; it rolls across the floor causing onlookers to move their feet to avoid it:

> Þe fair hede fro þe halve hit to þe erþe,
> Þe fele hit foyned with her fete, þere hit forth roled; (lines 427–8)

The Green Knight, to the amazement of all present, then bends down, picks up his severed head and leaves Camelot, reminding Gawain, with his parting words, of the bargain that he has made.

> 'Loke, Gawan, þou be grayþe to go as þou hetteȝ,
> And layte as lelly til þou me, lude, fynde,
> As þou hatȝ hette, in þis halle, herandeu þise knyȝtes. (447–9)

As can be seen from the above excerpts from the original text, the poem is written in a dialect very different from the Middle English of Chaucer–to the point of being often unintelligible to the modern reader. Chaucer's language, as the dialect of the economically and politically dominant south-east, and thus more directly traceable as an antecedent of modern English, is relatively accessible. That said, some parts of the poem are easier for the modern reader to understand than others. 'Bot Arthure wold not ete til all were served' (85) should cause few difficulties, whereas 'Queþer, leude, so lymp, lere oþer better' (1109) is a far trickier prospect. Most of the lines, however, lie somewhere in between these two extremes of comprehensibility. As Armitage (2007: xiii) puts it:

> [The lines] seem to make sense, though not quite. To the untrained eye, it is as if the poem is lying beneath a thin coat of ice, tantalisingly near yet frustratingly blurred. To a contemporary poet, one interested in narrative and form, and to a Northerner who not only recognises plenty of the poem's dialect but who also detects and echo of his own speech rhythms within the original, the urge to blow a little warm breath across the layer of frosting eventually proved irresistible.

Modern scholarship places the dialect as being from the region now known as the English West Midlands – South Lancashire, Staffordshire and Derbyshire (Barron 1998: 4) – or perhaps further north, from The Wirral (Kermode 2007). Armitage (2007: xii) has the author as 'broadly speaking, a Northerner'; indeed, as the quote above shows, it is partly a personal identification with this dialect that has inspired and influenced his particular restorying, a point that will be returned to shortly.

The poem, like *The Kalevala*, presents the translator with particular challenges due to its strict formal characteristics. Foremost here is the issue of alliteration, which Old English poetry uses more heavily than rhyme. In addition, the poet deploys a complex metrical form known as the 'bob-and-wheel'. Each stanza ends with a short half-line of only two syllables (the bob), followed by a quatrain (the wheel) which rhymes A-B-A-B and has three distinct stresses per line. In addition, the second and fourth lines of the wheel rhyme with the last syllable of the bob. The bob-and-wheel itself also contains alliteration:

> in stedde
> He brayde his bluk aboute,
> Þat vgly bodi þat bledde;
> Moni on of hym had doute,
> Bi þat his resounȝ were redde. (439–43)

To make matters even more complex for the translator, the bob-and-wheel summarizes the preceding stanza, a little like the final rhyming couplet of an English Sonnet, and, similarly, emphasizes this contrast in content and tone formally in comparison with the preceding alliterative verse structure. Finally, there is a strict pattern to the alliteration itself, with each line divided two halves, each containing two (or in the first half-line originally three) main stresses.

In short, this strict scheme is all but untranslatable into Modern English, without the risk of introducing lexical or syntactic anachronisms. Take the following example:

> Þe tulk þat þe **tr**ammes of **tr**esoun þer wroȝt
> watȝ **tr**ied for his **tr**icherie, þe **tr**ewest on erthe. (3–4)

This can be approximately rendered into modern English prose as follows ('O'Donogue 2006: xiii):

> The man who performed the machinations of treason there
> Was tried for his treachery, the most certain in the world.

Tolkien's (1995) versions maintain the alliteration at the expense of the stress patterning but suffers from the resulting mutations of natural syntax and lexis:

> When the siege and the assault had ceased at Troy
> and the fortress fell in flame to firebrands and ashes
> the **tr**aitor who the con**tr**ivance of **tr**eason there fashioned
> was **tr**ied for his **tr**eachery, the most **tr**ue upon earth. (1995: 19)

O'Donoghue, however, dispenses with the alliterative scheme altogether but, like Boroff (1967), maintains the syllabic stress pattern as rendered in Modern English in a roughly anapaestic metre:

> the **man** who'd betr**ayed** it was **brought** to **trial**,
> most **cer**tainly **guil**ty of **ter**rible **crimes**. (2006: 3, my emphasis)

He also dispenses with the rhyme scheme of the bob-and-wheel sections, prioritizing the formal structures of modern English. In short, the process of restorying *Gawain* necessitates compromises in terms of fidelity to the original: in alliteration, in meter, or in lexical choice and register. To build on Attridge's

(2004) definition: the linguistic and stylistic choices made by the translator are motivated by a specific artistic vision. To prioritize alliteration over metering and rhyme scheme is to attempt fidelity to Old English poetic conventions and thus to a particular vision of the language's inherent associations with its original context. Boase-Beier (2006: 12) highlights these particular challenges inherent in the translation process by referring to them as 'creative transposition'. 'On the face of it', she writes, 'translation would seem to demand that at least something is universal'. Otherwise, translation is all but impossible. The link between language, style and context would be too integral to allow transposition, and thus translation (whether of older varieties to modern or of one distinct language to another) and Type 3 restorying become chimerical ambitions.

Thus, Armitage's (2007) creative transposition remains faithful to the original alliterative scheme but goes far further than either Tolkien or O'Donoghue in his use of Modern English. However, he still seeks to maintain an explicit connection between sound and sense:

> [T]o me, alliteration is the warp and weft of the poem, without which it is just so many fine threads. In some very elemental way, the story and the sense of the poem is [sic] directly located within its sound. The percussive patterning of the word serves to reinforce their meaning and to countersink them within the memory. So in trying to harmonise with the original rather than transcribe every last word of it, certain liberties have been taken. ... The intention has always been to produce a living, inclusive and readable piece of work in its own right. In other words, the ambition has been poetry. (2007: iv)

Armitage's goal, then, is to restory, and restore, this poem with a view to broadening its appeal and accessibility. While staying true to its Old English roots through adherence to the alliterative scheme (which he sees as fundamental to the poem's overall effect), the updating of the register (making use of contemporary northern English dialect forms) aims to position the poem firmly within a particular sociolinguistic and ideological context, as it were to 'creatively transpose' it over as short an interval as possible. Tolkien's mention of 'political power' in the earlier quotation is significant; the dominant dialects of London and the South-East prevailed over other varieties. Armitage's affinity with its northern cadences gives this restorying its own ideological orientation, reasserting the primacy of the regional demotic as integral to the overall aesthetic effect of the poem. To lose the tie between region and voice is to lose a fundamental effect of the text.

Armitage's translation also remains true to the way that alliteration is patterned in Old English. In other words, it is not just the front syllable of each word that gives rise to the alliterative pattern (as in 'the **kn**ight that had **kn**otted the nets'), but rather the syllable's position vis-à-vis the overarching stress pattern. Straying, arguably, into the territory of the phonoaesthetic fallacy (Attridge 2004: 133; Nash 1986: 30; Simpson 2004: 69), Armitage cites the example of the following lines; note how the anapaestic metering acts as scaffolding, supporting and foregrounding the alliterative parallelisms:

> Next he fetches out the fillets of glimmering flesh
> and retrieves the intestines in time-honoured style. (1612)

Armitage writes:

> [The line] might not appear to alliterate at first glance. But read it out loud, and the repetition of that 't' sound – the tut-tutting, the spit of revulsion, the squirming of the warm, wet tongue as it makes contacts [sic] the root of the mouth – seems to suggest a physical relationship with the action being described. If the technique is effective, as well as understanding what we are being told we take a step closer to actually experiencing it. This is a translation not only for the eye, but for the ear and voice as well. (2007: xv)

In its use of contemporary demotic, Armitage's translation contains what Tolkien would doubtless have seen as linguistic anachronisms. Compare the original text, Armitage's translation, and then Tolkien's, of the moment the Green Knight arrives at Camelot:

> For wonder of his hwe men hade,
> Set in his semblaunt sene;
> He ferde as freke were fade,
> And oueral enker-grene. (147–50)

> Amazement seized their minds,
> no soul had even seen
> a knight of such a kind –
> entirely emerald green. (147–50)

> For at the hue men gaped aghast
> in his face a form that showed;
> as a fay-man fell he passed,
> and green all over glowed. (1995: 21)

The attempt to mimic more archaic lexis in Tolkien's version is clear ('hue', 'fay', 'fell'), arising from commitment to the strictures of the original form. Tolkien for the most part uses first-syllable alliteration (with the exception of 'gaped aghast'), whereas Armitage's alliteration is determined by stress patterning. Tolkien's version is, however, most faithful to the original (if by 'faithful' we mean linguistically and stylistically concurrent). There are many further examples of contemporary demotic in Armitage's translation. The Green Knight's weapon is described as 'the mother of all axes / a cruel piece of kit I kid you not' (208–9). Arthur is 'governor of this gaggle' (225), the Knight assures the court "'I'm spoiling for no scrap, I swear'" (279), and Arthur is described as 'keeping his cool' (251).

It is also important to note that the very anonymity of the poem, the fact that we know so little about its author, makes it attractive to the modern translator and ripe for restorying. It is almost as if the 'restory-er' can lay claim to it – as author. Each of these Type 3 restoryings of *Gawain*, then, differs wildly from one another, but each swears a different type of fidelity to the original. Tolkien's is scholarly in orientation, intent on retaining as many of the linguistic features of the original as possible. O'Donoghue prioritizes the syllabic stress patterning and removes archaic forms. Armitage wants the language to sound to the modern reader as it must have done to those who heard the original: fresh, vernacular, rooted in a region. It is the *sound* of the language which is of the utmost importance to Armitage; without that direct association between sound and sense, rooted in a locality, as he writes, then the work is no longer a poem.

2.5 Conclusion

This chapter has proposed that **from the point of view of the writer**, the term *restorying* may have more utility than the more generalized *intertextuality*, especially if subdivided into types according to the nature of the relationships between the pre-texts and the restorying. All three types of restorying also entail some form of *restoring* of the pre-text(s): a freshening, a reawakening, a creative appropriation, an injection of new energy, vitality, relevance or resonance. Restorying, then, is, as an essential aspect of creative practice, a tool which all writers make use of to a greater or lesser extent. Storytelling and story-making are intimately connected.

Furthermore, all types of restorying perform some kind of ideological function. Tolkien's legendarium drew on *The Kalevala* as a means of creating a mythic narrative that might relate to England as *The Kalevala* relates to Finland. Byatt sought to re-appropriate traditional mythic and folk structures as a feminist exploration of the hegemony of narrative archetypes. Armitage's translation of *Gawain* asserts the primacy of its original northern vernacular, claiming that without that regional association the poem fails to achieve its full expressive potential.

This proposal and illustration of three types of restorying is only a first step and is an appeal for further discussion and refinement. In any case, it is hoped that this chapter has provided some sense of the centrality of processes of restorying to creative practice and literary-linguistic mediation of the world. As Auden observed in his 1956 review of Tolkien, narrative archetypes like the quest are central to linguistic mediation in general, and not just literary texts:

> The difficulty in presenting a complete picture of reality lies in the gulf between the subjectively real, a man's experience of his own existence, and the objectively real, his experience of the lives of others and the world about him. … For objectifying this experience, the natural image is that of a journey with a purpose.

Notes

1. However, as is argued in Section 2.4, some repetition of narrative tropes is often unavoidable.
2. Tolkien used the term *Legendarium* to refer to his works set in Middle Earth, first using the term in a letter to Milton Waldman in 1951 (Carpenter 1981a).
3. However, a story from *The Kalevala* is retold directly in *The Story of Kullervo* (2015); this, however, is an example of Type 3 restorying in the terms of this chapter.
4. The issue of translation from one 'foreign' language to another is beyond the scope of this chapter to consider. See Boase-Beier (2006) for detailed discussion of the stylistics of translation.

References

Alfaro, M. J. M. (1996), 'Intertextuality: Origins and Development of the Concept', *Atlantis*, 18 (1/2): 268–85.

Armitage, S. (trans.) (2007), *Sir Gawain and the Green Knight*, London: Faber and Faber.

Attridge, D. (2004) Peculiar Language: Literature as Difference from the Renaissance to James Joyce, London: Routledge.

Auden, W. H. (1956), 'At the End of the Quest, Victory (Review of *The Return of the King* by J.R.R. Tolkien', *The New York Times*, 22 January 1956.

Bakhtin, M. (trans.) (1981), Caryl Emerson and Michael Holquist. *The Dialogic Imagination*, Austin, TX: University of Texas Press.

Bakhtin, M. (trans.) (1984), Hélène Iswolsky. *Rabelais and His World*, Bloomington, IN: Indiana University Press.

Bal, M. (ed.) (2004), *Narrative Theory: Critical Concepts in Literary and Cultural Studies*, London: Routledge.

Bardowell, M. R. (2009), 'J.R.R. Tolkien's Creative Ethic and Its Finnish Analogues', *Journal of the Fantastic in the Arts*, 20 (1): 91–109.
Barron, W. R. J. (ed.) (1998), *Sir Gawain and the Green Knight: Text and Facing Translation*, Manchester: Manchester University Press.
Barthes, R. (1957), *Mythologies*, Paris: Les Lettres Nouvelles.
Boase-Beier, J. (2006), *Stylistic Approaches to Translation*, London: Routledge.
Boroff, M. (trans.) (1967) *Sir Gawain and the Green Knight*, New York: Norton.
Boyd, B. (2009), *On the Origin of Stories: Evolution, Cognition and Fiction*, Cambridge, MA: Belknap Harvard.
Brooks, P. (1984), *Reading for the Plot: Design and Intention in Narrative*, New York: Random House.
Byatt, A. S. (1995), *The Djinn in the Nightingale's Eye*, London: Vintage.
Byatt, A. S. (1998), *Elementals: Stories of Fire and Ice*, London: Vintage.
Byatt, A. S. (2004), 'Happy Ever After', *The Guardian*, 2 January 2004. Available online: https://www.theguardian.com/books/2004/jan/03/sciencefictionfantasyandhorror.fiction (accessed 12 May 2019).
Carpenter, H. (ed.) (1981a), *The Letters of J.R.R. Tolkien*, Boston: Houghton Miffin.
Carpenter, H. (ed.) (1981b), *The Letters of J.R.R. Tolkien*, London: Mifflin Allen & Unwin.
Carpenter, H. (2000), *J.R.R. Tolkien: A Biography*, Boston, MA: Houghton Miffin.
Dawkins, R. (1976), *The Selfish Gene*, Oxford: Oxford University Press.
Flieger, V. (2002), *Splintered Light: Logos and Language in Tolkien's World*, Kent, OH: The Kent State University Press.
Flieger, V. (2005), *Interrupted Music: The Making of Tolkien's Mythology*, Kent, OH: Kent State University Press.
Fludernik, M. (1996), *Towards a 'Natural' Narratology*, London: Routledge.
Genette, G. (1983), *Narrative Discourse: An Essay in Method*, New York: Cornell University Press.
Genette, G. ([1987] 1997), *Paratexts: Thresholds of Interpretation*, trans. J. E. Letwin Cambridge: Cambridge University Press.
Goering, N. (2014), 'Lyg and Leuca: Elven-Latin, Archaic Languages and the Philology of Britain', *WoldCat*. 30 September 2015. 67–76.
Gooderson, S. (2005), 'Writing a Tale', *The Guardian*, 22 September. Available online: https://www.theguardian.com/books/2005/sep/22/fiction.asbyatt (accessed: 12 May 2019).
Gough, J. (1999), 'Tolkien's Creation Myth in *The Silmarillion* – Northern or Not?' *Children's Literature in Education*, 30: 1–8.
Herman, D. (2009), 'Narrative Ways of Worldmaking', in S. Heinan and R. Sommer (eds), *Narratology in the Age of Cross-disciplinary Research*, 71–87, Berlin: Walter De Gruyter.
Kermode, F. (2007), 'Who Has the Gall?' *London Review of Books*. 8 March. Available online: www.lrb.co.uk (accessed 8 August 2019).
Kocher, P. (1985), 'Ilúvatar and the Secret Fire', *Mythlore*, 12 (1): 36–7.

Kristeva, J. (1980), *Desire in Language: A Semiotic Approach*, New York: Columbia University Press.

Kristeva, J., Rey-Debove, J., and Umiker, D. (eds) (2010), *Essais de Sémiotique*, Berlin: De Gruyter Mouton.

Kullman, T. (2009), 'Intertextual Patterns in J.R.R. Tolkien's "The Hobbit" and "The Lord of the Rings"', *Nordic Journal of English Studies*, 8 (2): 37–56.

Lambrou, M. (2014), 'Narrative, Text and Time: Telling the Same Story Twice in the Oral Narrative Reporting of 7/7', *Language and Literature*, 23 (1): 32–48.

Lambrou, M. (2017), 'Dialogism in Journalistic Discourse: An Analysis of Ian McEwan's *Savagely Awoken*', in J. Mildorf and B. Thomas (eds), *Dialogue across Media*, Amsterdam: John Benjamins.

Lambrou, M. (2019), *Disnarration and the Unmentioned in Fiction*, Basingstoke: Palgrave.

Lanser, S. S. (1986), 'Towards a Feminist Narratology', *Style*, 20 (3): 341–63.

Leach, E. (1969), *Genesis as Myth*, London: Cape.

Lönnrot, E. (2008), *The Kalevala*, trans. Keith Bosley. Oxford: Oxford University Press.

Mason, J. (2014), 'Narrative', in P. Stockwell and S. Whiteley (eds), *The Cambridge Handbook of Stylistics*, 179–95, Cambridge: Cambridge University Press.

Mason, J. (2019), *Intertextuality in Practice*, Amsterdam: John Benjamins.

May, A. (2011), *Myth and Creative Writing: The Self-Renewing Song*, London: Routledge.

Mendlesohn, F. (2013), *Rhetorics of Fantasy*, Middletown, CT: Wesleyan University Press.

Moi, T. (ed.) (1986), *The Kristeva Reader*, New York: Columbia University Press.

Nash, W. (1986), 'Sounds and the Pattern of Poetics Meaning', *Linguistics and the Study of Literature*, Dutch Quarterly Review. Studies in Literature 1: 128–51.

O'Donoghue, B. (trans.) (2006) *Sir Gawain and the Green Knight*, London: Penguin.

Prince, G. (1974), *A Grammar of Stories: An Introduction*, Amsterdam: Mouton de Gruyter.

Prince, G. (2005), 'On a Postcolonial Narratology', in J. Phelan and Peter J. Rabinowitz (eds), *A Companion to Narrative Theory*, 372–81, London: Blackwell.

Propp, V. (1968), *The Morphology of the Folktale*, Austin, TX: University of Austin Press.

Riffaterre, M. (1987), 'Intertextual Unconscious', *Critical Enquiry. Special Issue: The Trial(s) of Psychoanalysis*, 13 (2): 371–85.

Riffaterre, M. (1990), 'Compulsory Reader Response: The Intertextual Drive', in M. Worton and J. Still (eds), *Intertextuality: Theories and Practices*, 56–78, Manchester: Manchester University Press.

Saussure, F. de. (1974), *Course in General Linguistics*, London: Collins.

Schauer, M., Schauer, M., Neuner, F., and Elbert, T. (2011), *Narrative Exposure Therapy: a Short-Term Treatment for Traumatic Stress Disorders*.

Shen, D. (2005), 'How Stylisticians Draw on Narratology: Approaches, Advantages and Disadvantages', *Style*, 39 (4): 381–95.

Simpson, P. (2004), *Stylistics: A Resource Book for Students*, London: Routledge.

Stanzel, F. K. (1986), *A Theory of Narrative*, Cambridge: Cambridge University Press.

Stockwell, P. (2002), *Cognitive Poetics: An Introduction*, London: Routledge.
Tiffin, J. (2006), 'Ice, Glass, Snow: Fairy Tale as Art and Metafiction in the Writings of A.S. Byatt', *Marvels and Tales: Journal of Fairy-Tale Studies*, 20 (1): 47–66.
Todorov, T., and Weinstein, A. (1969), 'Structural Analysis of Narrative', *NOVEL: A Forum on Fiction*, 3 (1): 70-6.
Tolkien, J. R. R. (1937), *The Hobbit, or There and Back Again*, London: George Allen and Unwin.
Tolkien, J. R. R. (1964), *Tree and Leaf*, London: George Allen and Unwin.
Tolkien, J. R. R. (1968), *The Lord of the Rings*, London: George Allen and Unwin.
Tolkien, J. R. R. (1977), *The Silmarillion*, Christopher Tolkien (ed.). London: George Allen and Unwin.
Tolkien, J.R.R. (1995), *Sir Gawain and the Green Knight*, London: The Clarendon Press.
Tolkien, J. R. R. (2010), 'On "The Kalevala," or Land of Heroes', *Tolkien Studies*, 7 (1): 246–61.
Tolkien, J. R. R. (2015), *The Story of Kullervo*, Veryln Flieger (ed.). London: Harper Collins.
Toolan, M. (2001), *Narrative: A Critical Linguistic Introduction*, London: Routledge.
West, R. (2004), 'Setting the Rocket Off in Story: The Kalevala as the Gem of Tolkien's Legendarium, in *Tolkien and the Invention of Myth: A Reader*, 285–94, Lexington, KY: The University Press of Kentucky..
Whittingham, E. A. (2007), *The Evolution of Tolkien's Mythology: A Study of the History of Middle-Earth*, Jefferson, MO: McFarland.

3

Adapting *Pride and Prejudice*: Stylistic choices as communicative acts

Anne Furlong

3.1 Introduction

Stylistic variation in retelling is not just a choice but a communicative act in its own right. If we examine the stylistic variations across a set of adaptations, or between adaptations and the source work, we see that stylistic differences give rise to implicatures which communicate the intended interpretation of the new work, as well as the relation of the new work to the source. An adaptor's stylistic choices are thus not merely aesthetic decisions: rather, they carry out a crucial communicative function. Whether an adaptation retells a narrative in ways that closely resemble the source, or comments on it, or repurposes the source to convey a radically distinct vision, stylistic variations provide critical contextual evidence and create powerful emotional and cognitive effects. In this chapter, I focus on Austen's *Pride and Prejudice*, since this work has been adapted within the same medium, as a mystery (*Death Comes to Pemberley*, by P. D. James) or as horror-comedy (*Pride and Prejudice and Zombies* by Seth Grahame-Smith), in other media (numerous film, radio, musical and television adaptations), and on other platforms (endless runner games such as *Stride and Prejudice* and card games such as *Marrying Mr Darcy* and its *Undead* expansion). I demonstrate how specific stylistic choices – including the selection, reshaping and retelling of narrative elements – help achieve the adaptor's communicative purpose.

3.2 Adaptation and retelling

Adaptations present canonical cases of retelling: by definition, an adaptation re-presents pre-existing intellectual content in a form or mode that differs to some degree from the source. However, much of the work on retelling narratives has emerged from work on first- and second language acquisition and literacy and in psychological studies of memory and retention, rather than from adaptation studies, which has been dogged by questions of fidelity, by complications of taxonomy and by the status of multimodal or transmedial adaptations.[1] In this section, I begin with some remarks on what constitutes retelling; I follow these by noting some overlap with adaptation. Finally, I make the case that any adaptation recognized as such[2] is an independent act of communication, regardless of its resemblance to the source.

Marsh (2007) quotes Gauld and Stevenson (1967: 40), who note that 'most people who retell a story are unlikely to care very much whether the story they retell is the same, detail by detail, as the story they originally heard' (2007: 16). The degree of 'accuracy' is affected by the communicative purpose of retelling; subjects who retold personal events to entertain or to gain sympathy tended to exaggerate or distort, while those aiming at informative retellings tended to omit material they deemed irrelevant (2007). Moreover, retellings varied depending on the audience; subjects addressing peers included more contextual information ('links to world knowledge' (2007: 17)) and evaluations than when speaking to the experimenters. Narratives retold to 'attentive audiences' were longer than those delivered to inattentive ones; narratives that aimed to entertain employed the historical present tense and included 'fewer story events' (2007: 17). 'Different ways of talking', Marsh argues, 'have consequences' (2007: 18) and 'impose structure on events' which 'can guide (and bias) later retrieval of events' (2007: 19).

While primarily concerned about the effects of retelling on accuracy of recall, Marsh notes the influence of audience, communicative situation and, above all, purpose. In the same way, stylistic (and other) choices in an adaptation are also determined by the adaptor's communicative purpose. If an adaptation's resemblance to a prior work is unrecognized, the audience will interpret the (new) work as they would any film, book, story, song or drama. If, on the other hand, the new work is recognized *as* an adaptation, it encourages the audience to entertain assumptions *from* or *about* the source work as part of the interpretive process. That relationship makes the adaptor's stylistic choices more salient and factors in to the audience's evaluation of *either* the source *or* the new work.

Audiences often anticipate that adaptations will retell source works, that is, communicate a close version of the manifestly intended interpretation of the source in a new mode. The more devoted audiences are to the source, the higher their standards of fidelity (literal and interpretive) and the lower their tolerance for any disparity or change. Thus Martin Amis takes Robert Leonard's 1940 film adaptation of *Pride and Prejudice* '(based on a script by Aldous Huxley, among others)' to task, calling it 'cold proof that any tampering will reduce the original to emollient inconsequentiality' (Amis 1996: 32). He is no more complimentary of the 1995 BBC TV miniseries, focusing on small changes of dialogue and arguing that 'these tiny precisions, these niceties, are the atoms that constitute Jane Austen's universe' (Amis 1996: 32). I argue (Furlong 2012: 183) that 'ultimately his aversion is rooted in the sense that the series does not present "his" Jane Austen' and that '[a]daptations which fall egregiously short in critics' estimation ... typically fail as representations of the *viewer's interpretation* of the source'.

Adaptations can and do accomplish much more than merely represent the generally accepted reception of a work or represent that view in a new medium. They may create new effects on the basis of the source text, or draw out and develop previously underdeveloped aspects or effects, or replicate the effect of the source work on their audience. A radio drama adaptation of *Pride and Prejudice* may achieve relevance by means of the actors' performances, by the use of sound effects, and through the presentation of narrative information as voice-over or in dialogue. The audience may find their views of the novel confirmed, expanded or altered, but audiences also look to identify the adaptor's communicative purpose, determine its acceptability and judge the final results accordingly.

3.3 Adaptation and stylistic choice

It is often assumed that adaptions are secondary to the work on which they are based, or on which they comment, or which they re-present. But as Hogan (2005), discussing Austen's influence on the twentieth-century Japanese writer Nogami Yaeko, notes, 'it is the *second* author or artist who has agency, not the first' (2005: 79, emphasis added).[3] That is, we ought to be concerned less with 'origin and source' (2005: 79) and more with the 'long chain of connections' between them (2005: 80). A similar shift, towards the adaptor's communicative purpose or intention (and away from questions of fidelity or reproduction), has yet to take place in adaptation studies. Standard treatments of adaptation, even as they resist fidelity as an evaluative criterion, return time and again to comparisons of source and adapted texts. The assumption underpinning much work in adaptation studies is that the new work is *at least* parasitic on the existing one so that adaptations are in some measure bound by the intentions, forms and effects of their sources. I do not accept this position; instead, I propose that an adaptor has no duty to 'respect' the source, except as this serves their communicative purpose.

It is true that many commercially produced adaptations (film, stage, television, limited series on a streaming service) measure their success (and are measured by their audiences) by the degree to which they create effects that are similar or analogous to those induced by audiences' encounters with the source.[4] Producers, writers and directors undertake fine-grained calculations intended to identify margins, not of error, but of tolerance: how far can they depart from the known or anticipated before their target audience rejects the new version? Film scripts must compress what the novels provide, though mise-en-scène can compensate for textual omissions by conveying critical information through visual images and metaphors, composition and cinematography; limited series may preserve more of the dialogue and action of the source, but the demands of continuity may simply bore the viewer. Above all, audiences may bring with them a strong expectation of similarity between the source and the adapted work (even if that 'source' is itself an earlier adaptation),[5] along with another, unstated and often unsuspected second assumption: the anticipation of amplification. In these circumstances, when retelling is anticipated, it is amplification, rather than fidelity or similarity, which functions as the criterion by which adaptations are typically judged.

From a relevance theoretic perspective, adaptations cannot achieve relevance simply by producing the same set of effects as the original in a new setting, medium or version: they must yield effects that could not be produced by the source. Some effects are created by the medium itself. So, for example, movies and plays provide rich visual, aural and somatic evidence for the intended interpretation in the form of costumes, setting, score, acting, mise-en-scène and so on. Novelizations of films supply detailed narrative commentary, authorial intrusions, supplementary dialogue or description, which complement the inescapable exteriority of film and stage with insights into psychological or emotional states which could not otherwise be perceived. Graphic novels, unlike stage or screen, are not temporally constrained; readers can abandon the forward movement of the written word or the moving image. Static images, unlike words, can be 'read' in any order, can be dwelt on at length and lack a grammar.[6] If we extend the category of adaptation to include fanfic, then a new work may address what the adaptor regards as deficiencies in the source. Thus, adaptations provide evidence for the intended interpretation of the new work that exploits its resemblance or debt to the earlier text. Irrespective of the final form, all of these adaptations constitute communicative acts independent of the source, unrestricted to or by the intended interpretation of the earlier text.

3.4 Adaptations of *Pride and Prejudice*

Austen's social comedy has provided the basis for a bewildering array of adaptations in every conceivable mode and medium. Ward (1996: 18–19) notes that the novel retains 'much of the moral force of the conventional romance, even as it moves away from stereotypical characterization'. Structurally as well as aesthetically and emotionally, *Pride and Prejudice* provides a well-bounded set of features that lend themselves readily to retelling and reworking. The outward-looking narrative of Austen's text, its free indirect reporting of motivation and its liberal provision of authorial attitude supply ample material for adaptors to compress, select and revise, confident of their interpretive choices.

In the following sections, I review a number of adaptations of *Pride and Prejudice*. Some, such as the 1940 (directed by Robert Leonard) and 2005 (directed by Joe Wright) feature films, emphasize certain assumptions and downplay others, challenging our views, perhaps encouraging us to understand the source novel as historically and culturally bound. Others, such as the 1995 BBC miniseries, confirm or amplify existing interpretations, communicating an expanded but otherwise unchanged reading of the text. Still others, such as the horror-comedy novel *Pride and Prejudice and Zombies*, demarcate a markedly distinct variation, presenting new works that recognizably and ostensively incorporate significant elements of the source. But though adaptations are clearly in *some* relationship to the source work, we should not always look to the source as the standard against which to measure the new text. So, for instance, an adaptation that endorses, critiques or amends a source work directs the audience to review the *source* in this expanded context. By contrast, an adaptation that exploits the structural or textual or literary components of the source encourages the audience to employ their knowledge of the source in order to arrive at the manifestly intended interpretation of the *new* work.

We can see how this plays out if we contrast abridgement with wholesale reimagining. Ollie Depew's 1952 abridged version helps unprepared readers – here, 'the less able high-school reader' (Groombridge 1952: 382) – appreciate the source novel more completely. Presuming his readers bring little or no previous experience with them, Depew minimizes the cognitive effort demanded by Austen's precise, elegant prose and thereby increases the likelihood that his readers will move on to the complete novel. His book is thus intended to be evaluated against the standard set by Austen's novel. On the other hand, the vlog series *The Lizzy Bennet Diaries* exploits the cultural capital of Austen's novel; viewers familiar with the source will appreciate the writer's inventiveness in discovering twenty-first-century equivalents for nineteenth-century characters. While Depew's adaptation endorses and illuminates the earlier work, in the case of the YouTube series, the source contributes to our enjoyment of the *newer* text. In the sections that follow, I discuss at more length how specific stylistic choices work to achieve the adaptor's communicative purpose.

3.5 Adaptations as *commentaries*

I have argued that an adaptation may influence our view of the source. Looser (2017) argues that our interpretation of *Pride and Prejudice* and particularly our opinions of the heroine have altered significantly over the past century. Adaptations, she writes, have 'shifted the focus of the reader-viewer away from envisioning the plot as centered on the admirable rebellion and growth of a witty, saucy heroine' and towards 'a sexy, misunderstood hero' (2017: 99). In early-twentieth-century stage dramatizations, duologues or excepts, she shows, 'Darcy seems almost beside the point, a fortunate afterthought, a just dessert [*sic*] for Elizabeth's cleverness, self-assertion, and confidence' (2017: 96–7). Olivier, Firth and MacFadyen originated, refined and confirmed this new Darcy; all three men deliver remarkably similar performances (when adjusted for preferred styles and cultural values), lending Byronic shade to a Regency aristocrat.

Both the 1940 and 2005 film adaptations establish Darcy as the focus of the narrative, and both put emphasis on courtship and marriage. While the prominence of the marriage plot is not surprising – the novel ends with a double wedding – the films' relentless emphasis on the importance of mating well represents a diminution of the novel's broader concerns as a *bildungsroman*: after all, in Austen it is Elizabeth's progress we follow, not Darcy's. The distinctions between the two films are largely superficial. The 1940 film truncated the plot, added new scenes and was set some fifty years after Austen's novel; the 2005 movie compresses the plot line, respects the novel's setting and interpolates new material. However, their respective treatments of Elizabeth stand in stark contrast, and it is here, rather than in decisions about costume and hairstyles, that the stylistic decisions serve distinctly different communicative purposes.

Adaptors working in commercial film must balance commercial and aesthetic requirements and so are acutely attuned to cultural preferences. The MGM film (1940), coming at the end of the Depression and at a time of increased discretionary spending, presented women 'in terms of consumption' (Brosh 2000: 148). However, 'women are both subjects and objects' in 'commercial interaction'

(2000: 148), which goes beyond 'attitudes to dress' (as 'markers of character and moral discernment' (2000: 150)) and towards the commodification that dominates the marriage market, for both men and women. To communicate a narrative about consumption, about romance and about men as objects of female competition, the film simultaneously 'represents glamour in its *mise-en-scène* and costumes' and 'satirizes those who seek money through marriage' (2000: 157). The stylistic choices do not merely reflect this dual purpose: they achieve it.

The Universal Studios adaptation, released in 2005, reframes the narrative with scenes that emphasize women as resisting, independent characters. However, in casting a twenty-year-old actress as Elizabeth, the producers hoped to appeal to a specific demographic: young women, certainly, but specifically audiences captivated by the 2003 *Pirates of the Caribbean* movie (directed by Gore Verbinski). That earlier film established Knightley not only as a bankable actress but also as a recognizable type: a woman representing contemporary values – particularly with respect to romance – in an historical context. I suggest that the film deliberately sets out to convey the contradictions within which twenty-first-century women operate. The contrast between the grubby chaos of the Bennet household and the eye-popping splendour of Chatsworth House (standing in for Pemberley) allows the film-maker to present the frankly materialistic benefits of marriage as earned (and therefore virtuous), rather than bestowed (and therefore undeserved). Elizabeth's petulance (or spirit) and sexual hunger (or self-directed desire) are attitudes and behaviours that are culturally valued in young and attractive twenty-first-century women, and through them she achieves a marriage which is presented almost as an apotheosis. The stylistic choices of the adaptors in casting, writing and mise-en-scène help convey this internally contradictory but seductive version of the source. Both films encourage us to reassess our reception of the source work and invite us to view the source as a product of its historical and cultural period and perhaps to undertake a stern re-evaluation of our own.

3.6 Adaptations as *illuminations*

An adaptation may amplify an existing interpretation. While in some cases, the interpretation communicated by the new version may usurp earlier views, it is more often the case (especially in transmedial adaptations) that the variant reshapes rather than supplants the interpretation altogether. In particular, when a text is presented in a different medium, such as film, television or theatre, a vast array of new contextual assumptions is made available. Importantly, these assumptions supply precisely those details which the writer leaves to the reader's imagination, details which performance or visual adaptations cannot do without. In fact, audiences anticipate this kind of illumination, and tend to evaluate the success of an adaptation on the degree to which these details line up with previous implicatures, or complement them or, more rarely, overturn and eliminate them.

Pride and Prejudice has been adapted for television a number of times, but the BBC TV series, aired in 1995, has eclipsed virtually all others. The lavish budget supported a six-hour running time, allowing Andrew Davies, the screenwriter, to retain much of the dialogue more or less intact. The producers went to extraordinary lengths to achieve historical accuracy, from costumes and sets to social niceties appropriate to the time and the characters' class. In keeping with the trends noted by Looser and others, Darcy occupies a narrative position of outsized importance and brooding sexuality. Elizabeth, in contrast to the feather-headed manhunter of the 1940 movie, is written to appeal to then-contemporary sensibilities while preserving some degree of historically appropriate demeanour.

Davies made no attempt to include the narrative voice (using, say, a voice-over), instead 'supplementing' the script 'with new dialogue in a convincingly Austenesque style' (Sørbø 2018: 529), and dramatized authorial comments by exploiting the communicative possibilities of cinema. So, for example, in the assembly when Darcy snubs Elizabeth, Austen writes:

> Darcy walked off; and Elizabeth remained with no very cordial feelings towards him. She told the story however with great spirit among her friends; for she had a lively, playful disposition, which delighted in anything ridiculous.
>
> (Austen 1813 [1938]: 18)

In this scene in the series, Elizabeth is shot in close-up for part of Darcy's remarks, and her 'no very cordial feelings' are conveyed by the expressions that cross the actress's face over five or six seconds of screen time. Hurt, embarrassment, disgust and shame give way to a small, sly smile that threatens to spill over into audible laughter. She rises – in this version, Darcy does not move – and crosses in front of him, her smile broadening. Darcy notes the smile and follows her with his eyes as she moves off screen. Within three seconds the sound of two women laughing rises over the music, and we are supposed to imagine that she is telling the story 'with great spirit'. Darcy appears mildly abashed or perhaps puzzled and put out. The camera cuts to a medium shot of Elizabeth and Charlotte in conversation; their renewed laughter and Darcy's reaction – he looks unsure of himself and moves hastily away in the opposite direction – strongly suggest that he, at least, feels he is being made to look 'ridiculous'. The true innovation here is to show Darcy's awareness of the offence he has given and of the spectacle he has made of himself; in the novel, Darcy's first recognition of Elizabeth's worth occurs a little while later, when he makes a series of 'mortifying' discoveries about her beautiful eyes, her 'pleasing form' and her 'easy playfulness'. Indeed, when Elizabeth roundly rejects his proposal of marriage, he betrays, not consciousness but 'anger', 'incredulity' and 'mortification'.

Most of these alterations are relatively subtle, but along with the compelling mise-en-scène they amplify existing interpretations with a wealth of visual and aural detail. But they also confirm the status of the source work as a masterpiece by demonstrating its continued relevance and its power to engage numerous, diverse audiences. Along with illustrations, abridgements and dramatized excerpts, these adaptations in part or whole populate Austen's fictional worlds and establish their décor. The direction of influence is back towards the source, rather than outwards towards the adaptation; the communicative act is an adjustment of, rather than a comment on, our understanding of the source text. The stylistic choices work to create the effects the adaptor is manifestly aiming for.

3.7 Adaptations as *original works*

In some cases, the adaptation exploits aspects of the source to create a variation that is intended to stand on its own merits. Here, similarities between characters, setting, plot, dialogue and so forth provide crucial premises for the context in which the audience is manifestly intended to process the new work. Three very different adaptations suggest the range of possibilities: P. D. James's *Death Comes to Pemberley* (2011a), Seth Grahame-Smith's *Pride and Prejudice and Zombies* (2009) and Helen Fieldings's *Bridget Jones's Diary* (1996). The first layers a murder mystery over a sequel, the second replaces parts of Austen's text with references to fighting the undead, and the third extracts characters, plot points and thematic elements in the service of a romantic farce. In truth, none of these versions, with the possible exception of Fielding's *Bridget Jones*, is likely to affect readers' interpretations of the source work; however, readers or viewers (all three have been reworked as films or mini-series) familiar with Austen may find their experience of the adaptations enriched by assumptions carried from the earlier to the later texts.

James's murder-mystery sequel is the weakest of the three. Despite the book's generally favourable reviews, one critic, reviewing the television mini-series made from it, commented that the cinematic version gave James's 'story space to unfold in a way' that the book had not (Crompton 2013), indicating that the devices and techniques of performance and film made the thinness of the text painfully clear. Crompton refers to the 'Rolls-Royce quality' of the 'period drama', its 'stately homes, lakes with fountains, verdant woods' (2013), which amplify James's novel. Above all, she focuses on the performances – Rebecca Front's 'comic relief', Trevor Eve's 'gruffly malign magistrate', Matthew Rhys's 'fierce-faced Darcy' (2011b) – suggesting that it is to these, and not to James, that she owes her understanding of these characters. She admits that Anna Maxwell Martin, though not 'the Elizabeth Bennet of my imagination', 'captures the heroine's key quality: her intelligence' (2011b). Most tellingly, however, she concludes that this Darcy and Elizabeth were neither 'the characters conjured up by P. D. James's nor 'Austen's creations', but 'honourable incarnations' (2011b).

Grahame-Smith's *Pride and Prejudice and Zombies* takes advantage of the popularity of zombie fiction in the 2010s but rises above the level of pastiche through deft stylistic touches and effective editing. Compare the following passages:

(a) <u>Her mind was less difficult to develop. She was a woman of mean understanding, little information, and uncertain temper. When she was discontented, she fancied herself nervous.</u> The business of her life was to get her daughters married; its solace was visiting and news. (Austen 1813 [1938]: 13)

<u>Her mind was less difficult to develop. She was a woman of mean understanding, little information, and uncertain temper. When she was discontented, she fancied herself nervous.</u> And when she was nervous – as she was nearly all the time since the first outbreak of the strange plague in her youth – she sought solace in the comfort of the traditions which now seemed mere trifles to others. (Grahame-Smith 2009: 12)

(b) <u>Lady Catherine was extremely indignant on the marriage of her nephew;</u> and as she gave way to all the genuine frankness of her character in her reply to the letter which announced its arrangement, she sent him language so very abusive, especially of Elizabeth, that for some time <u>all intercourse was at an end</u>. (Austen 1813 [1938]: 308)

<u>Lady Catherine was extremely indignant on the marriage of her nephew;</u> and her reply to its arrangement came not in written form, but in the

form of an attack on Pemberley by five-and-ten of her ladyship's ninjas. For some time after this was thwarted, <u>all intercourse was at an end</u>. (Grahame-Smith 2009: 320)

Grahame-Smith scrupulously imitates Austen's style in the interpolated or altered sections. But as the intended effect is created by the jarring incongruity of a zombie thriller embedded in a Regency comedy, only a *similarity* of style is necessary. Nothing in *Zombies* is likely to send us to the source text with the expectation of enriching, amplifying or altering our views; instead, our familiarity with Austen's novel supplies the adaptor with vital contextual premises. The stylistic choice – to relate shocking and inappropriate events in a close version of Austen's style – communicates, among other things, the relationship Grahame-Smith sets up between the source and the new text.

Helen Fielding reimagined *Pride and Prejudice* as the 1996 novel *Bridget Jones's Diary*. Here I discuss not the book, but the film adaptation (2001). The movie is noteworthy for its intimate relation with the 1995 BBC mini-series. Andrew Davies, the screenwriter for the series, was one of the credited writers for *Diary*, and Colin Firth, whose performance as Darcy set a new high-water mark,[7] played 'Mark Darcy'. This adaptation, then, encourages the viewer to use not one but two pre-existing works for vital contextual information. The expanded context allows the audience to compare the variations, to appreciate Fielding's choices and – if they accept the stylistic variations – to arrive at the manifestly intended interpretation and experience the intended aesthetic and intellectual effects of a romantic farce.

These three works could well be considered high-achieving fan fiction, which typically creates an immersive experience by projecting the writer or reader into the world of the source text where they interact intimately with the characters.[8] James wrote her sequel for the 'self-indulgent' pleasure 'of revisiting once again the world of Longbourn and Pemberley' and finding 'fresh insights and delights' (2011a). Allen Grove claims that *Zombies*, far from being a 'travesty', 'makes explicit' what Austen's novel implies: that the world of 'aristocratic gentility' 'was under attack … by larger and sometimes more violent and terrifying social and political forces' (Grahame-Smith 2009: 331). This pastiche takes advantage of a work long out of copyright, exploits the cachet of a 'towering work' of classic literature (Grahame-Smith 2009: 333) and capitalizes on the current upswing in horror-comedies featuring the undead. Finally, Fielding examines the complexities and challenges facing young working women at the end of the twentieth century. Within the constraints of the stereotypical romance novel, she chronicles the emotional and psychological stresses facing women at a time of rapid social change. She finds comedy in situations of acute humiliation, following Austen's example rather than attempting to replicate her accomplishment. Indeed, Page (2007) treats *Bridget Jones's Diary* from a feminist narratological perspective without any mention of Austen at all. Instead, she uses Hoey's (2001) notion of 'culturally popular, predictable patterns of text organisation' (2007: 99) to support her argument that 'the teleogical structure' of Fielding's work 'does not suggest feminist emancipation' (2007: 98).

3.8 Alternative platforms

The rise of new media has produced intriguing formal experiments. Pemberley Digital's YouTube series *The Lizzy Bennet Diaries* is 'purported to be the vlog (video diary) of a modern day Lizzie Bennet' (Russo 2018: 513), and though the series demonstrates a 'reverence for canonical female-authored texts' (2018: 518), viewers are directed not to Austen's novel, but to other novels by the series writers (2018: 519). *Stride and Prejudice*, an endless runner game in which a pixelated Lizzie Bennet runs and jumps across platforms of scrolling text, appeared in 2013. And the role-playing card game *Marrying Mr Darcy* (with 'Undead Extension' for fans of Grahame-Smith's adaptation) pits up to eight players in fierce competition for six suitors. The focus of the *Diaries* is on finding contemporary equivalents for the characters, relationships and tribulations recounted in Austen's work. Someone playing *Stride and Prejudice* is expected to read the entire novel on a small screen while a tiny figure leaps and tumbles. *Marrying Mr Darcy* provides some contextual information about eighteenth-century social mores and attitudes to assist competitors; in a concession to modern sensibilities, Old Maids can win the game under certain circumstances. These adaptations, despite their ingenuity, fall into what Russo calls 'the plethora of Austen spin-offs and sequels engage[d] in the commodification process' (2018: 516); none of them sheds much additional light on either Austen's novel or the process of adapting it.

3.9 Conclusion

Adaptations are communicative acts in their own right, forms of retelling in which stylistic choices are not incidental or ornamental, but crucial to achieving the adaptor's communicative aims, particularly when the source work is highly influential. As Halsey (2019) notes, Austen's influence is global. Adaptations and retellings of *Pride and Prejudice* are beyond counting: the story of a small set of upper-middle-class country families in Regency England is familiar to tens of millions of people in dozens of languages. The novel's appeal is due as much to its clever, versatile, indefatigable adaptors as to Austen herself. Their stylistic choices are crucial to communicating their attitude towards the source and to shaping the audience's experience. The complexity of the relationship between source, retelling, adaptation, reception and interpretation demonstrates both the robustness of the source work and the resources of audiences – readers, viewers and gamers.

Notes

1. Standard works in the field include Bluestone (1957), McFarlane (1996), Cahir (2006) and Hutcheon (2006), though these deal primarily with the adaptation of novels or texts into film. Leitch (2003) lays out some of the taxonomic and theoretical challenges facing the discipline, and Chatman (1980) draws attention to the limits of transmedial adaptations. Many theorists acknowledge Dryden (1913) as the seminal work on translation as explicating fundamental relationships between source and adaptation. For an overview of recent developments in adaptation studies, see Albrecht-Crane and Cutchins (2013).
2. I will expand on this remark in Section 3.4. I argue that audiences treat adaptations differently than they do 'original' or source works, but to do so they must recognize that a text is adapting (or responding to) a previous work.
3. Hogan quotes Baxandall's insightful remark about 'influence' in art criticism (1985: 58–9); he points to 'its wrong-headed grammatical prejudice about who is the agent and who is the patient … If one says that X influenced Y … one is saying that X did something to Y rather than that Y did something to X' (Hogan 2005: 79–80). I will return to this notion in my discussion of the 'directionality' of adaptation in Section 3.5.
4. Newell (2013: 78) points out that '[w]hile most major works on adaptation have dismissed fidelity as a matter of evaluation, analogies between source texts and adaptations continue to direct the reading and interpretation of adaptations'.
5. Looser (2017) demonstrates the degree to which Olivier (1940) set the template for the Darcys who came after him, as Firth (1995) did two generations later. She points out, moreover, that even Olivier was following a model set out by previous actors on stage and so was engaged – as Firth was later – in direct competition with their portrayals with a critical audience prepared for a particular interpretation and presentation of the character.

6   By 'grammar', I mean syntactic order, including deep and surface structures. Sentences must conform to the syntax of the language, including word order, inflections and so on. Visual imagery lacks a syntax, despite loose talk of the grammar of, say, paintings or photographs. This is not to say that composition is unimportant; it is instead to assert that composition, unlike language, is unrestrained by mental or psychological structures such as morphology.

7   Firth's Darcy is in the mould of Olivier's, but he is also a quintessentially millennial masculine hero, leavening Olivier's dour hauteur with barely concealed sensitivity. *Diary* gave Firth the opportunity to parody and thereby diminished his performance; against the famous (or notorious) swimming scene of the series, the writers set a preposterous fight that spills into and then out of a crowded Greek restaurant to a disco score.

8   Thomas (2011) identifies 'the centrality of metaleptic transgressions of diegetic levels, especially where the fans' extradiegetic desires are allowed to intrude or impose on the storyworld' (11).

References

Albrecht-Crane, C., and Cutchins, D. (eds) (2013), *Adaptation Studies: New Approaches*, Madison, New Jersey: Fairleigh Dickinson University Press.

Amis, M. (1996), 'Jane's World', *The New Yorker* (8 January): 31–5.

Austen, J. (1938 [1813]), *Pride and Prejudice*. Illustrated by Helen Binyon. Harmondsworth, UK: Penguin.

Austen, J., and S. Grahame-Smith (2009), *Pride and Prejudice and Zombies*, Philadelphia: Quirk Books.

Barcas, J. (2013), 'Pow!: Marvel Comics Adapts Jane Austen', *Eighteenth-Century Life*, 37 (2): 120–5.

Baxandall, M. (1985), *Patterns of Intention: On the Historical Explanation of Pictures*, New Haven and London: Yale University Press.

Bluestone, G. (1957), *Novels into Film: A Critical Study*, Baltimore: The Johns Hopkins Press.

Bridget Jones's Diary (2001), [Film] Dir. Sharon Maguire, UK: Working Title Films.

Brosh, L. (2000), 'Consuming Women: The Representation of Women in the 1940 Adaptation of *Pride and Prejudice*', *Quarterly Review of Film & Video*, 17 (2): 147–59.

Brown, L. (1986), '*Pride* and Prejudice by David Pownall (review), '*Theatre Journal*, 38 (3): 362–3.

Cahir, L. (2006), *Literature into Film: Theory and Practical Approaches*, Jefferson, NC: McFarland & Company, Inc., Publishers.

Chatman, S. (1980). 'What Novels Can Do That Films Can't (and Vice Versa), *Critical Inquiry*, 7 (1): 121–40.

Crompton, S. (2013), '*Death Comes to Pemberley:* Won Round by an Older and Wiser Lizzie', *The Telegraph*, 29 December. Available online: https://www.telegraph.co.uk/culture/tvandradio/10541753/Death-Comes-to-Pemberley-won-round-by-an-older-and-wiser-Lizzie.html (accessed 29 April 2019).

Dryden, J. (1913), *The Poems of John Dryden*, J. Sargeaunt (ed), London, New York: Oxford University Press.

Fielding, H. (1996), *Bridget Jones's Diary*, London: Picador.

Furlong, A. (2012), '"It's Not Quite What I Had in Mind": Adaptation, Faithfulness, and Interpretation', *Journal of Literary Semantics*, 41 (2): 175–91.

Gauld, A., and Stephenson, G. M. (1967), 'Some Experiments Related to Bartlett's Theory of Remembering', *British Journal of Psychology*, 58: 39–49.

Groombridge, A. C. (1952), '*Pride and Prejudice* by Jane Austen and Ollie Depew (review),' *The Clearing House*, 26 (6): 378, 382.

Halsey, K. (2019), 'Jane Austen's Global Influence', in *Oxford Research Encyclopedia of Literature*, Oxford: Oxford University Press. Available online: https://oxfordre.com/literature/view/10.1093/acrefore/9780190201098.001.0001/acrefore-9780190201098-e-279 (accessed 25 April 2019).

Hoey, M. (2001), *Textual Interaction: An Introduction to Written Discourse Analysis*, Abingdon and New York: Routledge.

Hogan, E. J. (2005), 'Beyond Influence: The Literary Sisterhood of Nogami Yaeko and Jane Austen', *U.S.-Japan Women's Journal*, 29: 77–98.

Hutcheon, L. (2006), *A Theory of Adaptation*, London: Routledge.

James, P. D. (2011a), *Death Comes to Pemberley*, New York: Random House Limited.

James, P. D. (2011b), 'PD James on *Death Comes to Pemberley*', *The Telegraph*, 4 November 2011. Available online: https://www.telegraph.co.uk/culture/books/authorinterviews/8870688/PD-James-on-Death-Comes-to-Pemberley.html (accessed 27 April 2019).

Kalmbach, J. R. (1986), 'Getting at the Point of Retellings', *Journal of Reading*, 29 (4): 326–33.

Leitch, T. (2003), 'Twelve Fallacies in Contemporary Adaptation Theory', *Criticism*, 45 (2): 149–71.

Limbacher, J. L. (1981), 'Feature Films to Teach Literature', *The English Journal*, 70 (1): 86–8.

Looser, D. (2017), *The Making of Jane Austen*, Baltimore: The Johns Hopkins University Press.

Marsh, E. J. (2007), 'Retelling Is Not the Same as Recalling: Implications for Memory', *Current Directions in Psychological Science*, 16 (1): 16–20.

McFarlane, B. (1996), *Novel to Film. An Introduction to the Theory of Adaptation*, Oxford: Clarendon Press.

Nagle, C. C. (2018), 'The Problem of the Jane Austen Musical', *Women's Writing*, 25 (4): 499–511.

Newell, K. (2013), '"We're Off to See the Wizard" (Again): Oz Adaptations and the Matter of Fidelity', in C. Albrecht-Crane and D. Cutchins (eds), *Adaptation Studies: New Approaches*, 78–96, Lanham, MD: Fairleigh Dickinson University Press.

Page, R. (2007), 'ced*Bridget Jones's Diary* and Feminist Narratology', in M. Lambrou and P. Stockell (eds), *Contemporary Stylistics*, 93–105, London: Continuum.

Pirates of the Caribbean (2003), [Film], Dir. Gore Verbinsky, USA: Walt Disney Pictures.

Pride and Prejudice (1940), [Film], Dir. Robert Leonard, USA: MGM Pictures.

Pride and Prejudice (1995), [TV series], Dir. Simon Langton, UK: BBC-TV.

Pride and Prejudice (2005), [Film], Dir. Joe Wright, USA: Focus Features.

Russo, S. (2018), 'Austen Approved: Pemberley Digital and the Transmedia Commodification of Jane Austen', *Women's Writing*, 25 (4): 512–24.

Sørbø, M. N. (2018), 'Interpretations of Jane Austen's Irony on Screen and in Translations: A Comparison of Some Samples', *Women's Writing*, 25 (4): 525–35.

Su, B., and Green, H. (2012–13), *The Lizzie Bennet Diaries*, [Web series], Los Angeles: Pemberley Digital.

Stride and Prejudice (2014), [Videogame], Dev. C. Fisher, USA: No Crusts Interactive, LLC.

Svanoe, E. (2013), *Marrying Mr Darcy: The* Pride and Prejudice *Card Game*.

Thomas, B. (2011), 'What Is Fanfiction and Why Are People Saying Such Nice Things about It?' *Storyworlds: A Journal of Narrative Studies*, 3: 1–24.

Ward, M. C. (1996), 'Adaptations in Nineteenth-Century Closure', *The Journal of the Midwest Language Association*, 29 (1): 15–31.

Wright, A. (1975), 'Jane Austen Adapted', *Nineteenth-Century Fiction*, 30 (3): 421–53.

4

Narrative retelling in McGahern's 'Swallows': The intensifying power of repetition and return

Michael Toolan

4.1 Introduction: Acceptable and unacceptable repeats

My chapter explores writers' recourse to retelling in the course of a single narrative, John McGahern's story 'Swallows', and the contribution such retellings may have to a story's effect. I will argue that intratextual retelling in literary narrative usually avoids the charge of redundancy since it comes with change of some kind: minimally, of tense and pronouns, as when direct speech is retold as indirect speech, but often also of speaker or tone or perspective or interpretation of the thing (re-)told. As a result it is a form of repetition that is welcome and immersive rather than egregious and irritating. Retellings also inevitably cause a reader to view the first telling in a new light, now more palpably 'just one version': the light may cause us to understand the first telling (and the first teller, if identified) differently. And now both tellings (or all, if more than two) contribute to the delineation of the narrative situation.

The first choral item of Bach's *St John Passion* begins with an intense and building thirty-six-bar orchestral introduction, followed by the first choral item, *Herr, unser Herrscher (Lord, our ruler ... Show us, through Your passion, That You, the true Son of God ... Have become transfigured!)*. And when this opening appeal is completed (it takes close to six minutes), the orchestral introduction is played through once more and almost the entire first choral item is sung through again too.

I cite this simply as one example of the kind of immediate repeating that is remarkably common in classical music, particularly of the pre-Romantic period, thus before 1800 roughly. This is the tyrannical power of the double dots, at the end of a section or movement, licensing a return Da Capo, back to the top, to go through the whole thing a second time – sometimes but not always with different performance dynamics or tempo. This is a kind of intra-compositional repeating, a presenting again, which in some other temporal art forms would be unconscionable. Imagine going to a production of *Hamlet* (or *La Traviata*, or *Les Sylphides*) where at the completion of Act 1 Scene 1 the performers took a moment to catch their collective breath … and then started again from the very beginning: *Who's there? / Nay, answer me: stand, and unfold yourself. / Long live the king! / Bernardo? / He.*

In music, under certain conditions, repetition not merely of motifs but of whole sections of a work is not only permitted but 'natural' and unremarkable. In most literary narrative forms – including narrative poetry, plays, stories and novels – such wholesale repeating of a scene or episode, whether adjacent or after intervening material, would usually be regarded as intolerable and aesthetically absurd. The repeated choric stanza in ballads and similar forms is scarcely an exception, being reflective of the ballad's roots in music. As for folk and fairy tales these too, despite their copious recurrence of structure and oral-formulaic fondness for repetition at the level of the phrase, eschew full repetition at the level of scene or episode. In 'Goldilocks', each bowl of porridge, chair and bed is different from the other two, as is each bear; there are similar recurrences without full repetition – no retelling – in 'The Elves and the Shoemaker'. The night the elves make one pair of shoes has to precede the night they make two pairs: this is the kind of sequential progression that full episode-retelling could undermine.

Intratextual retelling can be expected only quite sparingly in verbal narratives and in well-recognized conditions. In the course of evaluation, for example, a detail may be repeated two or three times, for emphasis and appreciation – not fundamentally different from what were once called Action Replays at sports stadia and in TV sports broadcasts. A goal is scored, and the recording of how this transpired is replayed to viewers numerous times. Or by way of abstract or trailer, the key event or key outcome of a story may be announced at the opening of the telling so that the fuller telling that follows is a form of retelling. And similarly a story-final coda may tell and then retell its message. But wholesale retelling within the compass of a single narrative text? Normally this would be highly questionable, if tolerated at all.

4.2 Ending a story with an HEI passage

By examining the forms of retelling deployed in one McGahern story, this chapter works towards making some generalizable points about story retellings, the telling again of an episode narrated before. Normally the short story is thought of as a model of brevity, fiercely focused on just one episode or strand in the life of an individual or community, all muscle no fat, compact and condensed, with every sentence, every word, rigorously assessed for relevance. Unlike the novel or even the five-act play, it is to be experienced at one sitting. And as Poe famously contended, 'During the hour of perusal [of the story] the soul of the reader is at the writer's control' (Poe 1902; see also Pratt 1981 for an interesting set of structural and functional differences between the short story and longer fiction; Abbott 2013: 136 on the comparative 'poetic' density of the story; and Lohafer 2003 for an original exposition of how reader intuitions about story closure shape our reception of stories).

Wonderful as that prospect is for the writer, it sets the bar high, in terms of needing to conclude the intense writer-reader encounter in some way that renders the reader satisfied at having experienced something worth their time and effort to take the measure of a whole small world, a distinct situation (Toolan 2016). I am far from alone in postulating that how stories end therefore becomes critical, albeit in many ways still mysterious and hard to reduce to a set of precepts or desiderata, let alone necessary conditions – almost as unfathomable as story beginnings. And my partial solution to this question – what is it that makes for a satisfactory story ending? – has been that, in many stories, a final or near-final passage of what I have proposed calling High Emotional Involvement (HEI) is deployed. A HEI passage is one with distinct form and function (Toolan 2016 presents a much fuller account). Formally, in terms of a number of stylistic parameters to which I will return in Section 4.9 below, it is text which intensifies or maximizes the texture found in the rest of the story, often to the point of transcending that surrounding text. The functional consequence is that the reader-text engagement is put on a different footing, usually with a deeper emotional and ethical confrontation, and a fuller reward for the empathetic commitment the reader has made to the situation or the characters they have to come to understand at some depth. But the HEI 'solution' to the problem of short story closure is by no means adopted by all twentieth-century literary stories, and one of the striking characteristics of 'Swallows' is that it resolves without benefit of an obvious HEI passage.

4.3 What happens in 'Swallows'

The events of the story occur on one rainy afternoon in winter, somewhere in the mid-west of Ireland, possibly in the 1960s although the precise period is immaterial. A young Surveyor from Dublin meets up with a slightly older police

Sergeant resident in the locality in order to take official measurements at the site of a boy's death in a traffic accident. Both male, they seem to get along, having a shared interest in violin music. The Surveyor is invited back to the Sergeant's home for refreshment, a home where the Sergeant is looked after by his housekeeper Biddy, who is old and deaf and devoted to her knitting machine. The Surveyor has a fine violin with him. He tells the Sergeant how he acquired it when on holiday in Avignon, competently plays both a Paganini piece and some folk tunes, and also tells him of Paganini's heroic life and censure by the Catholic Church. The Sergeant cannot reciprocate on an equal footing: his own neglected violin has a string broken, and he declines to play the Surveyor's. The Sergeant, who is drinking whisky liberally, presses the Surveyor to stay the night so that he might accompany him to the Catholic Workers' Association social in town and impress the unsophisticated locals with his rich cultural hinterland. Only belatedly does the Surveyor reveal he has a dinner commitment in Galway with an attractive young woman, a pianist with whom he will play sonatas. By comparison, the Sergeant has only memories to cling to – in particular a memory of playing his fiddle at dances some years ago when 'life was as full of promise as the smile of the girl with cloth fuchsia bells in her dark hair threw him as she danced past'. The Surveyor having departed for Galway, the story closes with the whisky-fuelled Sergeant bitterly predicting how a Mrs Kilboy will corner him at the social function and enrage him with her banal conversational topics: Jackson's thieving ass and whether Biddy's hens are laying. The Sergeant tells Biddy what he imagines he will say in response to such stultifying trivia, a reply that is jarringly different from Mrs Kilboy's gossip, being full of allusion to the Avignon palaces of the popes, and mentions of the great Paganini improvising marvellously on his Guarnerius even as death approached. Besides, deaf and with her back to him, Biddy hears not a word of the Sergeant's rant, being as absorbed as the three Fates in turning and turning the handle of her knitting machine, moving from heel towards the toe of the sock she is producing.

As may be apparent from this summary, 'Swallows' consists extensively of tellings and retellings: the Sergeant tells the Surveyor what happened to the road accident victim and what will likely happen to the offending motorist; the Surveyor tells the Sergeant about his violin, Avignon, Paganini and, belatedly, Eileen O'Neill. The Sergeant has little to tell in return, except of the pleasure of summer fishing; otherwise, drink taken, he is reduced to telling again the Surveyor's narratives or imagining doing so. Only Biddy has little time to tell things – other than that shopkeeper's ham was 'crawling' again – since she is too busy doing; she is on a journey of sorts, progressing towards the completion of the socks she is knitting, a voyage during which, at the story's end, she is enjoying 'plain sailing'.

4.4 Reported speech and narrative as retellings

The limited acceptability of intratextual or story-internal retelling is quite distinct from the abundance and indeed necessity of intertextual retelling that forges links between narratives. But before we contemplate the retelling of one text in another text, we should recognize how there is a doubling or a return, if not strictly a retelling, involved in the essence of narrative as in that of reported speech (just as it lies close to what is foundational in human language). The two are essentially very similar. Something happens or is said, and then someone reports the happening or the saying. Narratives and reported speech both exploit a double 'chronologic' (see, e.g., Sternberg 1990). There is a sequence of events or of dialogue, respectively, and then a discursive re-presenting, after the fact, of the events or speech, possibly in transformed sequence. The situational or 'deictic' shift is the same in both cases, from the event itself to the reporting of the event. Neither is strictly a retelling (because the original they report is a doing or saying, not a telling), but each is an implied repeating albeit a refracted repeating, loose (indirect or paraphrased) or tight (direct, notionally *verbatim*): reported speech is never the original dialogue in its total speech situation, nor is a narrative the original events themselves.

The crucial point about narrating now what happened then, or of reporting now what was said then, is that once the process is established, it can be iterated recursively. Once A can report what B said, then A can also report that B reported that C reported what D said. Likewise if A can tell what happened to them yesterday, A can also report what B reported that C reported happened to D. In all these situations of embedded telling or reporting, the recipient processing the information must understand the deictic- or world- or situation-shifting involved. A narrative projects a situation in which something happens, and part of what happens may be that a different situation, an embedded situation contingent on the first established situation, is also projected.

This situation-shifting is elegantly demonstrated early in the course of the compelling first sentence of 'Swallows':

> The wind blew the stinging rain from the Gut, where earlier in the bright weather of the summer the Sergeant had sat in the tarred boat, anchored by a rope to an old Ford radiator that clung to the weeds outside the rushes, and watched taut line after taut line cut like cheesewire through the water as hooked roach after hooked roach made a last surge towards the freedom of the open lake before landing slapping on the floorboards.
>
> (McGahern: 200)

There is the briefest projection of the 'current situation' by means of a simple nine-word opening main clause, before the phrase *where earlier* and one use of past perfect *had sat* (before resumption of simple past tense) are enough to pivot the description to a different time, albeit in roughly the same place. What is additionally clever but perhaps also tricky in this story opening is that the text continues with a repetition of the opening words (with only *stinging* removed) and even of the same following 'pivot' word *where* – except this time there is no pivot away from the current situation, but an elaboration of it:

> The wind blew the rain from the Gut against the black limestone of the Quarry, where on the wet tar, its pools ruffling in the wet wind, the Sergeant and the young State Surveyor measured the scene of the road accident, both with their collars up and hatted against the rain, the black plastic chinstrap a shining strip on the Sergeant's jaw.
>
> (McGahern: 200)

This is a fairly audacious rhetorical anaphora in view of normal narrative expectations but is also perhaps an early indication of the strategies of retelling – one might almost say a culture of retelling and recursion – that not only are adopted to structure this story and constitute its form but are also arguably the story's deepest message, its content. The pervasive retelling in 'Swallows' is a narrative iconicity, enacting the Sergeant's experience of life as a drudgery of recurrence mostly, with only the return each summer of a few fine days of fishing to look forward to.

4.5 'Swallows' as a three-act play

In some respects 'Swallows' approximates a play for three characters in three acts. Just two settings, occurring on a single afternoon, are directly represented in the story's present: an exterior near the Quarry, where the two men make measurements relating to the recent road traffic accident (RTA), and an interior, the kitchen in the Sergeant's home (the barracks), where the men sit drinking whiskey and tea and playing the violin and where Biddy works on her knitting, also. The narrative progresses straightforwardly from one scene or episode to the next, and these are fairly easy to summarize, as attempted in Table 4.1. In addition there are clear 'frame' boundaries marking the transition from one act to the next. Thus Act One ends when the two men leave the scene of the accident and drive back to the Sergeant's barracks; Act Two, the only act featuring all three characters, ends when the Surveyor leaves to drive on to Galway so that in Act Three only the

Sergeant and Biddy are present. On the printed pages, a wide blank space occurs between what I am calling Acts One and Two, while an asterisk, centred on the line, occupies a similar gap between Acts Two and Three (and these two are the only such inter-paragraph formatting features in the text). Table 4.1 should help to demonstrate how very extensive the retelling is that shapes this story.

Table 4.1 An act/scene analysis of 'Swallows'

	Act 1, 1200 words	Act 2, 2280 words	Act 3, 941 words
Scene 1	The Sergeant recalls roach-fishing in the Gut the previous summer	Biddy, knitting in the kitchen	**Biddy attends to the Sergeant.**
Scene 2	**The Sergeant and the Surveyor discuss the RTA and the driver's culpability.**	**The Sergeant pours whiskey for the Surveyor and himself.**	The Sergeant puts his fiddle away, recalls again the dances and the girl with cloth fuchsia bells in her hair.
Scene 3	The Sergeant asks about the Surveyor's violin, who tells how he bought it, in Avignon, where the papal palaces and the cafes and music are all 'wonderful'. The Sergeant imagines the Avignon just described.	**In the scullery, the Sergeant talks to Biddy about food items for tea.**	The Sergeant imagines the Surveyor and Eileen this evening, while (he imagines) he will be forced to listen to Mrs Kilboy's ramblings about everything including the woman who killed the boy in the RTA, ending with a remark about it being 'a long haul' to the summer.
Scene 4	The Surveyor asks the Sergeant about life 'in this place' and the Sergeant mentions his summer fishing.	The Sergeant takes whiskey while the Surveyor plays Paganini and then tells of Paganini's life and death.	The Sergeant (it is implied) thinks of the long haul to summer and fishing in the Gut.
Scene 5	**The Sergeant explains that while sometimes Biddy cooks the fish he catches, mostly he gives them away, not caring about the eating.**	The Sergeant takes his own fiddle out but it needs fixing; he recalls former days playing for dances, when 'life was as full of promise as the smile the girl with cloth fuchsia bells in her dark hair threw him as she danced past'.	The Sergeant plays at telling 'the unheeding Biddy' what he'll say to Mrs Kilboy in reply: about Avignon and its wonderful papal palaces and cafes and about Paganini who climbed out of the filth of Genoa to wealth and fame and 'stuck to his guns to the very end, improvising marvellously'.

Table 4.1 An act/scene analysis of 'Swallows' *(Continue)*

	Act 1, 1200 words	Act 2, 2280 words	Act 3, 941 words
Scene 6		The Sergeant tries to persuade the Surveyor to stop over, belatedly learns of the Surveyor's music date in Galway with Eileen O'Neill, who will 'probably wear the long dress of burgundy velvet with the satin bow in her hair as she plays'.	**The Sergeant finishes his whiskey and prepares to go out to the function, where he can 'put Mrs Kilboy on the straight and narrow'.**
Scene 7		The Surveyor forgoes saying goodbye to Biddy, as he sees she is too preoccupied adjusting the needles of her knitting machine to notice.	Biddy is too absorbed and happy using her knitting machine to notice the Sergeant leave.

In my segmentation of the story, there are nineteen scenes (five, seven and seven in each Act respectively), and by my calculation the majority of these participate in forms of retelling. Those scenes which are represented just once are in the minority: just two per act, six in all, highlighted in bold in Table 4.1. Even this calculation is generous in its inclusion of a scene like 1:2 (Act 1, Scene 2) among the non-repeated: in fact some of its commentary on the distress of the woman driver involved in the traffic accident is retold, in Mrs Kilboy's imagined speech, in 3:3. In terms of content the single-telling scenes are distinctive in being shorter than the retold scenes and often chiefly procedural: for example 2:3, where Biddy and the Sergeant discuss what she might buy at the shop to make a simple supper. They are needed to move the narrative forward, a necessary mechanics, but otherwise function as a background framework against which the lengthy passages of modified retelling stand out and attract the readers' attention.

4.6 Retellings in 'Swallows': Some examples

I will not attempt to itemize all the story's intratextual retellings, but I simply point to a few of what I see as the most significant ones. To begin at the beginning, as it were: I have already reproduced, above, the story's first, seventy-nine-word sentence. This can now be compared with lines which constitute what I am calling Act 3, Scene 4, where the Sergeant's free indirect thought is a near-verbatim repeating of the narrative content described at the opening:

> It would be a long haul to summer and the old tarred boat anchored to the Ford radiator in the mouth of the Gut, the line cutting the water as hooked roach after hooked roach made a last surge towards the freedom of the open lake.

The immediate trigger of these lines is the final observation in the long imagined direct speech monologue from Mrs Kilboy that we infer has been running through the Sergeant's mind (Act 3, Scene 3). This ends: '... *and did you ever see such a winter, torrents of rain and expectedness of snow, it'll be a long haul indeed to the summer*'.

The ingenuity of the Act 3:4 text lies in the way that what was previously presented (in 1:1) as a remembered past experience is now re-presented as a visualized future, the *irrealis* nicely supported by the use of temporally indefinite participles, *anchored* and *cutting*. These distinctions nicely demonstrate how cross-text retelling tends to come with differences added. But the multiple levels of repeating here are also significant: within the repeated sentence there is extensive local repetition, particularly in *taut line after taut line* and *hooked roach after hooked roach*. As a result across the story as a whole there are four mentions of *hooked roach*!

It is worth noting, also, that a third mention of the Sergeant's summer fishing occurs in Act 1:4, being the best he can offer by way of a counterpart to the Surveyor's continental vacations. In this retelling, the Sergeant's direct speech account uses interestingly different language from the other repeated version:

> 'I take out the old boat you see upside down there under the sycamore. Row it up into the mouth of the Gut and drop the radiator over the side. Time runs like lightning then, feeling the boat sway in the current, a few sandwiches and stout or a little whiskey, and unless there's a bad east wind you're always sure of fish. It's great to feel the first chuck and see the line cut for the lake.'
>
> (McGahern: 202)

The Sergeant's sole continuing recreational pleasure is thus first recalled narratorially as a past event, then described experientially in his 1:4 conversation and finally (3:4) imagined by him in the future. Only in the 1:4 telling, not the 1:1 or 3:4 versions, is the Sergeant accorded much agency: ('I take out the old boat ... row it ... drop the radiator'); in the 1:1 account he merely *sat* and *watched*. The Sergeant's only other memory, but a bitter-sweet one, is of the girl with cloth fuchsia bells in her dark hair who once smiled at him as she danced past, about whom we are told in 2:5 and again in 3:2. And this girl is herself a vanished repeat, a double, of the Eileen O'Neill with the satin bow in her hair, whom the Surveyor tells of at 2:5 and whom the Sergeant imagines again in 3:3. Besides the multiple mentions of the Sergeant's fishing, the Surveyor's violin-playing is also retold, albeit more distantly – as indeed is Biddy's knitting. But there are significant differences between the retelling of the Sergeant's fishing and of Biddy's knitting, which stem from the fact that in the case of the latter there is no deictic shift: her knitting is described as it proceeds, in the story's 'now', whereas it is only the memory or the prospect of the fishing that we are told of, with in each case a clear deictic shift to another situation, another time and place, than the story's present. In the story's present, Biddy is doing what she wants and likes to do (like the Surveyor), while the Sergeant sadly is not. This may be a more literary-critical point than a narratological one, let alone a stylistic one; but it may be part of the motivation for the story's different types of retelling.

4.7 Immediate repetition

In a narrative, the adjacent retelling or repeating of what has just been reported is an obvious kind of local foregrounding and can trigger reader inferences as to its purpose. An early example of such strictly adjacent retelling comes in Act 1:3. It comes immediately after the Surveyor has told at length the story of how he bought his violin from an old Italian musician working the café tables of Avignon, who was willing to sell in order to raise funds for his daughter's medical treatment ('who was consumptive or something', the Surveyor carelessly explains). This is immediately followed by a brief paragraph that, we infer, is some version of the Sergeant's envious private thoughts at this point, a retelling of what he has just been told, to which a final wry or bitter evaluative comment about the inhospitable present is added, to acknowledge the disparity between the Surveyor's romanticized story and the Sergeant's present reality:

> Streets of Avignon, white walls of the royal popes in the sun, glasses of red wine and the old Italian musician playing between the cafe tables in the evening, a girl dying of consumption, and the sweeping rain hammering on the windscreen.

A different kind of necessarily adjacent repeating is found in Act 2:3. These occur because the housekeeper, Biddy, is entirely deaf and also nervous in the presence of strangers like the Surveyor. Swinging a broom around in the scullery to drive out the hens, she is panicked when she nearly dislodges the Sergeant's shaving mirror (breaking of which would incur seven years' bad luck, according to folklore). The text continues:

> 'Never mind the mirror.' He turned her around by the shoulders.
> 'Never mind the mirror,' she shouted, frightened, to show him that she had read his lips.
> 'Keep your voice down.'
> 'Keep your voice down,' she shouted back.
> 'We want something to eat.'
> 'We want something to eat,' she shouted back, but she was calming.

Biddy's repeating here is itself a mirroring of the Sergeant, underscoring the general truth that the general pattern in discourse is for subordinates (servants, subalterns, the powerless) to retell the stories and repeat the instructions of the powerful. Still, Biddy's place in the structure of the story, traceable in Table 4.1, is more interesting than this might suggest. Although she is not an active participant in Act 1, she is mentioned and thus introduced at the close of it. Thereafter she appears, exercising her own creative agency, in the opening and closing scenes of both Acts 2 and 3 and almost only at these framing points. In fact, the structural symmetry is even stronger than this suggests: not only does the final scene of each act turn to Biddy, the final scenes depicting her in 2:7 and 3:7 are especially closely related, in some respects a retelling, only that in 3:7 it is the Sergeant who is the disregarded departing observer rather than the Surveyor as in 2:7.

Is Biddy an anti-Penelope (no suitors, ample progress with her knitting) to the Sergeant's stay-at-home anti-Ulysses? Even in the boat he fishes from, the Sergeant is anchored and does not move, whereas at the close of the story Biddy is in her own world, enjoying 'plain sailing'.

4.8 Retelling with switch of teller

The fullest and most oppressive retellings are those that occupy the bulk of Scenes 3 and 5 of Act 3. In 3:3, the Sergeant begins by imagining how Eileen O'Neill and the Surveyor will play music together, and interestingly in this internal retelling he adds details that were not in the Surveyor's earlier description: the Sergeant imagines *the delicate white hands of Eileen O'Neill would flicker on the white keyboard*. In the same sentence he contrasts this with his own foreseeable evening, more particularly the direct speech monologue that he predicts Mrs Kilboy will inflict upon him, the scatter of events she will allude to and give her opinion of:

> 'Something will have to be done about Jackson's thieving ass, Sergeant, it'll take the law to bring him to his senses, nothing less, and those thistles of his will be blowing again over the townland this year with him dead drunk in the pub, and is Biddy's hens laying at all this weather, mine have gone on unholy strike, and I hear you were measuring the road today, you and a young whipper-snapper from Dublin…'

Thus in 3:3 the Sergeant retells a monologue he has yet to hear.

But in Act 3, Scene 5, the retelling is much more extensive: here the Sergeant rehearses audibly to Biddy what he will say to Mrs Kilboy by way of reply to her predicted 3:3 contribution. Biddy hears nothing of course so that his words are particularly pointless, strictly speaking. Nearly all the substantive content of the Sergeant's 3:5 reply is a paraphrase of what the Surveyor told him earlier about Paganini, duly reported in 2:4 as follows:

> A man of extraordinary interest was Paganini, the Surveyor started to explain. He was born in Genoa in 1782, of a poor family, but such was his genius and dedication that he brought the world to his feet. In London, the mob used to try to touch him, in the hope that some of his magic might pass over to them, in the way they once tried to touch the hem of Christ's garments – like pop stars in our own day – but nothing could divert him from his calling. Even the last hours given to him in life were spent in marvellous improvisations on his Guarnerius. The Church proved to be the one fly in the ointment. She had doubts as to his orthodoxy, and refused for five years to have him buried in consecrated grounds. In the end, of course, in her usual politic fashion, she relented, and he was laid to rest in a village graveyard on his own land.

Now, in 3:5, the Sergeant merges much of this material and other earlier remarks of the Surveyor about Avignon and the papal palaces, along with much repeating of the name of his imagined addressee:

> Some of the palaces of the royal popes in Avignon are wonderful, wonderful, Mrs Kilboy, in the sun; and wonderful the cafes and wonderful, Mrs Kilboy, the music. Did you ever hear of a gentleman called Paganini, Mrs Kilboy? A man of extraordinary interest is Paganini. Through his genius he climbed out of the filth of his local Genoa to wealth and fame. So that when he came to London, Mrs Kilboy, the crowds there crowded to touch him as they once trampled on one another to get their hands on Christ; but he stuck to his guns to the very end, improvising marvellously, Mrs Kilboy, during his last hours on his Guarnerius.

As a consequence of such extensive repetition, there is a sense in which 'Swallows' is double its inherent length. This is something outrageous to perpetrate within the brief, concentrated compass of the short story form. But there is another sense in which without those retellings, we would have only half the story, and that would be a greater outrage.

4.9 No HEI passage in 'Swallows'

In the course of stylistic and narratological studies of near-contemporary short stories (see especially Toolan 2016), I have proposed that a significant number of them satisfy the reader's requirement of a satisfactory ending not chiefly by means of plot-resolution, but rather by a more textural means: a passage, sited near-finally and stylistically foregrounded in many respects, which draws the reader deeper into the ethical and emotional situation of one of the main characters. I have called such a passage a HEI passage (High Emotional Involvement or Immersion), offering a listing of what seem to be their ten most prominent and marked linguistic characteristics alongside discussion of stories by Munro, Carver and others which I believe exemplify this literary technique. I have also suggested that a HEI passage occurs in quite a few McGahern stories too, including 'All Sorts of Impossible Things', 'Gold Watch' and 'Creatures of the Earth'. To rehearse extremely briefly the stylistic features of HEI passages, they usually include a focalized character, in a particularized situation, whose thoughts and reactions are disclosed, thereby fostering reader understanding if not empathy (the verb *feel* is frequent; other projecting verbs like *think* and *see* and *want* are common too). By comparison with the bulk of the story's texture, in the HEI passage semantic negation is more frequent, sentence grammar is more complex (sometimes non-standard or ungrammatical), and sentence rhythm and intonation more tangible. Sentences have more temporal staging and simultaneity, with fundamental and absolute lexis relating to heat, light, extension prominent; on the other hand figurative language is scarce or hedged or conventional. But lexical and phrasal repetition is widespread, often with an 'arresting' effect.

Why should these HEIs have so much repetition in them; what is the attraction, the effect? First, and simply, there is a focusing of the reader's attention and a temporary arrest of the usual necessary forward momentum of narrative (Toolan 2009): a concentration through recurrence of description on one moment. Lexical repetition is neither necessary nor sufficient to create that arrested focusing, but the two seem to correlate. To repeat is to go over again, making no change, rather than to move on, to a new development.

Is there a passage in 'Swallows' that stands out by virtue of having a high frequency of most of the above features, relative to the rest of the story, and can such a passage be plausibly proposed to be a HEI one? My answer is that on this occasion there is not, precisely because in this story McGahern has opted for an atypical; one might even say contrarian, strategy of closure, commensurate with the story's theme. As a consequence, in 'Swallows' there is no HEI passage – at least no orthodox version of such a resolving and 'reader-rewarding' passage.

Granted, there are towards the end of the story a couple of brief paragraphs with some of the characteristics of HEI closural writing, but these are too short and too disjunct temporally and affectively to foster reader immersion:

> The smell of porter and whiskey, blue swirls of cigarette smoke, pounding of boots on the floorboards as they danced, the sudden yahoos as they swung, and the smile of the girl with the cloth fuchsia bells in her hair as he played, petrified for ever in his memory even as his stumblings home over the cold waking fields.
>
> It would be a long haul to summer and the old tarred boat anchored to the Ford radiator in the mouth of the Gut, the line cutting the water as hooked roach after hooked roach made a last surge towards the freedom of the open lake.

Instead the entire final phase of the story puts the Sergeant, the protagonist, in the background and, in so doing, is at odds with the first noted characteristic of HEI passages. As we have seen, it is largely occupied by one long paragraph in which the Sergeant fluently imagines what Mrs Kilboy's speech to him that evening will be; another long paragraph of his imagined verbatim reply, extensively recycling the Surveyor's self-satisfied commentary of earlier that afternoon, and a final short paragraph about Biddy. In a sense, in the two long paragraphs of imagined speech, the Sergeant becomes a detached narrator or author: not a character speaking and thinking in the narrative present but a narrator reporting what 'his' character and Mrs Kilboy's character will say to each other in the near future. But the Sergeant is not the narrator in fact; he is and remains a character. There is a pretence at deictic shift, situation shift, to the evening's CWA function, but in reality there is no shift and the story here-and-now remains the early evening in the Sergeant's kitchen, with the Sergeant now dressed to go out and Biddy preoccupied with her knitting.

4.10 Plain sailing

The final two paragraphs of the story show the Sergeant leaving and Biddy staying, and together these create an anti-climactic resolution, a resumption of the *status quo*. With his hat and overcoat on, the Sergeant is as ready for foul weather as he was at the story's opening. But even here this downbeat ending is given depth and resonance by means of many subtle cross- and intra-paragraph repetitions, which suggest a connectedness between the two protagonists' lives and circumstances, alongside the evident differences and disconnections. Among the latter, the most immediate is that the Sergeant speaks to Biddy at the close of the first paragraph but she does not reply – does not even realize she has been spoken to – at the beginning of the second.

> The Sergeant tired of the mockery and rose **from the chair**, but he **finished** the dregs of the glass with a flourish, and placed it solidly **down** on the table. He put on his hat and overcoat. 'We better be **making a start**, Biddy, if we're ever going to put Mrs Kilboy on the straight and **narrow**.'
> Biddy did not look **up**. She had **turned** the heel and would not have to adjust the needles again till she had to **start narrowing** the sock **close to the toe**. Her body swayed happily **on the chair** as she **turned** and **turned** the handle, for she knew it would be all plain sailing till she got **close to the toe**.

Among the lexical repetition links between or within the two paragraphs, I have bolded some of the most noticeable (including among these repetitions via antonymy, such as the pairing of *down* in paragraph 1 and *up* in paragraph 2). Nor need the repetitions be limited in size to a word or two: arguably the entire statement that *she knew it would be all plain sailing till she got close to the toe* is largely a reformulation of what is reported in the previous sentence, that *she would not have to adjust the needles again till she had to start narrowing the sock close to the toe*. A particular spatial convergence that would further unite the two paragraphs is left unconfirmed, however: is the table on which the Sergeant solidly places his whisky glass the same table on which Biddy's knitting machine is set up? It hardly matters – certainly not to Biddy, who is happy in her repetitions, her turning and turning of the handle, repeating the same stitch knowing that *it would be all plain sailing till she got close to the toe*. Biddy, then, can foresee and tell the future just as well as the Sergeant, except in her case – perhaps affected by her hearing disability – the future is one of language-free productiveness, not language-enmeshed entrapment.

References

Abbott, H. Porter. (2013), *Real Mysteries, Narrative and the Unknowable*, Ohio: Ohio State University Press.

Lohafer, S. (2003), *Reading for Storyness: Preclosure Theory, Empirical Poetics, & Culture in the Short Story*, Baltimore/London: Johns Hopkins University Press.

McGahern, J. (1992), 'Swallows', in *Collected Stories*, 200–10, London: Faber.

Poe, E. A. (1902), 'Hawthorne's *Twice-Told Tales*', in James A. Harrison (ed.), *The Complete Works of Edgar Allan Poe*, Vol. 11, 104–13, New York: Thomas Y. Cromwell.

Pratt, M. L. (1981), 'The Short Story: The Long and Short of It'. *Poetics*, 10: 175–94. Reprinted in Charles E. May (ed.), *The New Short Story Theories*. Columbus: Ohio University Press, 1994, pp. 91–113.

Sternberg, M. (1990), 'Telling in Time (I): Chronology and Narrative Theory', *Poetics Today*, 11 (4): 901–48.

Toolan, M. (2009), *Narrative Progression in the Short Story: A Corpus Stylistic Approach*, Amsterdam: Benjamins.

Toolan, M. (2016), *Making Sense of Narrative Text: Situation, Repetition, and Picturing in the Reading of Short Stories*, London & New York: Routledge.

5

Modern retellings of Jane Austen

Joe Bray

5.1 Introduction

Over two hundred years since her death, Jane Austen remains one of literature's most adapted and reworked authors. Recent versions include Whit Stilman's 2016 film *Love & Friendship*, *Pride and Prejudice and Zombies* (Seth Grahame Smith's 2009 novel followed by Burr Steers's 2016 film) and Andrew Davies's 2019 *Sanditon* on ITV, which is one of many attempts to extend her last, unfinished work. All adaptations of Austen must negotiate the pride and prejudice of the dyed-in-the-wool Janeites, some of whom refuse to countenance any kind of updating of their beloved's originals. One particular kind of reworking has come in for particularly negative criticism. In this chapter I will focus on a recent project which aimed to retell Austen's major novels in novelistic form. That the project has been largely unsuccessful is evident both from the fact that only four retellings of the six major novels have been published so far (with no sign of the other two) and from the mixed reviews of those that have appeared. I will ask whether stylistics can shed any light on why these and other retellings of Austen tend to be poorly received. I will thus revisit the thorny issue of whether stylistic analysis can in fact be entirely separated from assessments of value and if not what form these assessments often take in stylistic work. I will suggest that stylisticians often participate, however unwillingly, in complex games involving value judgements. These can take them, I will argue, far beyond the textual or aesthetic object in question. An understanding of the variety of factors which may influence the evaluation of works of art can help explain why any kind of retelling, especially of a beloved author, is so open to hostile criticism and attack.

5.2 The Austen Project

The Austen Project was commissioned by HarperCollins in 2011. The volumes published so far are (in order): *Sense & Sensibility* (2013) by Joanna Trollope (note the ampersand), *Northanger Abbey* (2014) by Val McDermid, *Emma* (2014) by Alexander McCall Smith and *Eligible* (2016) by Curtis Sittenfeld (a retelling of *Pride and Prejudice*). Each takes the original characters and the basic elements of the story and updates them within a twenty-first-century context; McCall Smith's *Emma* and Sittenfeld's *Eligible* are subtitled 'A Modern Retelling'. Though the extent of divergence from Austen's original plot varies (with *Eligible* the least faithful), common social and technological indicators of the contemporary context tend to recur. In McDermid's *Northanger Abbey*, for example, the heroine Cat is an avid user of social media, constantly updating Facebook with her adventures at the Edinburgh Fringe (which is the modern version's equivalent of Catherine Morland's introduction to society in Bath). Henry Tilney's famous mockery of the obsession of young ladies of fashion for keeping a journal ("'this delightful habit of journalizing which largely contributes to form the easy style of writing for which ladies are so generally celebrated'" (2006: 19)) in Austen's novel is replaced in McDermid's retelling by a dig by the same character at social media:

> You're female and, I'm pretty sure, under twenty-one. If you don't do Facebook, how are your sisters and your cousins and your best mates going to be provoked to teeth-gnashing jealousy of your trip to Edinburgh? How else will they know you're having the time of your life while they're doing whatever it is they do in Dorset? All you girls do it all the time – Facebook, Twitter. I have this theory. It's why you've all suddenly got so good at writing novels. Chick lit and the serious stuff. It's because of all the practice you get spinning yarns on your phones and iPads.
>
> (2014: 28–9)

Reality television is also a common theme; after his rejection by Emma in McCall Smith's retelling, Philip Elton is introduced to 'a popular contestant in a television talent show, *Look at Me!*' (2014: 279). The future Mrs Elton is 'a dancer and Edith Piaf impersonator', despite the fact that 'she could not really sing, least of all in French, which she sang with the American accent that bad British singers for some reason feel they must adopt' (279). Although she thinks that 'Non, je ne regrette rien' is a song about declining a social invitation, she 'under[stands] very well, though, that her C-list celebrity status [is] best exploited by finding a man who was capable of supporting her in the style to which she aspired' (279).

The reality show contestant in Sittenfeld's *Eligible* is a more sympathetic character. The retelling's opening sentence 'Well before his arrival in Cincinnati, everyone knew that Chip Bingley was looking for a wife' is explained by the fact that Chip had two years previously 'appeared on the juggernaut reality-television show *Eligible*' (2016: 3), an obvious reference to the American TV series *The Bachelor*. In the final episode, with two of the twenty-five single women who started the series vying for his attentions remaining, Chip 'wept profusely and declined to propose marriage to either. They both were extraordinary, he declared, stunning and intelligent and sophisticated, but toward neither did he feel what he termed "a soul connection"' (3–4). Despite her protestations, it is clear from her knowledge of Chip's life story that Mrs Bennet has watched the show, as indeed have all her daughters, with the exception of Jane, with whom of course he falls almost immediately in love.

Readers of novels in The Austen Project have frequently complained that these contemporary elements seem artificially bolted on. While acknowledging the 'deft modern touches' in Trollope's *Sense & Sensibility* (which include Marianne's public rejection by John Willoughby ('Wills') being spread via social media), the novelist and critic Amanda Craig (2013) argues that overall the effect of such contemporary touches is underwhelming: 'All of this is ingenious but serves to remind us how much of Austen's genius lies in her style and elegance of mind.' Readers on Goodreads, a website for book enthusiasts which allows readers to leave reviews of books they have read and discuss them in groups, have come to similar conclusions, often expressed more vehemently. Alisha, reviewing McDermid's *Northanger Abbey*, comments:

> I understand. You're trying to do a modern retelling, but there's only so many times I can see words like 'LOL' before I start to lose my mind. The teen slang was just too overblown. Quite blatantly an older person imitating their view on younger people. I could make a drinking game of the clichés. The 'young person narrative' was wrong, unrealistic and incredibly hard to relate to.

Reviewing Trollope's *Sense & Sensibility*, Rikke is even more scathing: 'As one of the reviewers before me have asked: **why**? Why was this book necessary? Why was it introduced as a modern retelling, when it in reality is the exact same story with an iPod and a Facebook profile thrown in once in a while? What is the point of this book? Why does it claim to be anything new?' The prevailing view, on this website at least, is summed up by Kim:

> I had really high hopes for The Austen Project, but after reading Val McDermid's take on *Northanger Abbey* and McCall Smith's take on *Emma*, I think that it's safe

to say that this project is not for me. There really is no author like Austen, and these retellings are quite weak. [...] If you want to get into Austen, just read her novels. The Austen Project is just a very pale imitation.

5.3 Stylistics and value

I want to ask whether stylistics can shed any light on why modern retellings such as The Austen Project are hard to pull off and whether it can aid understanding and assessment of the value of retellings as a genre. Stylisticians have largely shied away from value judgements, with the excuse that they are not their province. Noting the focus of stylistics on formal features and their functional significance, Katie Wales adds that while 'intuitions and interpretative skills are just as important in stylistics and literary criticism [...] stylisticians want to avoid vague and impressionistic judgements about the way formal features are manipulated' (2001: 373). Despite Wales's caveat that 'not that good literary criticism is necessarily vague or impressionistic' (373), some stylisticians have indeed identified this as the traditional distinction between stylistics and literary criticism, claiming that the former is less reliant on subjective, impressionistic assessments of value. Henry Widdowson outlines this foundational opposition, asserting that in contrast to the value-laden terminology of literary criticism, stylistics is concerned with the patterning of language in texts and makes no presupposition as to artistic value:

> In brief, stylistics takes the language as primary and artistic values are regarded as incidental to linguistic description: literary criticism, on the other hand, takes artistic values as primary and refers to language in so far as it serves as evidence for aesthetic assessments.
>
> (1996: 140)

Yet behind what look like neutral, objective analytical statements about language in stylistics often lurk implicit value judgements. An example from my own recent work on Austen can clarify:

> As the rest of this chapter will demonstrate, the complexity of this relationship between narrator and character is developed further in the novels usually considered to have been written towards the end of Austen's career. In *Mansfield Park*, *Emma* and *Persuasion* FIT [free indirect thought] and NP [narrated perception], in combination with other categories, enable a depth and subtlety of representation of character psychology which was unprecedented in the

English novel at the time, allowing intimate access to each character's mind as she reasons and debates with herself. The ambiguity of perspective that is the hallmark of these techniques is again crucial.

(Bray 2018: 65)

There are several keywords here that contain implicit value judgements: complexity, depth, subtlety, intimate, ambiguity, hallmark. Each in the context is positive; indeed some have a long history of use as terms of approbation in criticism (especially 'ambiguity'; see, for example, Empson (1930)). It is hard, in Widdowson's terms, to see this author's appreciation of the 'artistic values' of Austen's writing as 'incidental'. If not exactly the starting point, it certainly seems to underpin the analysis of her stylistic technique.

According to some critics, any claim of a purely objective criticism is illusory. Northrop Frye argues:

Value-judgements are subjective in the sense that they can be indirectly but not directly communicated. When they are fashionable or generally accepted, they look objective, but that is all. The demonstrable value-judgement is the donkey's carrot of literary criticism, and every new critical fashion, such as the current fashion for elaborate rhetorical analysis, has been accompanied by a belief that criticism has finally devised a definitive technique for separating the excellent from the less excellent. But this always turns out to be an illusion of the history of taste.

(1957: 20)

Frye even claims that value judgements cannot be supported by concrete evidence:

Shakespeare, we say, was one of a group of dramatists working around 1600, and also one of the great poets of the world. The first part of this is a statement of fact, the second a value-judgement so generally accepted as to pass for a statement of fact. But it is not a statement of fact. It remains a value-judgement, and not a shred of systematic criticism can ever be attached to it.

(20)

This seems however a somewhat extreme position. Most stylisticians, along perhaps with many literary critics, would argue that 'systematic criticism' can go some way to providing a basis for a judgement of Shakespeare's greatness or at least to explaining how such a judgement might arise. Widdowson, for example, notes that 'by investigating the way language is used in a text, it can make apparent those linguistic patterns upon which an intuitive awareness of artistic values ultimately depend' (140). In this view then stylistics should not shy away from the use of value-laden terms but rather investigate how they arise, the 'linguistic patterns' which generate them. In his discussion of a passage from Terry Eagleton's criticism, Michael Toolan notes:

> It is stylistics that undertakes to be precise, analytical and verifiable about the grammar that underlies and creates the literariness effects which in turn induce readers to reach for such complex evaluative terms as *shambling, strident, alienated, terse, passionate, placid* and so on. Stylisticians should not be dismissive of these powerfully synthesising and summarising evaluative terms – their existence makes stylistics possible, and wide agreement that a particular passage is strident or shambling or restless helps allay anxieties about conflictingly various textual interpretation. They have an important place in literary reading, but one that stylistics endeavours to keep distinct from that of analysis.
>
> (2014: 15)

Thus although Toolan attempts to separate the business of stylistics from Eagleton's use of 'complex evaluative terms', he acknowledges their power and their importance for the stylistician, and the word 'endeavours' suggests that they are not always as distinct from analysis as he or she might think or hope.

5.4 Evaluating retellings

The analysis of any retelling is indeed inextricably bound up with complex questions of value. Take the following example from Joanna Trollope's *Sense & Sensibility*:

> Marianne's abilities were, in many respects, quite equal to Elinor's. She was sensible and clever; but eager in everything; her sorrows, her joys, could have no moderation. She was generous, amiable, interesting: she was everything but prudent. The resemblance between her and her mother was strikingly great.
>
> Elinor saw, with concern, the excess of her sister's sensibility; but by Mrs. Dashwood it was valued and cherished.

This is a very flat description of Marianne's character. Her qualities are listed very matter-of-factly, with the positive balanced by her lack of moderation and prudence. Two adversative 'but's counter positive aspects of her character by introducing less favourable qualities. The second and third sentences are structured to reflect this balance, divided by a semicolon and a colon. The effect is rather repetitive and bland; the narrator is setting out Marianne's good and bad points bluntly and without elaboration. The fourth sentence is also lacking in nuance, while the next paragraph sums everything up rather crudely by invoking one half of the novel's title.

Compare this with a passage on Marianne from the original *Sense and Sensibility*:

> It must be extraordinary, Elinor thought, to be able to surrender oneself so completely, not just because it would feel so exhilarating but also because it meant that one was – oh, how unlike me, Elinor thought regretfully – able to trust. Marianne could trust. She trusted her instincts; she trusted those dear to her; she trusted her emotions and her passions. She drank deep, you could see that; she squeezed every drop of living out of all the elements that mattered to her. It made her careless sometimes, of course it did, but it was a wonderfully rich and rapt way to be.

The major difference here is that this is Elinor's view of Marianne rather than a flat external description. The first sentence gives a clear indication of Elinor's presence in 'Elinor thought', before brief slipping into her first-person perspective following Austen's characteristic use of the dash: '[O]h, how unlike me, Elinor thought regretfully'. What follows is Austen's classic stylistic technique of free indirect thought: Elinor's impression of Marianne, yet retaining the overall third person and past tense of narration. Signs of Elinor's subjectivity here as she considers her sister's ability to trust admiringly include the repetition of 'trusted', the use of the second-person 'you' and the evaluative language, especially the adverb 'wonderfully'. To use terms from my own appreciation of Austen's style, this passage is altogether more complex, subtle and ambiguous than that in the Trollope retelling, hence better stylistically and indeed better overall.

As readers familiar with Austen's work will have already noticed however, there is a problem with the above analysis. The first passage is in fact from her *Sense and Sensibility*, the second from Trollope's modern retelling. For those who are unwilling to acknowledge the superiority of Trollope over Austen, one option is to search for previously unnoticed nuances in the original passage from *Sense and Sensibility*. A critic who is trained to look for hidden meanings and ironies would indeed need very little encouragement to read in this way. Perhaps for example what we are being presented with here is not simply a single external point of view. The sentence 'The resemblance between her and her mother was strikingly great' in particular might hint at some kind of group perspective, which is observing the family from a distance. There may be a hint here that the truth of each character is more complex than these first impressions suggest. The first paragraph could also be Elinor's opinion of her sister, which would suggest a frustration at the younger sister's lack of moderation and prudence, as well as a sense of superiority, which perhaps does not reflect well on the elder. There are no doubt other possible interpretations which would bring out previously hidden tensions and nuances. It is possible, in other words, if one rereads and re-analyses the text closely enough, to find evidence which would justify an initial preference for Austen over Trollope.

One could also look again at the Trollope passage and argue that in its somewhat forced inclusion of many of the classic signs of free indirect thought it is striving too hard to be Austenian. A frequent criticism of the novels in The Austen Project is in fact that they 'ape' both her plot and her style too closely. McCall Smith's *Emma* is particularly attacked on this front. Leah Price's 2015 review, for example, notes that 'good adaptations capture the spirit of the original', praising Amy Heckerling's 1995 film adaptation *Clueless*. In contrast McCall Smith's retelling, according to Price, 'reads like a too literal translation. His reluctance to alter now anachronistic details forces him to spend pages explaining why, in an age of universal schooling, Emma would have a governess, and why, at a time when overscheduling afflicts even the erstwhile leisure class, she wouldn't have a job'. Viv Groskop (2014) similarly observes that McCall Smith's version 'is faithful to the original in a very literal way, which causes all sorts of practical problems'. After running through some of these she concludes that '[u]ltimately it's impossible to avoid the pastiche feel of these Austen retakes and it all becomes a slightly exhausting academic exercise'.

Readers on Goodreads also point to the over-literalness of McCall Smith's 'translation'. Koeeoaddi comments, 'Sorry. I really wanted to love this but could not get past page 75. I think the author's decision to try to stay close to the storyline and even the language of the original while updating it with jeans, iPods and artsy smocks just didn't work for me.' Kate also gave up well before the end:

> I'm quitting this a third of the way through. I'm not sure what exactly the point is of a modern adaptation of Austen if so much of the language feels as though it's trying to ape her style. I assumed the point would be to retell these stories in a modern context, and, for me, that should include the voice of the novel as well. I wanted to quit when I was 15% in and still on Mr. Woodhouse, a good background character but one that should stay there, and I finally had to give up.

An extract from McCall Smith's novel can perhaps illustrate the closeness to, verging on mimicry of, Austen's style that these and other readers have identified:

> He got into the Land Rover, waved – unenthusiastically, thought Emma – and

drove off. She had not felt it during their sparring, but now she felt the rawness that followed from the argument. Disagreements, even with people she knew, made her feel like that – shocked, perhaps, at the animus that can be behind mere words. She was surprised, though, by the intensity of her dismay over the fact that George had expressed disappointment in her. Why should she care what he thought? Why should she bother if she had somehow fallen short of whatever standards he had mentally created for her? It was as if she had been *moved* in some way by the encounter, and that made her feel uneasy in a way that she neither expected nor fully understood. It was unease, yes, but it was something else, she thought – and she was not quite sure what that something else was.

(2014: 172)

This again bears many of the hallmarks of Austenian free indirect thought, including the questions ('Why should she care what he thought?'), the epistemic modality ('perhaps', 'not quite sure'), the repetition ('Why should she care … ?' 'Why should she bother … ?'), the italics ('It was as if she had been *moved*'), the parenthetical indications of thought ('unenthusiastically, thought Emma'), the adverb 'yes'. There is even an example of what is often cited as the most prototypical marker of the style, the combination of past tense with proximal deixis: 'now she felt the rawness that followed from the argument'.

From a subjective point of view though there is something not quite right about the passage. The abundance of indicators of Austen's key stylistic technique creates, for the author of this chapter at least, a jarring effect, as does the inclusion of the Land Rover and, perhaps most crucially, Mr Knightley's first name. Austen's Emma never refers to the hero as 'George' and would be unlikely to do so even in her head. Instead, even in her most heightened emotional moments, his surname prevails: 'It darted through her, with the speed of an arrow, that Mr. Knightley must marry no one but herself!' (2005: 444). My objection to 'George' is therefore based on my knowledge of *Emma* and perhaps reflects a snobbish attempt on my part to demonstrate this knowledge. It also seems designed to suggest that McCall Smith's apparent ignorance on this point reflects badly on his retelling as a whole.

This example suggests then that the assessment of value of any kind of literary work may be based on more than simply what is there on the page. My resistance to the passage is partly based on my opinion of the cultural value of Austen herself, and what I expect is a suspicion, shared by many readers, of the worth of *any* kind of retelling. As we have seen, less obviously faithful adaptations are frequently praised by readers (Heckerling's 1995 *Clueless* is the most common example). For this reason, Sittenfeld's *Eligible*, which sticks least closely to its

Austenian template, has been by far the best received of the novels in The Austen Project. In Sittenfeld's retelling the heroine Liz has been involved in a long on-off relationship with the married Jasper Wick by the start of the novel when she returns to the family home in Cincinnati after her father's heart surgery. There she meets the snooty neurosurgeon Mr. Darcy, with whom she indulges in various bouts of 'hate sex' until the two recognize their feelings for each other. Readers have largely praised Sittenfeld's ingenious, free-wheeling updatings of Austen's plot. In a *New York Times* review, for example, Sarah Lyall (2016) observes:

> Taking the story out of England and bringing it to America has allowed Sittenfeld to draw back the curtains, throw open the windows, and let the air in, along the way lightly touching on such current topics as the cost of health care, artificial insemination, transgender and interracial relationships, and the unreality of reality television. The characters can be raucous and the situations ungenteel, but not since 'Clueless,' which transported 'Emma' to Beverly Hills, has Austen been so delightedly interpreted.

For the other novels in The Austen Project which do attempt a more literal retelling, a common question on Goodreads is why they were undertaken at all. Rikke's comment on *Sense & Sensibility*: '**why**? Why was this book necessary?' is echoed by Lisa's observation, under the heading '**Why???**':

> The Austen project is a strange little idea to rewrite all the Austen novels for a modern age. Why? It certainly can't be because the originals are unreadable – I'd imagine they are more popular today than they have ever been. One can only assume they see it as a money-spinner. I'm delighted to say I got this book free – and even then it was too expensive.

Davna's review of *Sense & Sensibility* is even more colourful: 'It gets one star just because it got published, which is something I have never done, so hooray for you. But this was just a complete pile of crap. Just don't touch Jane Austen, go stick a fork in an outlet next time you have the urge.'

Responses to the retellings of Austen's novels suggest then that the forming and expressing of value judgements is a complex social activity and that more than analysis of the words on the page is involved. The evidence so far indicates that evaluation takes place within social groups, whether they be online communities such as Goodreads, or academic circles such as Austen scholars, and that it is significantly affected, if not determined, by this context. Some philosophers have been concerned to explore the relationships and negotiations that can underpin this kind of activity. In the remainder of this chapter I will turn to one particularly influential philosopher of language who has shed light on the games that can take place in evaluating works of art, including literary texts.

5.5 Judgement games

In his early work, for example the *Tractatus Logico-Philosophicus* (1921), Ludwig Wittgenstein focused on the logical form of propositions, in the belief that language consists of propositions which picture the world. In his later thought, from roughly the early 1930s onwards he became more interested in the philosophy of mind and the relationship between thought and language. In this period he developed the concept of language games, which are defined by Anthony Kenny as follows:

> Words, Wittgenstein now insisted, cannot be understood outside the context of the non-linguistic human activities into which the use of the language is interwoven: the words plus their behavioural surroundings make up the language-game. Words are like tools: their functions differ from one another as much as those of a saw and a screwdriver.
>
> (1973: 14)

In Wittgenstein's writing collected in *Philosophical Investigations* examples of language games include obeying and giving orders, making up stories, telling jokes, thanking and swearing. They can also be applied to the realm of aesthetics (always one of his central concerns), where they are especially complex. So evaluating, and evaluating a work of art in particular, is also a kind of language-game.

Wittgenstein's acknowledgement of the complexity of aesthetic language games is apparent in Lectures on Aesthetics (which was compiled after his death from notes taken by students during his lectures in the 1930s in Cambridge). Here he observes that 'we don't start from certain words, but from certain occasions or activities' (1966: 3). He notes that the very varied ways in which we express value judgements will depend on the occasion or activity and might not be verbal at all:

> What does a person who knows a good suit say when trying on a suit at the tailor's? 'That's the right length', 'That's too short', 'That's too narrow'. Words of approval play no role, although he will look pleased when the coat suits him. Instead of 'That's too short' I might say 'Look!' or instead of 'Right' I might say 'Leave it as it is'. A good cutter may not use any words at all, but just make a chalk mark and later alter it. How do I show my approval of a suit? Chiefly by wearing it often, liking it when it is seen, etc.

(5)

The words themselves which are typically used in the expression of value are thus of little interest:

> We are concentrating, not on the words 'good' or 'beautiful', which are entirely uncharacteristic, generally just subject and predicate ('This is beautiful'), but on the occasions on which they are said – on the enormously complicated situation in which the aesthetic expression has a place, in which the expression itself has almost a negligible place.

(2)

Jane Austen recognizes too this enormous complexity. At the tense dinner thrown by the Dashwoods for the Middletons in volume II of *Sense and Sensibility*, at which Elinor finally meets Edward's mother Mrs. Ferrars, the attention of the party is caught by a 'very pretty pair of screens' which Elinor had painted for her sister-in-law Fanny before her departure from Norland. These are now handed 'officiously' by her brother John to Colonel Brandon for his admiration:

> 'These are done by my eldest sister,' said he; 'and you, as a man of taste, will, I dare say, be pleased with them. I do not know whether you ever happened to see any of her performances before, but she is in general reckoned to draw extremely well.'
>
> The Colonel, though disclaiming all pretensions to connoisseurship, warmly admired the screens, as he would have done any thing painted by Miss Dashwood; and the curiosity of the others being of course excited, they were handed round for general inspection. Mrs. Ferrars, not aware of their being Elinor's work, particularly requested to look at them; and after they had received the gratifying testimony of Lady Middleton's approbation, Fanny presented them to her mother, considerately informing her at the same time, that they were done by Miss Dashwood.
>
> 'Hum' – said Mrs. Ferrars – 'very pretty,' – and without regarding them at all, returned them to her daughter.
>
> Perhaps Fanny thought for a moment that her mother had been quite rude enough, – for, colouring a little, she immediately said,
>
> 'They are very pretty, ma'am – an't they?' But then again, the dread of having been too civil, too encouraging herself, probably came over her, for she presently added,
>
> Do not you think they are something in Miss Morton's style of painting, ma'am? – *She does* paint most delightfully! – How beautifully her last landscape is done!

Beautifully indeed! But *she* does every thing well.

Marianne could not bear this. – She was already greatly displeased with Mrs. Ferrars; and such ill-timed praise of another, at Elinor's expense, though she had not any notion of what was principally meant by it, provoked her immediately to say with warmth,

This is admiration of a very particular kind! – what is Miss Morton to us? – who knows, or who cares, for her? – it is Elinor of whom *we* think and speak.

And so saying, she took the screens out of her sister-in-law's hands, to admire them herself as they ought to be admired.

(2006: 267–8)

A myriad of relationships and hidden social nuances is revealed here. The social climber John Dashwood is trying to impress Colonel Brandon, who admires anything created by Elinor's hand, partly out of his love for her sister. There is a complex interplay between Fanny, her mother and Elinor, which has the absent Edward at its heart; Fanny wonders at first if her mother has been too harsh in her judgement of Elinor's work, then if she herself has been too civil, and compensates by invoking Miss Morton, the family's preferred suitor for Edward. Marianne is rather baffled by the whole exchange and keen to get the focus back on to her sister. The passage constitutes an astute representation of how value judgements are arrived at in a social setting, illustrating the importance, in Wittgenstein's terms, of the activity and the occasion. Austen cleverly highlights how we admire things 'as they ought to be admired', depending on the relationships between the artist, the viewer(s) and the various other participants involved. It is notable here that the screens themselves are not described; their appearance is incidental to the subtle nuances between the characters that they bring out and illuminate.

This example suggests then that Austen recognizes the complex games that are involved in evaluating a work of art. Fanny's comparison of Elinor's style of painting with Miss Morton's, though meant maliciously, also indicates the difficulty, if not the impossibility, of judging in isolation. It tallies with Wittgenstein's observation that 'what we really want, to solve aesthetic puzzlements, is certain comparisons – grouping together of certain cases' (1966: 29). He is very critical in particular of what he sees as reductivist attempts to explain aesthetic judgements according to a scientific model of cause and effect: '[Y]ou might think Aesthetics is a science telling us what's beautiful – almost too ridiculous for words' (11). He reserves most scepticism for the claim of experimental psychology that works of art can be understood, or valued, through any kind of scientific theory about how particular forms are perceived by the human brain, arguing that 'aesthetic questions have nothing to do with psychological experiments, but are answered in an entirely different way' (17). He emphasizes instead that complex language games, including that of evaluation, need to be considered in their social and institutional context.

This approach poses challenges for the evaluation of literary texts. How can the critic account for the complexity of the games that are played with value judgements when so much beyond the text is involved? Retellings pose an especially difficult challenge given the variable, often complicated relationship they have with their originals, and the values that are attached to these. It is possible though that ongoing dialogue and engagement with other disciplines will be of benefit, especially sociolinguistics and the social sciences more generally. Among the many applications of Wittgenstein's thought in recent years, one of the most stimulating looks at intersections between his philosophy and social psychology, especially as concerns human behaviour. Emilio Ribes-Iñesta, for example, has argued that 'human behaviour cannot be understood if we separate language and social practice. Language without social practice and social practice without language are senseless' (2006: 110). In this view language is not exclusively a psychological phenomenon, an expression of inner thought. Rather all human behaviour, including seeing, feeling and thinking, is linguistic, and 'language provides meaning and sense to all human behaviour to the extent that things, events, persons, values, goals, and any conceivable element in human life is dealt with through language and as language' (120).

5.6 Concluding remarks

Evaluating retellings of Jane Austen such as those attempted in The Austen Project is a complex process. For many readers, the closer the retelling comes to the original the worse it is. This appears to reflect a widely held belief not that Austen's style is inimitable (as the authors involved in The Austen Project have shown, it can in fact be copied very precisely), but rather that it should not be imitated. As we have seen, this leads into questions surrounding the social and cultural value of authors such as Austen which take us far beyond what is there on the page. The games that we all (stylisticians included) engage in when evaluating works of art are, like those in Austen's novels, varied, fascinating and unavoidable.

References

Austen, J. (2005) [1816], *Emma*, R. Cronin and D. McMillan (ed.), Cambridge: Cambridge University Press.
Austen, J. (2006) [1811], *Sense and Sensibility*, E. Copeland (ed.), Cambridge: Cambridge University Press.
Austen, J. (2006) [1818], *Northanger Abbey*, B. M. Benedict and D. Le Faye (ed.), Cambridge: Cambridge University Press.
Bray, J. (2018), *The Language of Jane Austen*, London: Palgrave Macmillan.
Craig, A. (2013), Review of *Sense & Sensibility* by Joanna Trollope. *The Independent*. Available online: https://www.independent.co.uk/arts-entertainment/books/reviews/book-review-sense-sensibility-by-joanna-trollope-8887105.html
Empson, W. (1947 [1930]), *Seven Types of Ambiguity*, 2nd edition, London: Chatto & Windus.
Frye, N. (1957), *Anatomy of Criticism: Four Essays*, Princeton and Oxford: Princeton University Press.
Groskop, V. (2014), Review of *Emma: A Modern Retelling* by Alexander McCall Smith, *The Guardian*. Available online: https://www.theguardian.com/books/2014/nov/24/emma-alexander-mccall-smith-review-exhausting-implausible
Kenny, A. (1973), *Wittgenstein*, London: Penguin.
Lyall, S. (2016), '"Eligible," Curtis Sittenfeld's Update of Jane Austen'. *The New York Times*. Available online: https://www.nytimes.com/2016/05/01/books/review/eligible-curtis-sittenfelds-update-of-jane-austen.html
McCall Smith, A. (2014), *Emma: A Modern Retelling*, London: The Borough Press.
McDermid, V. (2014), *Northanger Abbey*, London: The Borough Press.
Price, L. (2015), 'Review of *Emma: A Modern Retelling* by Alexander McCall Smith'. *The New York Times*. Available online: https://www.nytimes.com/2015/05/31/books/review/emma-a-modern-retelling-by-alexander-mccall-smith.html
Ribes-Iñesta, E. (2006), 'Human Behaviour as Language: Some thoughts on Wittgenstein', *Behaviour and Philosophy*, 34: 109–21.
Sittenfeld, C. (2016), *Eligible*, London: The Borough Press.
Toolan, M. (2014), 'The Theory and Philosophy of Stylistics', in P. Stockwell and S. Whiteley (eds), *The Cambridge Handbook of Stylistics*, 13–31, Cambridge: Cambridge University Press.
Trollope, J. (2013), *Sense & Sensibility*, London: HarperCollins.
Wales, K. (2001), *A Dictionary of Stylistics*, 2nd edition, Harlow: Pearson.
Widdowson, H. (1996), 'Stylistics: An Approach to Stylistic Analysis', in J. J. Weber (ed.), *The Stylistics Reader: From Jakobson to the Present*, 138–48, London and New York: Arnold.
Wittgenstein, L. (1921), *Tractatus Logico-Philosophicus*, New York: Harcourt.
Wittengenstein, L. (1966), *Lectures and Conversations on Aesthetics, Psychology and Religious Belief* (ed.), C. Barrett, Oxford: Basil Blackwell.

6

Rewriting misdirection: A stylistic approach to crime fiction writing

Christiana Gregoriou

6.1 Introduction and background

Though a well-loved genre, it was only in 2018 that crime fiction became *the UK's most popular* fiction genre for the first time (London Book fair data, cited in Harding 2018). Despite, or perhaps even because of, this genre's popularity, it has only recently begun to attract the academic attention it deserves. By stylistically analysing previously unexplored contemporary UK crime novel production data, this chapter contributes to discussions surrounding the increasing value of a relatively neglected genre, while allowing insight into its genre making and the mechanisms contributing to crime fiction remaining a genre with popular appeal. In doing so, such research can not only feed into aspiring crime writers' efforts to newly understand and ultimately improve their craft but, as Clark (2012: 157) demonstrates, also provide 'opportunities for pedagogical activities which help students to develop their understanding of how texts give rise to effects'. The chapter is relevant to a volume on narrative retellings given that it is concerned with how a crime fictional written narrative gets 'retold' in the process of an author's editing and redrafting of an early version of a manuscript. In turn, such engagement sheds light into the creative writing process that leads to the end book-product.

Crime fiction is the art of 'misdirection'. I here define misdirection as a genre-typical set of techniques through which the crime fiction reader is very often deliberately misled away from the precise nature of the circumstances surrounding the crime the fiction features. Although not limited to crime fiction, misdirection is crucial for the genre formula and a major factor determining the genre's positive reception and success. In other words, for readers to be typically pleasurably surprised at the encounter of crucial revelations when reaching the end of crime novels they read, they must be misdirected away from evidence to start with. To name but a few examples, characters, who readers are meant to read as suspicious, turn out to be innocent (and known as 'red herrings') and vice versa. Despite this set of misdirecting techniques having attracted some language specialist academic attention (see Emmott and Alexander 2010, 2014; Gregoriou 2017, 2020; Seago 2014), the techniques have not yet been investigated through modern crime fiction writing production data. Rather than theorize as to the nature of the genre's writing process, this chapter instead engages with actual data in the form of crime fiction author archive material to offer hands-on analysis of the makings of misdirection in modern crime fiction creative writing.

When discussing the makings of misdirection, Emmott and Alexander (2010: 329) draw on the helpful analogy of crime fiction writers as conjurers who employ various strategies with which to control readers' attention, hence 'cognitively misdirecting' them away from evidence pointing to crime fiction 'puzzle' 'solutions'. The techniques in question could be non-linguistic where, for instance, a character uses a physical disguise, or rhetorical, where an author buries information to encourage shallow processing, uses supposedly reliable characters to vouch for the reliability of other characters, sets false trails to distract readers and, finally, authenticates the solution (Emmott and Alexander 2010). Stylistics offers a set of tools with which to unpick the authors' manipulative linguistic devices and elucidate the misdirecting strategy. Among others, one could study repetition; schema-oriented language; gendered language; unclear, ambiguous and polysemous lexical choices and their associated pragmatic inferences and associations, including early references to who turns out to be a killer; various language-specific grammatical restrictions that relate to matters of agency/responsibility and so on. (For an introduction to 'schema theory', which explains how readers' knowledge about given subjects comes to influence literary processing, see chapter 5.2 in Gregoriou 2009.) Of relevance here is Emmott's (1997: 225) concept of frame repair/reconstruction, according to which readers of crime fiction are often invited to rethink their understanding of previously visited scenes or circumstances at the discovery of these having been insufficiently processed at first read. Though such reconstructions could be the result of the reader being careless – not having first read the text closely enough – crime fiction reconstructions are often intended by the author. What misdirection effectively does is mislead readers into deliberately misprocessing settings and situations, only for them to repair their understanding of the relevant circumstances at the encounter of important revelations later on.

As argued in Gregoriou (2020), essential to the misdirecting narrative device is what is known as the genre's 'fair play rule' (Sayers 1947: 225), that is, the notion that observant readers should be able to solve the crime at the detective story's heart despite the author's determined attempt to direct them away from evidence. The fair play skill 'lies in mentioning [plot-significant] items without drawing attention to them or to their significance so that they are not suspected of being relevant to the solution' (Emmott and Alexander 2014: 333) too soon. What the present chapter addresses is the crucial concern of how crime writers confront the challenge of securing fair play. It does so through a stylistic approach to a hitherto unexamined archive pertaining to contemporary crime writers' creative process materials in the form of annotated early drafts and notebooks. In so doing, I address the question of how a crime author's misdirection-making *changes tact* in order to uphold the generic fulcrum of 'fair play'. The matter of fairness is linked to that of credibility. Put differently, crime fiction burying depends on readers being confused as to the significance of information in both the foreground and background of a text; while some information which proves to be plot-significant gets buried in the background, that which proves plot-insignificant gets foregrounded, with the writer needing to manage the reversal in significance in such a way that the solution proves ultimately credible (Emmott and Alexander 2014) and hence 'fair'.

The University of Leeds' Brotherton library allows access to unpublished material that can help illuminate the authors' negotiation of fairness. It hosts an extensive contemporary crime fiction special collection, inclusive of material that relates to the critically acclaimed crime series from the published work of award-winning contemporary authors, one of whom is Peter Robinson, whose Detective Chief Inspector Alan Banks crime series' first novel (2004) [1987] *Gallows View* I turn to next. Before exploring Robinson's (re)making of this novel's misdirection and clue-burying, I start with a necessary plot outline, focusing only on the relevant novel aspects that relate to the misdirecting devices in question.

In *Gallows View*, Banks is called to investigate a number of crimes, including a 'peeping Tom' who terrifies the women he spies on; two young men, Trevor and Mick, involved in breaking into homes of (mostly) old people, raping a woman and even an apparent break-in ending in one old woman, Alice Matlock, accidentally dying. The book opens with a short extract from the yet-unknown male (notice the use of 'he' and 'his' in 'His whole body tingled as he watched' on p. 2) peeping Tom's viewpoint. Certain chapters later being written from each of Trevor and Mick's perspectives unequivocally show them to be breaking into, and vandalizing, people's homes looking for things to steal and sell and even raping a resident. It is for this reason that readers are led to believe that it is these two young men who were involved in Alice's passing too though, ultimately, readers discover that it was Graham Sharp, Trevor's father, who was the culprit instead. It is in an effort to protect young Trevor and silence Alice, who was threatening to report Trevor's wrongdoings to the police, that Graham kills her by accident, after which he vandalizes her place so as to link her passing to the burglaries the police is investigating. The novel featuring numerous viewpoint shifts, including those into the perspectives of Alice, Alan and Graham, contributes to the book's misdirection, as will later be explained.

The chapter will answer the following research questions: What are the stylistic means through which Robinson operates the workings of reader misdirection in *Gallows View* while responding to the challenge of playing 'fair'? In what ways does his editor feed into the crime author's misdirection, and what does engagement with notebooks and different versions of carefully selected crime novel extracts reveal about the nature and (re)making of the misdirection of the crime writing process'?

6.2 Misdirection-(re)making in *Gallows View*

To respond to the challenge of 'playing fair', crime authors ought to ensure that criminal characters are suspicious enough to be noticed, but not so much so that the reader dwells on them far too much and/or knows them to be guilty from the start.

6.2.1 Robin Allott's peeping on unsuspecting women

One such suspicious character in *Gallows View* (2004) [1987] is Robin Allott, a photography friend of the Inspector's wife, Sandra, who is revealed to be the 'peeping Tom' Banks's investigative team is after. In the novel's unpublished early draft (available through the Leeds crime fiction archive) the reader is first introduced to Robin as one of six characters having a drink in a pub, having just attended a photography lecture:

> Sandra found herself sitting between Harriet and Eric Clough, a rather intense young man who would as soon slit his throat as crop one of his photographs. Opposite were Julia Sloane, a young married woman, who, Sandra thought uncharitably, was only there because she was blatantly chasing Robin Allott, the

shy, handsome, recently-divorced schoolteacher beside her; and finally, Norman Chester, who always seemed more interested in the scientific process than in the photographs themselves. Normally, of course, such an oddly-assorted group would never have come together, but they were united in the need for a real drink – especially after a longish lecture.

(*Gallows View* early draft, p. 32–3)

According to Emmott and Alexander (2014: 332), items (and their significance) can be buried through a number of techniques, including 'Mention the item as little as possible'; 'Use linguistic structures which have been shown empirically to reduce prominence'; 'Place the item next to an item that is more prominent, so that the focus is on the more prominent item'; 'Make the item apparently unimportant in the narrative world (even though it is actually significant)' and so on. Besides, '[t]he more information is compressed into short text units, the shallower the reader processes this information – i.e. the reader skims over items, does not remember all details or does not differentiate between potentially relevant and irrelevant detail' (Seago 2014: 210).

'Peeping Tom' Robin is an item 'buried' when first introduced to us readers in this scene communicated through Sandra's viewpoint (see the reference to the description of Julia as one which 'Sandra thought uncharitably'). This burying is achieved in a number of ways. To begin with, Robin appears unimportant and is backgrounded when introduced in the midst of as many as six pub characters. Four of these six, namely Eric, Julia, Robin and Norman, are characters newly introduced to the reader and hence take focus, with Sandra and Harriet being backgrounded, having been introduced previously. Three of the 'new' characters are male (notice the novel's previously described p. 2 opening text suggesting a male peeper), and two of these three male ones, that is Eric and Norman, are more linguistically and thematically prominent and indeed appear far more suspicious than Robin. Unlike Robin who is 'shy' and passive, Eric is 'intense', having been introduced through Sandra's throat-slicing metaphor making him appear as potentially physically dangerous to others. The means through which Eric is described in particular triggers the schema of a psychologically 'intense' character who struggles to control his overwhelming emotions and might, as a result, be capable of socially deviant behaviour. The language hence triggering a potentially criminal interest in Eric deflects attention away from the actual criminal featuring in the scene, Robin. Even more so, Robin is buried through being listed in the middle, rather than the start/end of the given excerpt's rather long list of new pub characters. Notice that he features in the *second* of the excerpt's three sentences and is also the *second* in a list of three newly introduced characters in the excerpt's second sentence, meaning that he is buried through the order in which he is listed, and features, too.

Just as importantly, Robin features in a grammatically subordinate clause (starting with 'because she was blatantly chasing') itself embedded within yet another subordinate clause (starting with 'who [...] was only there'), as opposed to appearing in a main clause of his own. What Robinson here manipulates is the fact that information in main clauses is more easily remembered than information in subordinate clauses (see supportive research by Sanford and Sturt 2002: 386). This is in line with an Emmott and Alexander (2010: 345) manipulation guideline advising whodunit writers to '[b]ury key information by grammatical embedding, by surrounding it with more interesting material, and by manipulating the overall focus of the discourse so that the buried information is not the main rhetorical point'. Robin is here 'buried' when presented as having few defining or notable personality-related characteristics compared to the similarly newly introduced others. Though Eric is 'intense', Julia is defined by her infatuation with Robin, and Norman is presented in terms of his scientific process-related interests, Robin is merely described in terms of his good looks, school-teaching profession and divorced status. Robin's 'shyness' hints at a personality of sorts, but not one that is distinguishable or remarkable like that of the others. In other words, readers arguably learn less about Robin than they do about all the other newly introduced characters, for which reason they are likely to think of him as unimportant to any of the story's criminal plots. Even more so, Robin gets to be introduced to readers incidentally as a character mentioned only because he is someone another more prominent, and hence focused-on character, Julia, takes a romantic/sexual interest in. It is for this reason that he first features in a grammatically 'object' position ('she was blatantly chasing Robin Allott') rather than a 'subject' position in the clause in question; he is first mentioned as the 'object' of Julia's affection not only metaphorically but also grammatically, which again backgrounds him in readers' suspicions even further.

Later in this early draft, Robin is said to 'blushingly [continue] to fend off Julia's persistent advances' (p. 33) while, when discussing the peeping incidents, Julia subsequently says she would not mind being peeped on while glancing sideways at Robin, at which point he becomes 'reddened' and 'flashe[s] Sandra a long-suffering smile' (p. 36). Further to such references suggesting that he is uninterested in Julia altogether, the references even point to Robin feeling victimized, even preyed on, by her. Note that later, when Julia stops attending the group gatherings, Robin is said to be relieved at her absence (p. 205). References of this kind invite sympathy for Robin's character. This itself is key in generating the impression of him as likeable and someone to be viewed not as a potential (physically powerful) perpetrator of any kind and not least a perpetrator of the kind he ultimately proves himself to be (i.e. a 'peeping Tom'), but even a victim on his own accord, because of Julia's somewhat predatory behaviour. The draft suggests that he is an appealing ('handsome', Sandra's narrative voice says) man who is actually finding himself resisting a young, married and attractive woman's advancements (Julia is later described as an 'attractive twenty-five year old' on p. 37). He is not portrayed as a man that women would object to the advances of or should be wary of. The means through which he is described are even somewhat fitting for the 'ideal victim' (see Christie 1986) schema, in line with which victims of crime are weak and blameless (he is 'blushingly' 'shy' and 'suffering') and respectable ('schoolteacher'), not to mention sexualized (he is 'attractive', someone a woman pines over and so on). In short, him being somewhat victimized suggests that he could not possibly be criminalized.

Just as importantly, Robin is mentioned very little throughout this early novel draft and even remains silent through all early draft scenes previously mentioned. He does not speak at all until the early draft's p. 206, where he makes a passing and insignificant photography-related comment in a conversation the photography group has. Readers of the early draft do not come to the realization of him being the peeper the police are after until he visits Sandra in her home towards the end of the early book draft, at which point his 'peeping' and dangerous tendencies come to be revealed. He threateningly forces Sandra to strip, only for him to collapse in tears, and have Sandra attack him in self-defence, saving herself from possible harm. Here, readers 'repair' their understanding of the previous scene circumstances and come to interpret the previously visited scenes differently to how they first read them. The early reference to Julia wanting Robin to 'peep on' her is read ironically in retrospect, for instance. Similarly, descriptions alluding to Robin's evident shyness can now be read in terms of a man who kept himself unnoticed, so as to 'peep' on unsuspecting women without suspicion.

In any case, as a result of Robin having been overly buried in this early draft manuscript, early draft readers (including myself, and also Robinson's editor 'Cynthia', according to annotations on the manuscript) are arguably *overly* surprised to discover him to be ultimately dangerous at this draft's end. In a margin annotation on the early draft's first introduction to Robin, the editor asks, '[A]re all these [characters] necessary?' and, in one of the author's notebooks, Robinson scribbles, 'Make Robin more memorable' (see Figure 6.1), presumably because he does not behave in an incriminating way at all in the early draft.

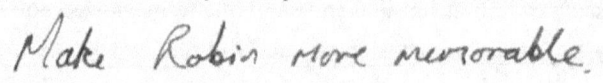

Figure 6.1 'Make Robin more memorable' excerpt

As a result, the published book places Robin in a much more prominent storyline position, all the same still in keeping with fair play regulations which require him to be *somewhat* buried still.

When we first encounter Robin in the published novel, he is in a group of four rather than six pub characters:

> As usual, Sandra, Harriet, Robin Allott and Norman Chester, all preferring stronger refreshments, adjourned to the Mile Post across the road.

> Sandra found herself sitting between Harriet and Robin, a young college teacher just getting over his divorce. Opposite sat Norman Chester, who always seemed more interested in the scientific process than the photographs themselves. Normally, such an oddly-assorted group would never have come together, but they were united in the need for a real drink – especially after a longish lecture.

(Gallows View (2004) [1987]: 29)

We have now lost the early draft's 'intense' Eric Clough and, also pining Julia Sloane, characters who no longer appear in the published novel altogether. Early draft annotations slashing out initial mentions of Julia and Norman indicate a surplus of characters though, as it so happened, it was ultimately Norman who made the final 'cut' at Eric's expense. It was in the early manuscript's p. 37 that Eric talks about the peeper maybe being a member of the photography club, for instance, as opposed to Norman doing so in the published version. Notably, the editor crosses out the narrative voice adding 'They all felt that if they responded, they would be opening a can of worms they would far rather keep closed' (early draft, p. 37) which Robinson eliminated from the published book so as not to foreground this possibility any further. Also, lines such as Robin saying 'I sometimes have a devil of a job keeping things to myself' in the published book's p. 193 were ones originally ascribed to Eric in the early draft's p. 209, these ultimately being read as potentially incriminating for Robin instead. In short, Robinson comes to do away with characters and reallocate lines both of which contribute to Robin being more prominent in the published book compared to the early draft.

To return to the p. 29 excerpt's smaller character list above, notice that Robin is here not characterized as 'shy', 'handsome' or the object of anyone's affection. Perhaps describing him as such would subsequently seem odd then; besides, readers' 'peeping' schema would most likely suggest someone altogether unappealing for women, and descriptions of Robin as someone 'handsome' would prove contrary to those expectations. In fact, though Robin is said to be attractive/handsome according to various women's perspectives in the early draft, he is not described so at all in the published book. Also note his newly divorced status and teaching profession, which too feature in the early draft's 'Robin Allott, the shy, handsome, recently-divorced schoolteacher' (p. 32). Notice, however, the published book's Robin now being 'a young college teacher just getting over his divorce', which suggests a struggle to do so, and victimizes him, also inviting sympathy from readers perhaps, particularly when compared to the early draft's 'recently-divorced' reference which does not necessarily suggest him to be struggling to accept his newly divorced status at all. As for his profession, notice the change from 'school' to 'college' teacher, possibly implemented to take away the paedophile element (i.e. any implication that his later revealed peeping sexual interest in adult women might possibly extend to children). Lastly, note that – unlike the book's early draft – he is here described as 'young', a description that later fits a psychological profiler's assessment of the peeper he ultimately turns out to be ('find [...] men between the ages of about twenty and thirty-five', on published book's p. 119). Even more tellingly, the published book also features added scenes that hint at Robin's criminal behaviour, particularly as his speech now features in them. In discussing the peeper with others in the group, Robin asks: 'Do you think he understands [what he is doing] himself?' (p. 33), which was maybe added as a clue to him not fully understanding his own criminal doings when readers read on. A series of notebook scribbles showcases several other additions to the published book version (see Figures 6.2–6.4):

> 'Add a scene where Robin, Sandra etc. go somewhere photographing for a day (coast?) Then Robin says he knew [the unrelated murder victim] Alice'
>
> (see Figure 6.2).

> 'Sandra suggests on first hearing that Robin should talk to [Banks] [about Alice's unrelated murder] He seems nervous but she convinces him – he won't bite you – and he agrees. Banks sees him at home, mother there [...]'
>
> (see Figure 6.3).

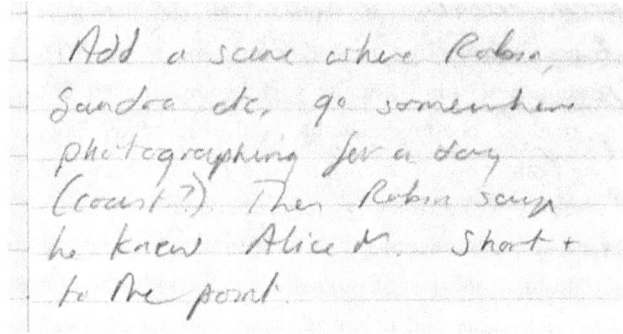

Figure 6.2 'Add a scene where Robin, Sandra etc. go somewhere' excerpt

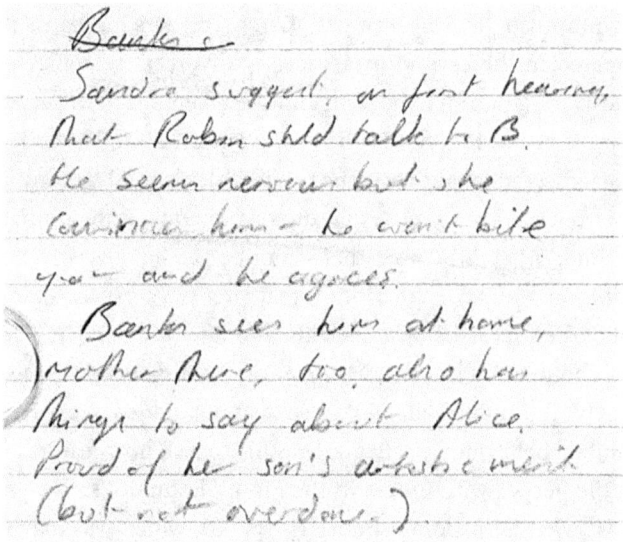

Figure 6.3 'Sandra suggests on first hearing that Robin should talk to [Banks]' excerpt

'Don't really create any suspicion in Bank's mind that Robin killed Alice, but he seems (very subtly) to be telling Sandra it wasn't kids – enough that we wonder if he's going to confess' (see Figure 6.4).

These scribbles point to the addition of scenes that prove useful in creating 'fairness' in the crime fictional game the author plays with his readers, all the while bringing Robin to the narrative foreground *a little*. In the added scene where Robin mentions knowing Alice, he later says, '[I]t sometimes seems to me as if we're looking outside through a clear window at some idealised

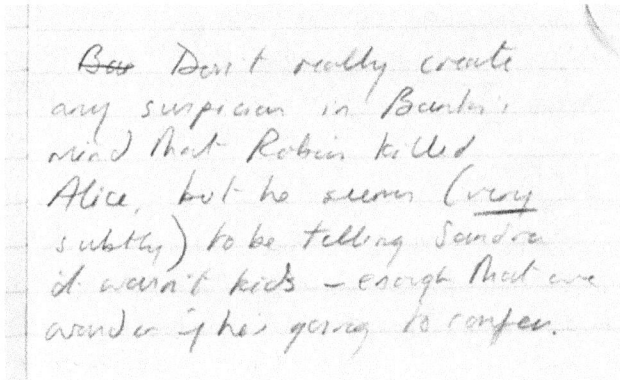

Figure 6.4 'Don't really create any suspicion in Bank's mind that Robin killed Alice' excerpt

image' (p. 127), a photography-related comment differently interpretable at the realization of him being a peeper later. The Robin-visiting scene is added so as to make Robin more fitting for the psychological profiling constructed of him elsewhere; Banks finds him single and living with a parent, as the profiler predicted ('find [...] men either alone or with a single parent, most likely a mother', published book's p. 119). His mother being present when Banks comes to visit proves key, as is her mentioning Robin's father being an 'invalid' (p. 156), hence not featuring in the scene, or his life much. Even more so, it is during this added scene where Robin brings Alan's attention to there not having been 'senseless damage to Alice's sentimental possessions' (published book's p. 303), hence signalling that this supposed burglary was likely staged. Robin's nervousness on the day of Banks's visit is explainable as he caught sight of Alice's killer, even though he cannot explain how to Banks, at least not without incriminating himself in his own 'peeping' behaviour. Robin hence appears somewhat suspicious in the published book, but not guilty of the crime he turns out to have committed, that is, 'peeping'. Interestingly, Sandra also comes across as much less flirtatious with Robin in the published book's p. 252 rewriting (with Robinson doing away with references she makes to him being attractive/handsome in the early draft's p. 272, for instance) to eliminate any potential indication that his subsequent threatening actions to her were in any way welcoming.

All in all, through alterations made to the final *Gallows View* draft, Robinson manages to bring Robin to the narrative foreground *enough* but does so while still burying Robin-specific information. Since Robin is brought to the foreground in conjunction with the separate crime of Alice's murder, Robinson can be said to accord to the burying strategy that Emmott and Alexander (2014: 334) refer to as Strategy 1-2-ALT, that is, attaching displaced or false significance to a plot-significant item. Here, rather than foregrounding something unimportant (Strategy 1) or backgrounding something important (Strategy 2), what Robinson does is combine the two, that is, draw attention to an aspect of Robin (his knowing Alice) which is not the aspect that is relevant to solving the crime he proved guilty of (his peeping on women). Therefore, readers attach significance to Robin that ultimately proves false; since his acquaintance with her proved irrelevant to her murder, the connection the two had was a red herring misleading the reader away from thinking of him as involved in a crime other than her murder. In so doing, Robinson's published book, on the whole, diminishes the importance of crucial plot-relevant details and encourages some shallow processing (Emmott and Alexander 2014) of Robin much more effectively than the early draft does.

6.2.2 Graham Sharp's manslaughter/murder of Alice

Mick saying that Trevor and he should 'stop' it with the 'old dears' (published book's p. 36 and early draft's p. 41) fairly leads readers into thinking that the two of them are admittedly elderly people burglars. Since Trevor is shown to be a rapist, and Mick an accomplice to rape during one such burglary, they prove capable of committing crimes far worse than breaking, entering and thieving. And since Alice's killing is linked to one such burglary, readers are led to believe that they could also be elderly people killers, too. Besides, the early draft does mislead readers into thinking that it was burglars who killed Alice (see p. 62's 'Same pattern as the other break-ins'), as does the published book on p. 58, though, as noted, it was Graham Sharp who proved to be Alice's actual, if accidental, killer in both versions' endings. The early draft does feature some clues to Graham's criminal misbehaviour, clues which remained intact in the final version. See, for instance, the early draft's (p. 11) reference to Graham not knowing 'if he was going about things the right way or not' with Trevor, also found in the published book's p. 11, a reference which is interpretable differently at the realization of what it was that Graham actually did to protect his son from harm, that is, kill Alice. The published book also retains references to Graham's 'worried' reaction to the police officer on his door (p. 65, also on p. 71 in early draft) and to him saying that Trevor was with him on the night of Alice's murder (p. 66, also on p. 72 in early draft). In the first reading of this text, these references suggest Graham is worried about his son's vulnerability, for which he is quick to offer

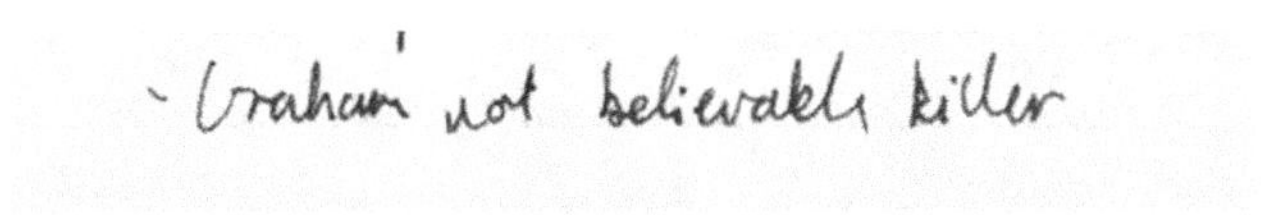

Graham not believable killer

Figure 6.5 'Graham not believable killer' excerpt

him an alibi for murder, 'binding' him into the home frame in conceptual frame theory (Emmott 1997) terms. Having said that, these suggestions are ultimately 'repaired' as inferences to Graham's own vulnerability and him wanting to give himself an alibi, instead. The same goes for the Sharps finishing their dinner in silence on the final book's p. 90. Taken altogether, though both versions invite readers to become aware of Graham having lied to the police about being with his son on the night of Alice's murder, readers are not fully meant to appreciate him doing so to protect his own tracks until much later.

Despite such clues though, a Robinson notebook scribble suggests that 'Graham [is] not [a] believable killer' in the early draft (see Figure 6.5).

Scribbles with respect to Graham self-instruct the writer to rework this character; he must be ultimately less innocent-looking than in the early draft, despite the few clues to him being suspicious that the early draft is already peppered with. An author notebook features references to Graham needing to be 'more ferocious in love-making' with his lover Andrea, which 'show[s] some tension, preoccupation in him', 'he's not [the] same as usual', which would explain his later 'then release of confession' (see Figure 6.6), while elsewhere there is a reference to Andrea needing to ask Graham 'what's wrong' (see Point 2 in Figure 6.7).

As a result, Robinson adds a short post-sex exchange with Andrea, not featuring in the early draft, and meant to function as a clue to Graham's later admission to having killed Alice. This shows Andrea saying 'See how much better you feel now', followed by Graham's 'I was just a bit preoccupied, that's all', to which she replies with: 'You were all tense […] Whatever it was, it certainly made you wild, though' (p. 81). The latter published book line implies that something as yet unspecified has just happened (i.e. he killed Alice, we later realize), which generated Graham's tension before he and Andrea had sex. Other scribbles similarly indicate this need '[t]o make Sharp guilty […] Hands shake as he does dishes', for instance (see Point 1 in Figure 6.7). On the published book's p. 11, readers indeed find a reference to Graham's shaking hands when picking up the breakfast dishes not found in the early draft's p. 11, where instead the author himself hand-wrote 'his hands shook as he' over the line referring to the

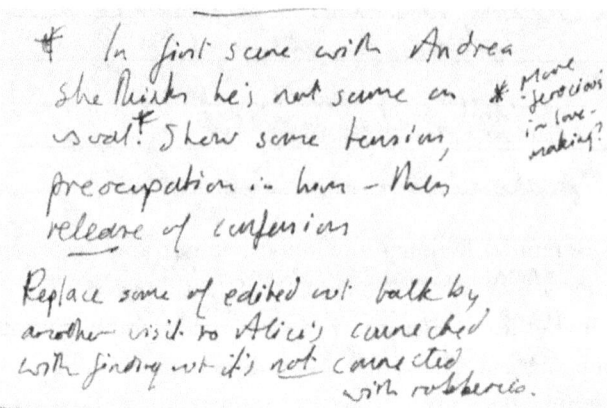

Figure 6.6 'In first scene with Andrea' excerpt

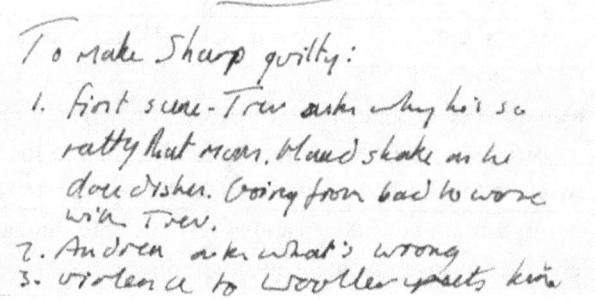

Figure 6.7 'To make Sharp guilty' excerpt

father picking up dishes. The author here self-instructs to add the relevant guilt-signalling shaking-hand reference later. Lastly, a series of notebook scribbles refers to an altercation that Sharp has with his neighbour Wooller, who appears to be threatening to reveal his affair with Andrea: 'Violence to Wooller upsets him' (see Point 3 in Figure 6.7), 'Sharp with Wooller – violence reminds him of killing [Alice Matlock] (not overtly)' (see Figure 6.8).

As these scribbles propose the addition of text which is meant to hint at Graham struggling to cope with his guilt, they counter the *unfair play* of the early draft where Graham appears to feel less guilty throughout. The published book features the following added bit of narration in the midst of Graham threateningly confronting Wooller, narration meant to signal Graham being upset by his own violence, readers later realizing that this confrontation reminds him of this violence having previously come to cause Alice's death. I use underlining to mark the bits of text which were added

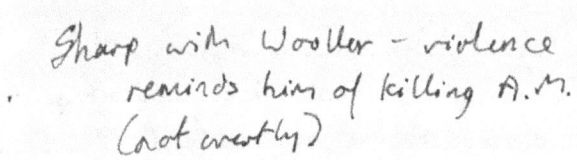

Figure 6.8 'Sharp with Wooller' excerpt

when the excerpt was reworked into the final draft, normal font indicating early text bits which the final draft retained:

> '"Stop it," Wooller whined, putting his hand to the back of his head. "You've split my skull. Look, blood". […] <u>Sharp felt a sudden lurch of fear in his stomach. He let go of Wooller and leaned against the doorway, pale and trembling. Wooller stared at him with his mouth open.</u>
> <u>Quickly, Graham made the effort to pull himself together. He grabbed a glass from the draining-board and, without even bothering to see if it was clean or not, filled it with cold water from the tap and gulped it down.</u>
> <u>Feeling a little better, he ran his hand through his hair and faced a confused Wooller</u> […] "I'm not going to tell you again," […]'
> (*Gallows View* (2004) [1987]: 182–3)

Here, Robinson adjusts the description of Graham's attack to signal the latter being reminded of the harm he is actually capable of causing (note also Graham's 'snarl[ing]' in the early draft's p. 188, which becomes 'quiet menace' in the published book's p. 183). In short, the published book shows Graham trying to control his own menacing behaviour, whereas no such attempt at control is found in the early one.

When officers hypothesize as to the peeper potentially being Alice's killer, with 'she threatened to report him and he killed her?' (early draft's p. 78), the editor handwrites 'by mistake' on the side, leading Robinson to change this text into 'she threatened to report him, they struggled, and he pushed her? Manslaughter' (published book's pp. 73–4), reframing Alice's murder into the lesser crime of manslaughter instead, alleviating Sharp of some guilt to some extent. This impression of somewhat reduced responsibility is also suggested through notebook scribbles which self-instruct the writer to dramatize the killer's confession, also showing remorse and relief on his part: 'Sharp's confession – dramatize [and] visualize murder, his horror, conflict, [r]emorse. It's a relief to tell it' (see Figure 6.9).

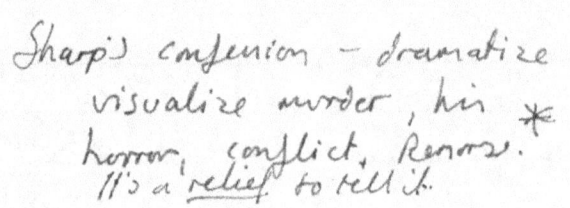

Figure 6.9 'Sharp's confession' excerpt

See, for instance, added references to Sharp being 'on the verge of a nervous collapse' (p. 304), crying ('Sharp put his head in his hands and sobbed' on p. 305) and saying 'It's just a relief. You've no idea what a burden this has been for me' (p. 305) while admitting to his part in an 'accident' (p. 305), all of which do not appear in the early draft. All in all, a comparison of the early draft to the published book, and also relating these versions to notebook scribbles, reveals how the writer came to eventually make Alice's killer a bit more suspicious-looking, even though his crime is recast as an accidental murder of sorts. In Alice's murder case too, the published book also plays 'fairer' than the early draft.

6.3 Conclusion

As Emmott and Alexander (2014: 343) argue, '[w]riters of plots with surprise endings use foregrounding and burying to carefully direct readers in the hope of controlling their attention and thereby achieving rhetorical manipulation'. Stylistic study of unpublished material in such formats as notebooks and annotated early novel drafts can allow an analyst to interrogate *how* this happens and, hence, trace how a novel's published version came to misdirect a reader away from characters who turn out to be criminally and appropriately significant. Engaging with archival material that established writers share can offer readers, analysts and writers the opportunity to gain not only an insight into the crime fiction (re)writing process but also a clearer sense of how crime writers specifically negotiate the precise challenge of the 'fair play' device. What exploring the archival material relating to *Gallows View* more precisely enabled was an engagement with the ways in which, with respect to the characters of both Robin and Graham, the book's published version came to play 'fairer' than the earlier draft. This 'retelling' is arguably one that contributed to the book's popularity and success, particularly given that this 1987 book is but one, and the first, in a series featuring over twenty-six Banks novels, many of which have also been adapted for television (British ITV's *DCI Banks*, 2010–16). The University of Leeds Peter Robinson crime fiction special collection currently extends to material relating to the first twenty-five of these novels (published to date). It also relates to Robinson's other, and also Frances Brody's and Sophie Hannah's own, crime writing. This archive allows a researcher to further explore the ways in which a writer's misdirection strategizing changes and develops over time and as a series develops, all while the author collaborates not only with intervening editors and readers but also in line with 'fair play' being firmly complied with.

Acknowledgement

I would like to thank the Leeds University Crime Fiction archive (housed in the Brotherton Library) for giving me permission to reproduce images from Peter Robinson's notebooks in my chapter.

References

Christie, N. (1986), 'The Ideal Victim', in E. A. Fattah (ed.), *From Crime Policy to Victim Policy*, 17–30, London: Palgrave Macmillan.
Clark, B. (2012), 'Beginning with "One More Thing": Pragmatics and Editorial Intervention in the Work of Raymond Carver', *Journal of Literary Semantics*, 41 (2): 155–73.
Emmott, C. (1997), *Narrative Comprehension: A Discourse Perspective*, Oxford: Oxford University Press.
Emmott, C., and Alexander, M. (2010), 'Detective Fiction, Plot Construction, and Reader Manipulation: Rhetorical Control and Cognitive Misdirection in Agatha Christie's *Sparkling Cyanide*', in D. McIntyre and B. Busse (eds), *Language and Style: In Honour of Mick Short*, 328–46, Basingstoke: Palgrave Macmillan.
Emmott, C., and Alexander, M. (2014), 'Foregrounding, Burying, and Plot Construction', in P. Stockwell and S. Whiteley (eds), *The Handbook of Stylistics*, 329–43, Cambridge: Cambridge University Press.
Gregoriou, C. (2009), *English Literary Stylistics*, Basingstoke: Palgrave Perspectives on the English Language.
Gregoriou, C. (2017), *Crime Fiction Migration: Crossing Languages, Cultures, Media*, London: Bloomsbury.
Gregoriou, C. (2020), 'Untranslatable Clues: Reader Manipulation and the Challenge of Crime Fiction Translation', in S. Sorlin (ed.), *Stylistic Manipulation of the Reader in Fiction*, 215–33, London: Bloomsbury.

Harding, L. (2018), 'Crime Becomes Most Popular Fiction Genre for First Time in UK'. *The Sunday Post*, 11 April. Available online: https://www.sundaypost.com/fp/crime-becomes-most-popular-fiction-genre-for-first-time-in-uk/ (accessed 11 April 2019).

Robinson, P. (2004) [1987], *Gallows View*, London: Macmillan.

Sanford, A., and Sturt, P. (2002), 'Depth of Processing in Language Comprehension', *Trends in Cognitive Sciences*, 6 (9): 382–6.

Sayers, D. L. (1947), *Unpopular Opinions*, New York: Harcourt, Brace.

Seago, K. (2014), 'Red Herrings and Other Misdirection in Translation', in S. Cadera and A. P. Pintaric (eds), *The Voices of Suspense and Their Translation in Thrillers*, 207–20, Amsterdam: Rodopi.

Part Two

Factual retellings

7

Siegfried Sassoon, autofiction and style: Retelling the experience of war

Marcello Giovanelli

7.1 Introduction

On 7 February 1930, Siegfried Sassoon wrote the first letter in a short but intense and quite remarkable series of correspondence with his fellow First World War poet-soldier Robert Graves. Graves and Sassoon had first met in France in November 1915 with Graves playing an influential role in the development of Sassoon's poetic style. Over time, however, the two grew apart. Their correspondence in 1930 was precipitated by the publication in 1929 of Graves's memoir *Goodbye to All That*, a book which angered Sassoon because Graves had included, without permission, one of Sassoon's private poems and an account of his stay at Sassoon's family home where Graves claimed that he had heard Sassoon's mother attempting to make spiritual contact with Sassoon's dead brother. The poem and part of the description were removed, at Sassoon's request, before publication. Sassoon was further irritated by what he felt were Graves's more general inaccurate and sensationalist representations of the events of the war. In fact, Graves had written the book to ease his own financial troubles and seemed quite willing to use it literally to leave the past behind; earlier in 1922, he had written to Sassoon to stress the difference between his war and post-war selves: 'You identify me in your mind with a certain Robert Graves now dead […] Don't' (Graves 1982: 134). Graves further defended his writing and method by arguing:

> I would even paradoxically say that the memoirs of a man who went through some of the worst experiences of trench warfare are not truthful if they do not contain a high proportion of falsities. (Graves 1930: 354)

This chapter examines the process and nature of retelling by situating it within the specific context of Sassoon's own reconstructions of his war experiences. Unlike Graves, Sassoon found it difficult to resist his 'queer craving to revisit the past' (Sassoon 1938: 140) and reshaped and retold large parts of diary entries, letters and poems in his two trilogies of prose memoirs written and published between 1928 and 1945 (see Giovanelli 2019a for discussion from a literary linguistic perspective). In this chapter, I explore one such retelling of his 1917 poem 'Lamentations' (Sassoon 1918) in *Memoirs of an Infantry Officer* (henceforth *Memoirs*) (Sassoon 1930). I compare the poem and its revision by examining *Memoirs* as an example of autofiction (Doubrovsky 1977), a genre where the conflation of author and main protagonist-as-narrator gives rise to a series of ontological distortions, combining the recounting of real events, places and characters with various degrees of fictionality. I specifically draw on the Cognitive Grammar notion of a construal relationship (Langacker 1987, 2008) to suggest that *Memoirs*, rather being a sanitized, detached representation of previously narrated material (see for example Campbell 1999; Thorpe 1966), offers a more complex treatment of events viewed from the distinctive vantage point that Sassoon's shifting concerns and reflections on his experience between 1917 and 1930 allow. My approach thus allows for an examination of how narrative events are retold across time and different genres and how, for Sassoon, such retellings form important concerns regarding the reconstruction of the past, the reshaping of earlier material for a new context and the re-evaluation of previously narrated events.

7.2 The First World War: Retelling and direct experience

In the late 1920s, the 'war books controversy' (see for example Falls 1930) debated both the validity of different kinds of war experience and how such experiences might best be told (and retold). A boom in war memoirs and fictional novels led to a rise in what Watson (2004: 195) calls the 'soldier story', the prototype of which downplayed the British military victory and instead foregrounded the narrative of the individual in the midst of a landscape of slaughter, incompetent commanders and a legacy of disillusionment. These overarching narratives of personal experience were grounded in what Hynes (1990: 158) terms 'the authority of direct experience', a term which captures the fact that the First World War was the first conflict where those who fought in it were also those who came to represent it most powerfully in art forms. Hynes (1990: 158) argues that 'a new poetry [...] a point of rhetoric: of truth-telling' emerged from 1916 onwards written by those who had actively participated in the war. He suggests that such writing both exemplified and legitimized the claim that a war narrative had value if that story had been directly experienced. The 'aesthetic of direct experience' then becomes a starting point for and a way of perpetuating the 'Myth of the War [...] an imaginative version of it, the story of the war that has evolved, and has come to be accepted as true' (Hynes 1990: ix).

War experiences, however, were not homogenous or consistent in any way since participant roles were varied and consisted of different kinds of 'war work' (Watson 2004: 2). Equally, the narrative representation of direct experience is not the same as the direct experience itself since any retelling is always framed within a different context and usually at some temporal distance from the experience. Watson (2004: 4) thus argues that we need to distinguish between 'war experience' (the experience itself) and 'war memory' (the reconstructed narrated version of that experience). This focus on the situational aspect of retelling aligns with studies that more generally position narratives as social constructs (Hatavara and Mildorf 2017) and emphasize that the perception of the self at a particular moment in time influences the remembering of past experiences (Wilson and Ross 2003). In this way, the presentation of *truth* at any one time remains a distillation of moments of retrospective observation and reflection (Linde 1993). In other words, to compare reconstructions of experience is to compare writing from distinctive time periods that represents the war from specific vantage points.

My analysis of Sassoon's retelling begins with a poem that both clearly draws on a direct experience and which then becomes material for Sassoon's subsequent narrative in *Memoirs*. In Section 7.3 below, I offer a short general analysis of the poem that then provides a reference point for my more sustained analysis of the *Memoirs* extract in Section 7.4.

7.3 Retelling direct experience: 'Lamentations'

> I found him in the guard-room at the Base.
> From the blind darkness I had heard his crying
> And blundered in. With puzzled, patient face
> A sergeant watched him; it was no good trying
> To stop it; for he howled and beat his chest.
> And, all because his brother had gone west,
> Raved at the bleeding war; his rampant grief

Moaned, shouted, sobbed, and choked, while he was kneeling
Half-naked on the floor. In my belief
Such men have lost all patriotic feeling.

(Sassoon 1918)

Sassoon wrote 'Lamentations' while at Craiglockhart Hospital in Edinburgh in July 1917. The poem was first published on 29 December 1917 in the *Cambridge Magazine* before appearing in Sassoon's 1918 collection *Counter-Attack*. The incident outlined in the poem is not mentioned in a diary entry but its later retelling in *Memoirs* and surrounding diary entries place the event as occurring on 16 February 1917 following Sassoon's return to France after five months of sick leave. 'Lamentations' is in the form of a sonnetina tre, a ten-line poem with an ababccdede rhyme scheme and relays the speaker's encounter with a soldier who has suffered a physical and psychological breakdown following the news of his brother's death. The soldier is being watched over in the guardroom by a sergeant who is unable – or unwilling – to alleviate the man's suffering. The poem foregrounds the immediacy of the situation, retold in the simple past, the clause structure inverting the order in which the speaker experiences the events so as to emphasize the dramatic opening impact of 'I found him'. The soldier himself is referred to simply as 'him' and then, later, through variations of third-person pronominal forms, 'his' and 'he'. The choice of the pronominal form over a noun is an emerging stylistic trait of Sassoon's poetry from early to mid-1916 (see Giovanelli 2014, 2019b). Within discourse, such forms either point to a more universal referent or 'generalized participant' (Langacker 2009: 115) or else acknowledge greater accessibility (Ariel 1990) and a more easily retrieved referent. In such cases, although an exact identification of the individual involved is denied, the form intimates some kind of recognition on the part of the hearer or reader and thus has the potential to 'refer to an individual of whom we *sense* that we are aware' (Giovanelli 2014: 153, added emphasis).

Sassoon draws on several other conventions that appear across his work in the mid-1916 to late 1917 period. For example, the verb choice 'blundered' echoes the description of soldiers in the trenches in poems such as 'A Working Party' and 'Counter-Attack', their clumsy movements a consequence of the constraints placed on their bodies by the inhuman conditions of the trenches. There is also a balance between movement and stasis. In 'Lamentations', the speaker's activity contrasts with the more pensive nature of the sergeant whose passivity and helplessness are emphasized in the behavioural verb 'watched' and in phonological patterning of plosive /p/ and diphthong /eɪ/ in 'puzzled, patient face'. The sergeant's stasis is, in turn, contrasted with the actions of the solider, who 'howled and beat his chest'. Later, 'his rampant grief' acts as the clausal subject of the verbs 'moaned' 'shouted', 'sobbed' and 'choked', a kind of non-language that makes understanding difficult and which culminates in the pathos of the dehumanized solider lying 'half-naked on the floor'. The difficulty in understanding the soldier is not confined to the sergeant since the speaker also appears to find the events described difficult to assess. It is for this reason, I think, that the disengagement of the speaker from the middle of line 2 to line 9 is so interesting. The scene as it stands presented here minimizes the speaker's presence and perspective; the 'I' of the narrating voice disappears and instead the attention of the reader is directed on the soldier.

When the speaker reappears, his detachment is equally striking. At this point in the poem, we might expect a reaction that is sympathetic to some degree but, instead, the speaker's response is arguably dismissive; the formal register of 'In my belief' and the distant 'such men' project a largely unsympathetic voice even if the final judgement on the soldier is read as an ironic one. Unable, like the watching sergeant, to respond, the speaker merely provides a clinical assessment of the scene that he has witnessed.

'Lamentations', then, presents a scene in which the subjectivity of the speaker is downplayed and the attention afforded to the soldier maximized so that the reader is positioned to focus their attention on the events of the poem rather than the narrating voice. It is unsurprising therefore that literary-critical readings tend to emphasize the power of objectification and description in the poem. In his lengthy analysis Hipp (2005) reads 'Lamentations' as a grittier counter-response to Sassoon's 1915 poem 'To My Brother', written shortly after his was killed during fighting at Gallipoli. In this earlier poem, the speaker's loss is mitigated by his patriotic beliefs, which in turn are foregrounded through a clearer emphasis on the speaking 'I' and a backgrounding of the death itself. In contrast Hipp, adopting a biographical stance, reads a lack of subjectivity together with the speaker's self-removal from the scene in 'Lamentations' as a form of self-protection to avoid any further personal distress (he equates the speaker here directly with Sassoon, of course). Hipp's interpretation is an interesting one and the comparison, though speculative, provides a neat insight into the ways in which the de-centring of the speaking voice may be contextualized and understood; similar although much more tentative interpretations are offered by Sillars (1999) and Sternlicht (1993) which suggest that this is a typically preferred literary-critical reading of the poem.

It is interesting, however, that the retold version of 'Lamentations' in *Memoirs* has received relatively little critical attention. In the remainder of this chapter, I draw on Cognitive Grammar and examine *Memoirs* as autofiction to suggest that Sassoon's retelling of the events of Rouen in his later work is more nuanced.

7.4 Retelling Rouen: *Memoirs of an Infantry Officer*

7.4.1 Memoirs of an Infantry Officer *as autofiction*

Twelve years later, Sassoon revisited and retold the experience of 'Lamentations'. In contrast to his later trilogy, Sassoon's three 'Sherston' memoirs, *Memoirs of a Fox-Hunting Man* (Sassoon 1928), *Memoirs of an Infantry Officer* and *Sherston's Progress* (Sassoon 1936), are not autobiographical in the strictest sense. Instead they may be read as examples of autofiction (Doubrovsky 1977), a genre that distorts 'reality and textuality by conflating the authorial signature of the self (*auto-*) with a character (*-fiction*)' (Gibbons 2018: 75–6). Although the term *autofiction* significantly post-dates Sassoon's writing, the genre's concerns with blurring fact and fiction, questioning 'selfhood, ontology, truth and memory' (Gibbons 2018: 76), and functioning as 'a form of autobiographical writing that permits a degree of experimentation with the definition and limits of the self, rather than the slavish recapitulation of known biographical facts' (Dix 2018: 3), all apply to these three texts which despite being based on real events incorporate various significant fictional aspects. The narrating 'I' is George Sherston who, unlike Sassoon, is an orphan without any siblings and is brought up by his Aunt Evelyn. Sassoon also downplays or omits other parts of his own biography. Sherston is a reader of literature but not a writer, and references to his sexuality are omitted entirely. The names of places and characters, despite being drawn from Sassoon's own experiences, are almost exclusively changed (an important exception is Sassoon's physician at Craiglockhart, W. H. Rivers) and key events are omitted (for example Sassoon's initial meeting with Graves who appears in *Memoirs* as the distant and unlikeable 'David Cromlech' rather than the close friend and confidant of Sassoon's diaries). Sassoon himself seemed aware of the experimental nature of his writing and its hybrid and intertextual nature. In defence of his own method, he wrote to Graves that 'Sherston is only 1/5 of myself, but his narrative is carefully thought out and constructed' (Graves 1982: 208). In his second volume of his later trilogy *The Weald of Youth*, which he called 'this "real autobiography" of mine' (Sassoon 1942: 70), Sassoon remarks that part of his life story has already been 'monopolised by a young man named George Sherston' (1942: 70), that he 'is a little shy of trespassing on Sherston's territory' and that 'to assert he was "only me with a lot left out" sounds off-hand and uncivil' (1942:70). In a conflation of fact and fiction, Sassoon later depicts a scene where 'grey-haired Aunt Evelyn [is] coming out into the garden with my mother' while Sherston himself 'has somehow been mysteriously embodied in his author' (1942: 71). The passage ends with a lengthy description of Sassoon/Sherston as a young child from the perspective of Aunt Evelyn before returning to describe the entire episode as a 'collision between fictionalized reality and essayised autobiography' (1942: 73). In the final volume of his second trilogy, *Siegfried's Journey*, Sassoon justifies omitting any reference to the final year of his war experience through an intertextual reference that once more highlights the ontological conflation of himself-as-narrator and Sherston:

> The inveterate memorizer George Sherston has already narrated a sequence of infantry experiences – from the end of July 1917 – which were terminated on July 13th, by a bullet wound in the head. His experiences were mine, so I am spared the effort of describing them.
>
> (Sassoon 1945: 69)

Finally, although Sherston explicitly mentions that 'those who expect a universalization of the Great War must look for it elsewhere' (Sassoon 1930: 17), Sassoon's bleaching of many of his own idiosyncrasies (a point he explicitly critiques in *Sherston's Progress*) means that Sherston's power comes from presenting 'himself as typical of the young officers of his day' (Watson 2004: 230). This kind of appeal to a wider universal set of experiences is what Jensen (2018: 69–70) terms a form of 'self-erasure', inherent in autofiction and typically functioning to arouse readerly interest since it 'aims to formulate a distinct kind of human subject, one whose intersubjectivity (I, me, us) generates a kind of aesthetic intimacy'.

7.4.2 Autofiction: Style and Cognitive Grammar

In a cognitive-stylistic account of Ben Lerner's (2014) novel *10:04*, Gibbons (2018: 81–4) replaces *autofiction* with *autonarration*, a term that she argues facilitates a more explicit analysis of 'stylistic features' (2018: 82). Gibbons utilizes the following aspects of perceptual, composition and textual deixis (see Stockwell 2002: 45–6) to provide a text-driven analysis of autonarration:

Perceptual deixis: related to reference and the text's use of the pronoun system
Composition deixis: signals that refer to the text's fictional status
Textual deixis: references to writing as a process and intertextual references to 'real-world' aspects of writing (e.g. texts and authors). (adapted from Gibbons 2018: 84)

In the discussion that follows and in my analysis in Section 7.3, I build on Gibbons's discussion of perceptual deixis and pronouns using the Cognitive Grammar notion of construal. A construal is a particular representation or packaging of conceptual content that is inherently meaningful. In a prototypical action clause, for example, the use of the active voice, 'The man kicked the ball', construes the agent 'The man' as the focal point; in contrast, the passive voice, 'The ball was kicked by the man', construes the patient 'The ball' as clausal subject and focus of attention and defocuses (Shibatani 1985) agency to the end of the clause; agency may also be deleted entirely as in 'The ball was kicked'. Each of these construals thus consists of a form that is a meaningful construction in its own right (see Langacker 2008: 383–4).

One specific construal phenomenon (Langacker 2008: 55) relates to perspective, specifically the viewing arrangement that profiles 'the overall relationship' (Langacker 2008: 73) between subjects of conceptualization (writer/reader or speaker/hearer) and the object of conceptualization (the scene) within the ground (the immediate context in which discourse occurs). In an optimal viewing arrangement (Langacker 1987: 129), the subject of conceptualization invests all of their attention on the object of conceptualization. In this instance, a theatre analogy is often used whereby the subject, like an audience totally absorbed in the play onstage, has minimal or no self-awareness. Here, the role of the subject in the 'construal relationship' (Langacker 1987: 128) is maximally subjective and the role of the object maximally objective so that 'what S [subject of conceptualization] observes is O [object of conceptualization], not S observing O' (Langacker 1987: 129). This arrangement generally is known as an objective construal.

The construal relationship, however, can be reconfigured so that it becomes more egocentric (Langacker 1987: 130). A conceptualizer may position themselves onstage as a focus of attention with various degrees of prominence and consequently objectified to the extent that they are now profiled as both subject *and* object of conception. Drawing once more on the theatre analogy, the conceptualizer's scope of attention now takes into account their role as observer and their immediate surroundings as well as the performers onstage. This type of arrangement is known as a subjective construal, having its most noticeable linguistic realization in the use of first-person pronoun which positions its referent onstage. An egocentric, subjective construal may also arise when a conceptualizer draws attention to aspects of the ground through the use, for example, of the second-personal pronoun 'you', spatial or temporal adverbs such as 'here' or 'now', any type of modality, or the explicit use of evaluative lexis which encodes 'the speaker's attitude towards an onstage element [...] or its limitation to particular social contexts' (Langacker 2008: 262). These two construal relationships are shown in Figure 7.1

In practice, absolute subjective and objective construals are unusual (see for example Langacker 2008: 262; Verhagen 2007 for discussion) and may, instead, be understood as representing two ends of a continuum with the majority of instances falling at some intermediate point. The construal relationship in any extended stretch of discourse is also dynamic rather than static, so attention is often redistributed between subject and object of conception as the viewing of a scene unfolds and progresses. Nuttall (2018: 47) uses the metaphor of a seesaw in acknowledging how this inverse relationship operates: 'allocating attention to one reduces attention to the other; like a see-saw, one goes up as the other goes down'.

In the following section, I draw on the notion of a construal relationship to examine the degrees to which the point of view adopted by the conceptualizing narrator of *Memoirs* is objectified through self-positioning onstage. Here, I examine how various distributions and redistributions of attention may shed light on some of the ontological distortions and conflations in Sassoon's retelling of 'Lamentations'.

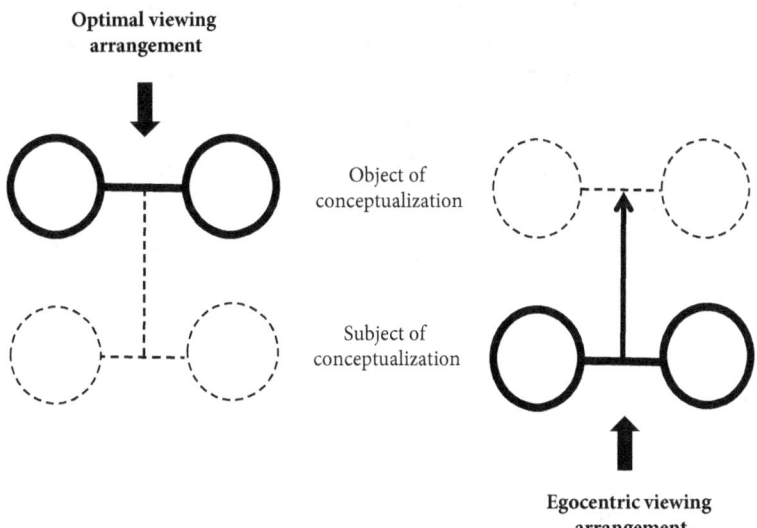

Figure 7.1 Construal relationships (adapted from Verhagen 2007)

7.4.3 Identities and selves in Memoirs

A feature of 'Lamentations' is that the subject of conceptualization is largely off-stage in a non-egocentric viewing arrangement apart from at the beginning and very ending of the poem. Although the use of evaluative lexis means that there is some degree of subjectivity, the disappearance of the first-person pronoun from the middle of line 2 until line 9 means that the poem's events appear relatively more objectively construed. In *Memoirs*, however, the construal relationship is more complex as my analysis that follows demonstrates. The first extract below is the opening to Part 7, which precedes the description of the soldier.

> Sometime in the second week of February I crossed to Havre on a detestable boat named *Archangel*. As soon as the boat began to move I was aware of a sense of relief. It was no use worrying about the War now; I was in the Machine again, and all responsibility for my future was in the haphazard control of whatever powers manipulated the British Expeditionary Force. Most of us felt like that, I imagine, and the experience was known as 'being for it again'. Apart from that, my only recollection of the crossing is that some-one relieved me of my new trench-coat while I was asleep.
>
> At nine o' clock in the evening of the next day I reported myself at the 5th Infantry Base Depot at Rouen. The journey from London had lasted thirty-three hours (a detail which I record for the benefit of those who like slow-motion war-time details). The Base Camp was a couple of miles from the town, on the edge of a pine forest. In the office where I reported I was informed that I'd been posted to our Second Battalion; this gave me something definite to grumble about, for I wanted to go where I was already known, and the prospect of joining a strange battalion made me feel more homeless than ever. (Sassoon 1930: 167)

In the first instance, the retelling in *Memoirs* provides an initial greater context: Sherston's return to France, details of his journey, reporting at the Base Depot in Rouen including a specific time and place that fix the spatio-temporal parameters of the narrative, his thoughts on being transferred (from the First Battalion) to the Second Battalion and general descriptions of the surroundings and evaluations of his feelings. This more personal description results in a scene that is construed more subjectively, evident in the use of the first-person pronoun that maintains the egocentric viewing position as well as markers of modality such as 'imagine', 'wanted' and generally evaluative lexical choices such as 'detestable', 'relief', 'manipulated', 'grumble', 'strange' and 'homeless'. Since this extract is the opening to Part 7, the part and section headings, text alignment and graphology (the initial 'S' in 'Sometimes' is a drop cap) are all characteristics of an authorial presence that in turn explicitly signal the objectification of the subject of conceptualization.

The authentic nature of the events described (Sassoon did indeed arrive back in France in 1917 and report to the Infantry Base Depot at Rouen) together with the fact that they are narrated to us by Sherston, a fictional entity, whose own 'biography' is both the same as and different to Sassoon's, thus distorts the ontological boundaries between versions of the self. Sherston-as-narrator is understood as the conceptualizing presence at the opening of the passage, although the use of the past tense makes it clear that the participant of the clause is a prior version of him. When Sherston addresses the reader in the present tense, however, greater attention is drawn to his role as a mediator of the narrative. Here, the act of conceptualizing itself is objectively construed.

> <u>My only recollection is</u> that someone relieved me
> Most of us felt like that, <u>I imagine</u>
> [...] <u>which I record</u> for the benefit of those who like slow-motion war-time details.

This new Sherston – albeit a temporary one – appears to speak from a more proximal vantage point, more aligned to the reader as a co-participant in the ground than as a fictional entity. The embedded construal gives rise to an egocentric viewing arrangement with discrete layers of perspective. As Nuttall (2018: 58) explains, 'the more conceptualisers which mediate a construal, the more distributed our attention, and the less objective or vividly simulated the ultimate conceived situation or text world'. Here, our attention shifts to extricate past and present versions of Sherston, placing onstage, through markers of narration: 'my only recollection', 'I imagine' and 'I record', a closer narrating 'I' more explicitly. The construal relationship thus gives prominence to the acts of remembering and writing through which the present remembering self is construed objectively. For the reader, however, assigning who is onstage involves navigating the different narrating Sherstons as well as considering the various ways that these Sherstons may or may not correspond to the authorial presence, Siegfried Sassoon.

The events detailed in 'Lamentations' are then directly retold in the following passage.

> The 5th I.B.D. Adjutant advised me to draw some blankets; the storeroom was just round the corner, he said. After groping about in the dark and tripping over tent ropes I was beginning to lose my temper when I opened a door and found myself in a Guard Room. A man, naked to the waist, was kneeling in the middle of the floor, clutching at his chest and weeping uncontrollably. The Guard were standing around with embarrassed looks, and the Sergeant was beside him, patient and unpitying. While he was leading me to the blanket

store I asked him what was wrong. 'Why, sir, the man's been under detention for assaulting the military police, and now 'e's just 'ad news of his brother being killed. Seems to take it to 'eart more than most would. 'Arf crazy 'e's been, tearing 'is clothes off and cursing the War and the Fritzes. Almost like a shell-shock case, 'e seems. It's his third time out. A Blighty one don't last a man long nowadays, sir.' As I went off into the gloom I could still hear the uncouth howlings. (Sassoon 1930: 168)

The inverted clause structure of 'Lamentations' is now replaced with a more iconic construal mirroring the chronology of events as experienced by the narrator: he stumbles in the dark, opens the door and finds himself in the Guard Room. In contrast to 'Lamentations', some of the description of the soldier is now omitted and greater prominence is afforded to the perspective of the Sergeant. Initially, this is marked through Sherston's more evaluative description of the Sergeant as 'patient and unpitying', replacing a previous lack of empathy with what would appear to be a crueller lack of sympathy. In contrast to 'Lamentations', the backstory of the soldier is recounted through the free direct speech of the Sergeant, another embedded construal. In this example, although attention is on the speaking Sergeant, his words are clearly framed within Sherston's construal, or in other words, they are *part of* Sherson's construal. The perception of authenticity that the use of free direct speech may evoke is countered by the fact that the reader has no way of accounting for the reliability of the narrator's reporting – a fact made more complex by the fact that Sherston may or may not be equivalent to the authorial figure of Siegfried Sassoon. Indeed the Sergeant's words, despite their nod towards authenticity (the frequent h-dropping, the use of 'Fritzes' for German soldiers, 'Blighty one' for a minor wound and 'sir' as a mark of respect to a senior officer), are as crafted as, if not more so than, the narrative summary of 'Lamentations'. In turn, Sherston is himself onstage as the addressee of the Sergeant's free direct speech and therefore construed objectively as a salient participant in the speech act itself, as well as in the evaluative, more explicit subjectivity of 'I could still hear the uncouth howlings' with which the extract ends. In effect we are asked to construct and follow a series of nestled viewpoints: 'Sassoon observing Sassoon/Sherston observing Sherston observing the scene' rather than the greater prominence given to the observation of the object of conceptualization in 'Lamentations'.

The objectification of multiple conceptualizing presences in *Memoirs* thus results in a stronger emphasis on the act of remembering rather than the remembered. This emphasis is realized through greater contextualization of the first extract, the use of the Sergeant's free direct speech in the second section and the overall layered subjectivity which moves between different levels of mediation and highlights the ontological fuzziness inherent in Sassoon's autofictional account.

7.5 Conclusion

This chapter has examined how the autofictive nature of *Memoirs* affords a more layered and arguably more complex retelling of 'Lamentations', evident through my analysis that highlights the construal relationship that is given prominence in each of the texts. In *Memoirs*, a more explicit objectification of the conceptualizer or overall subjective construal draws attention to the telling and tellers of the event in contrast to the more objective construal of 'Lamentations'. The differences between the two versions are thus both striking and informative.

In a moment of reflection towards the beginning of *Memoirs*, George Sherston acknowledges that '[m]oments […] are unreproduceable when I look back and try to recover their living texture' (Sassoon 1930: 45). Despite his criticism of Graves, it seems that Sassoon (and Sherston) seemed aware of the complexities inherent in refashioning the past to make sense of experiences that occurred over ten years earlier although the very act of writing, of course, suggests that such retellings are also desirable and inevitable. The retelling in *Memoirs* may also be contextualized within Sassoon's own literary journey from war poet of direct experience to autofictive writer, averse to the ethos and traits of Modernist verse yet still keen to experiment within the popular and relatively recent literary genre of the war memoir. Sassoon's use of Sherston distorts the ontological boundaries between narrating and authorial presences and presents a more carefully mediated or construed version of the events in Rouen in 1917. This autofictive strategy may be therefore read, as Linde (1993: 105) argues is the case for all narrative retellings, as a method to 'observe, reflect, adjust the amount of distance, and correct the self that is being created'.

References

Ariel, M. (1990), *Accessing Noun Phrase Antecedents*, London: Routledge.
Campbell, P. (1999), *Siegfried Sassoon: A Study of the War Poetry*, Jefferson, NC: Macfarland.
Dix, H. (2018), 'Introduction: Autofiction in English: The Story So Far', in H. Dix (ed.), *Autofiction in English*, 1–23, London: Palgrave.
Doubrovsky, S. (1977), *Fils*, París: Gallimard-Folio.

Falls, C. (1930), *War Books: A Critical Guide*, London: Peter Davies.

Gibbons, A. (2018), 'Autonarration, I, and Odd Address in Ben Lerner's Autofictional Novel *10:04*', in A. Gibbons and A. Macrae (eds), *Pronouns in Literature: Positions and Perspectives in Language*, 75–96, London: Palgrave Macmillan.

Giovanelli, M. (2014), 'Conceptual Proximity and the Experience of War in Siegfried Sassoon's "A Working Party"', in C. Harrison, L. Nuttall, P. Stockwell and W. Yuan (eds), *Cognitive Grammar in Literature*, 145–60, Amsterdam: John Benjamins.

Giovanelli, M. (2019a), 'Construing and Reconstruing the Horrors of the Trench: Siegfried Sassoon, Creativity and Context', *Journal of Literary Semantics*, 48 (1): 85–104.

Giovanelli, M. (2019b), 'The Language of Siegfried Sassoon's 1916 Poems; Some Emerging Stylistic Traits', *Siegfried's Journal*, 26: 22–8.

Graves, R. (1929), *Goodbye to All That*, London: Jonathan Cape.

Graves, R. (1930), 'Correspondence: The Garlands Wither', *The Times Literary Supplement*, 26 June, 354.

Graves, R. (1982), *In Broken Images: Selected Letters of Robert Graves 1914–1946*, P. O'Prey (ed.), London: Hutchinson.

Hatavara, M., and Mildorf, J. (2017), 'Fictionality, Narrative Modes and Vicarious Storytelling', *Style*, 51 (3): 391–408.

Hipp, D. (2005), *The Poetry of Shellshock: Wartime Trauma and Healing in Wilfred Owen, Ivor Gurney and Siegfried Sassoon*, Jefferson, NC: McFarland.

Hynes, S. (1990), *A War Imagined: The First World War and English Culture*, London: Pimlico.

Jensen, M. (2018), 'How Art Constitutes the Human: Aesthetics, Empathy and the Interesting in Autofiction', in H. Dix (ed.), *Autofiction in English*, 65–83, London: Palgrave.

Langacker, R. (1987), *Foundations of Cognitive Grammar: Volume 1 Theoretical Prerequisites*, Stanford, CA: Stanford University Press.

Langacker, R. W. (2007), 'Constructing the Meaning of Personal Pronouns' in G. Radden, K-M. Kopcke, T. Berg and P. Siemund (eds), *Aspects of Meaning Construction*, 171–88, Amsterdam: John Benjamins.

Langacker, R. W. (2008), *Cognitive Grammar: A Basic Introduction*, Oxford: Oxford University Press.

Langacker, R. W. (2009), *Investigations in Cognitive Grammar*, Berlin: Mouton De Gruyter.

Lerner, B. (2014), *10:04*, New York, NY: Granta Books.

Linde, C. (1993), *Life Stories: The Creation of Coherence*, Oxford: Oxford University Press.

Nuttall, L. (2018), *Mind Style and Cognitive Grammar*, London: Bloomsbury.

Sassoon, S. (1918), *Counter-Attack and Other Poems*, London: Heinemann.

Sassoon, S. (1928), *Memoirs of a Fox-Hunting Man*, London: Faber and Faber.

Sassoon, S. (1930), *Memoirs of an Infantry Officer*, London: Faber and Faber.

Sassoon, S. (1936), *Sherston's Progress*, London: Faber and Faber.
Sassoon, S. (1938), *The Old Century and Seven More Years*, London: Faber and Faber.
Sassoon, S. (1942), *The Weald of Youth*, London: Faber and Faber.
Sassoon, S. (1945), *Siegfried's Journey*, London: Faber and Faber.
Shibatani, M. (1985), 'Passives and Related Constructions: A Prototype Analysis', *Language*, 61: 821–48.
Sillars, S. (1999), *Structure and Dissolution in English Writing 1910–1920*, Houndmills, Basingstoke: Macmillan.
Sternlicht, S. (1993), *Siegfried Sassoon*, New York, NY: Twayne Publishers.
Stockwell, P. (2002), *Cognitive Poetics: An Introduction*, London: Routledge.
Thorpe, M. (1966), *Siegfried Sassoon: A Critical Study*, London: Oxford University Press.
Verhagen, A. (2007), 'Construal and Perspectivization', in D. Geeraerts and H. Cuyckens (eds), *The Oxford Handbook of Cognitive Linguistics*, 48–81, Oxford: Oxford University Press.
Watson, J. (2004), *Fighting Different Wars: Experience, Memory and the First World War in Britain*, Cambridge: Cambridge University Press.
Wilson, A., and Ross, M. (2003), 'The Identity Function of Autobiographical Memory: Time Is on Our Side', *Memory*, 11 (2): 137–49.

8

Retelling catastrophe through translation

Jean Boase-Beier

8.1 Introduction

When people experience terrible events, they need to shape them into stories and to tell someone else about them (Lambrou 2014: 13). This need can arise out of trauma (see Caruth 2013: 5–6), or it can – often in addition – be a more considered response, a way of making sure others know what happened (Nader 2007: 16). Henry Greenspan, in his work with Holocaust survivors, notes the importance of listening so that survivors' memories become stories told to an audience and hence something that others can engage with (Greenspan 2010: 42–3). Toolan (2014: 90) notes that we often narrativize in order to help us deal with our own death and that of others.

As the catastrophic events of the 1940s, that we now refer to collectively as the Holocaust, were unfolding, many people suffered trauma from the loss of home and possessions, the death of friends or family members, and many were aware that even more terrible events were yet to come. We might expect people under such circumstances to give straightforward reports, or write journals, and there are indeed many journals arising from the Holocaust, Anne Frank's being perhaps the best known (Frank 2007). Others told stories, for example, in concentration camps and ghettos and achieved in this way a measure of mental escape (see Reiter 2000: 58–69).

Many people told their stories in poems. Poetry, perhaps more than other literary forms, is often used to respond to catastrophe, because it can give a sense of order and individual control in chaotic times (Heaney 1995: 189; Nader 2007: 16–17) and it is less likely to be treated as fiction. Poems can be memorized or written on small scraps of paper. Poetry was for many writers during the Holocaust a natural expression of anger, fear or despair, and it allowed them to speak of almost unbearable events: an example is Abraham Sutzkever's 'Tsum kint' (To the Child), which recounts the death of his newborn baby, killed at birth in the Vilna ghetto (Boase-Beier and de Vooght 2019: 51). For religious writers, poetry could stand in place of prayer, with God as its intended audience, as in Dietrich Bonhoeffer's poem 'Who Am I?' with its final words: 'You know my name' (Boase-Beier and de Vooght 2019: 91).

Even in the case of religious poetry, there is always the hope that human beings might also read it. One of the greatest fears of the Holocaust writers was that there would be no one to listen to their story after they had died: that, as in Selma Meerbaum-Eisinger's poem 'Tragedy', 'no-one will know or care' (Boase-Beier and de Vooght 2019: 28). The fear that their stories might never be heard led writers to go to extraordinary lengths to preserve their work: Sutzkever and many other ghetto poets buried their poems to be retrieved later, and others had them smuggled out of camps, ghettos or prisons (see Boase-Beier 2017: 152–4).

When Holocaust poems are translated, they undergo an act of retelling, whereby the poem appears in a different language, for a new audience, with a context very different from that in which it was written or indeed was first read. In many cases – indeed, today, in most cases – the poet will no longer be alive, even if he or she survived the Holocaust. Translating the poems can thus be felt by translators to be a necessary act of prosopopoeia, or speaking for the dead, though there are always ethical concerns about speaking for others (see Gubar 2003: 201–6). But one could argue that, without translation, many people's stories would be forgotten.

Holocaust poems relate to real events and indeed often precisely describe such events while they are happening. From the stylistician's point of view, it therefore makes sense to consider them in terms of the characteristics they share with more obviously narrative texts, such as short stories.

One such characteristic is that poetry communicates (Phelan 2014: 52), and this may be particularly true of Holocaust poetry (Boase-Beier 2017: 153–4). Many Holocaust poems, like Sutzkever's poem to his dead child, address family members, or even the oppressors, as does Fania Żorne's 'Oh, deutsche Mutter' (Boase-Beier and de Vooght 2019: 103). Many poems present a sequence of events, told from a particular perspective (see Hühn and Schönert 2005: 1–3), and Holocaust poems in particular are often characterized by a specific event or 'episode', which is thematically distinct and requires 'a shift in the reader's understanding' (Miall 2007: 148); such a shift is one of the possible cognitive effects, including a feeling of empathy (Boase-Beier 2015: 23–32) that arises from the reader's 'intense identification' (Phelan 2004: 629) with the characters in poems.

In narratological terms, an event is 'something that happens' (Kafalenos 2006: 1), but it needs to be worth telling, to have what is called 'tellability' (Baroni 2014). It is likely that the popularity among poetry readers in general of collections and anthologies with a specific topic (love, the environment, war) has to do with the tellability of such stories. Holocaust poetry, too, is commonly anthologized.

It has frequently been noted that lyric poetry, in particular, is likely to have a first-person narrator, and to describe an inner state (Furniss and Bath 2007: 213; Hühn and Schönert 2002: 287), and it is often distinguished from narrative poetry, where there is a more obvious story. But even narrative poems exhibit many characteristics typical of poetry (Bal 2009: 10), such as being written in lines or having poetic 'shape' more generally (Boase-Beier 2011: 113–37).

However, I would argue that almost all poetry will exhibit some narrative characteristics (see also Hühn and Schönert 2002) and that this is especially true of Holocaust poetry, though it still has many of the typical characteristics of poetry, including poetic shape, rhythm and sound repetition, and it often has a first-person narrator. It is not just that it exhibits both narratological and poetic qualities, but that narrative and style interact, whereby the style may 'corroborate or counterpoint' the narrative (McHale 2009: 17). It has been observed by several scholars (e.g. Klimek 2013) that we can therefore usefully combine narratological with stylistic insights when we analyse poetry. My concern in this chapter is to examine how such insights can explain the interaction of narrative and style in a Holocaust poem and how that interaction changes when the story is retold in translation.

8.2 A Holocaust victim's story

In writing literary works that relate to the Holocaust, the writer must wrestle with questions of truth and ethical appropriateness, and the fear that to respond aesthetically to such traumatic and grotesque events is morally questionable, quite aside from the legitimacy of speaking on behalf of victims. It has become something of a commonplace to quote philosopher Theodor Adorno's warning from the 1950s that it is barbaric to write poetry 'after Auschwitz' (Adorno 2003: 30), a view that seems to be based on an understanding of the aesthetic as that which is detached from life and does not take a moral stance (see Furniss and Bath 2007: 451–3). Michael Rothberg coined the term *traumatic realism* for writing that does justice to both truth and aesthetics by incorporating 'traces of trauma' (Rothberg 2000: 9, 139).

Clearly, someone writing in the midst of tumultuous or life-threatening events is unlikely to be worried by such considerations, which are in any case mainly relevant for post-Holocaust poets writing later. But the translator of Holocaust poems automatically becomes a post-Holocaust poet and needs to be aware of them. Above all, when a text is translated, the context in which the original text was read will change, and a translation has to take into account how, in a changed context, the stylistic links to the new context can be preserved and how effects on the reader can be assured, while making sure that ethical appropriateness is maintained.

Readers, including translators, of any story, whether told in a poem or other text, will have to reconstruct both the story itself and the way it has been told: its mediation (Hühn 2013a). When the story is told in poetry, it is the link between the way it is mediated to make a narrative and the particular poetic means of expression used to do this that constitute the poetics, the style-narrative link that drives the poem. A translator of poetry will always have to be concerned with that link. And a translator of Holocaust poetry also needs to be aware of Holocaust poetics in a broader sense, including the connotations of words typically used to write about the Holocaust and what types of expression are generally deemed appropriate (see Boase-Beier 2015).

The poem 'O seltsam lichtes Leben dicht am Tod' (literally: O strangely light life close to death) was written in 1943 by musician and teacher Alfred Schmidt-Sas (whose real name was Alfred Schmidt) in Berlin's Plötzensee prison, when he had been condemned to death for anti-Nazi activity. Here is the original poem, with a word-for-word gloss that should enable the reader to see roughly what the German means. The translation itself is discussed in Section 8.3.

O seltsam lichtes Leben dicht am Tod

1   Fast   neun   Schritte   lang
    almost   nine   paces   long
2   ist meine letzte weißgetünchte Welt
    is my   last   whitewashed   world
3   vielleicht neun Tage   noch,
    perhaps   nine days   still
4   dann   fällt
    then   falls
5   mein   Kopf,
    my   head
6   der jetzt noch denkt und spricht und hört.
    that now still thinks and speaks and hears

7	So nahe	wartet	schon	der	große	Schlaf
	so near	waits	already	the	big	sleep
8	mit seiner	dunklen	Schwinge	überschattend		
	with its	dark	wing	overshadowing		
9	die grelle	Glut	von	Wünschen	oder	Ängsten.
	the glaring	glow	of	wishes	or	fears
10	Er sänftigt	die	längsten,	allerbängsten,		
	it calms/will calm	the	longest	most-fearful		
11	die Augenblicke	bitt'rer	Menschennot.			
	the moments	of-bitter	human-emergency			
12	O seltsam	lichtes	Leben	dicht am Tod.		
	o strangely	light	life	close to death		

Though Schmidt-Sas was accused by the Nazis of leading a Communist group, he was not a Communist, but simply someone who believed in principles of common sense and freedom and that such principles would help him, when in fact they were exactly what made him a threat. He was arrested for storing a photocopier for friends who had been producing anti-Nazi leaflets and was subjected to a sham trial in October 1942. He was executed by guillotine in April 1943.

While waiting several months for his execution, he wrote a number of poems, diary entries and letters in his prison cell, addressed to his fiancée Marga Dietrich, to whom they were delivered by the prison chaplain. Dietrich married Schmidt-Sas posthumously and preserved his work, which was handed to the archive of the *Institut für Zeitgeschichte* (Institute of Contemporary History) in Munich after her death. Since this poem appears at the end of his last letter to his fiancée, it is clear that she was his main intended audience and that the poem was meant to reassure her. But in the preceding letter he already assures her of his love, his calm state of mind and his conviction that 'Nothing can disappear, that once existed' (Gollwitzer et al. 1954: 122; my translation). His poem must therefore have been meant to do more: to order his thoughts and make sense of his approaching execution, to help his reader experience some of the feelings he was experiencing. He might also have felt that a poem, unlike a letter, would later find a wider audience.

He was not to know that he would be taken up as part of the memorialization of resisters after the war, and both letter and poem published in a book of writings of the condemned, only eleven years after his execution. The 1954 book explicitly frames resistance as an act that carries out the divine will, even for those who, like Schmidt-Sas, believe in humanity rather than God

(Gollwitzer et al. 1954: 7). In the book's Foreword we can sense the shock of the editors at the vast numbers of resisters who were killed, at a time when the full extent of the murder of millions, and particularly of the genocide of Jews, was still not known. The editors explain that the collection is not just a 'memorial, reminder and warning' (Gollwitzer et al. 1954: 7) but is an essential element in the healing of people and nations, giving hope for a future Europe based on common values.

The narrator in the poem, whom the reader of the 1954 book is likely to have identified unequivocally with Schmidt-Sas himself, both because of the context provided by the anthology and the fact that the poem is preceded by his final letter and followed by the note 'Written with hands bound' (Gollwitzer et al. 1954: 23), says he feels a sense of peace and euphoria. As he was an atheist, his euphoria, also expressed in the accompanying letter, does not come from a belief in the afterlife or confidence in a joyful reunion with his fiancée, but from a belief that death marks the highest point of life and of their love.

In terms of its narrative characteristics, we note that, besides a precise description of the location in lines 1 and 2, there is a temporal sequence of events: the time of writing, and an imagined time nine days hence, when the speaker will be executed. The narrative returns in the second stanza to the present to consider the effects of the knowledge of his impending execution on his current state of mind, thus adding 'evaluation' (Labov 2013:30) and thereby making it clearer why the story in the poem is being told.

One obvious event in narratological terms (see Hühn 2013b) is the narrator's imagined execution by beheading, which is described with a sense of horror and of the difficulty of grasping that his head will soon be separate from his body. The way the head is described ('that now still thinks and speaks and hears', line 6) is as though it is already separate, as though it is not (even now) the whole person thinking and speaking and hearing; in German this effect is underlined by the use of the present tense of 'fallen' (to fall), which also has a future meaning in German. There is a second event, perhaps even more surprising, in the mental change that occurs in lines 10 and 11, as the narrator describes, and the reader realizes, that the 'dark wing' of death in line 8 is not something to be feared but something that banishes fear. It is the unexpectedness of the change from horror to calm that is the main 'point' (Labov 1972: 366) of the narrative.

In order to see what happens when we translate, we need first to consider how the narrative sequence in the original poem interacts with its stylistic features, and with the original historical context, and how it would have achieved cognitive effects on its original readers.

Schmidt-Sas uses many typical stylistic features of poems, such as internal rhyme and end-rhyme (längsten – allerbängsten; -not – Tod), assonance or half-rhyme (noch – Kopf; wartet – Schlaf), and alliteration (weißgetünchte Welt; lichtes Leben). These stylistic features are not merely embellishments added to an expression of extreme emotion to make it more striking, or more controllable, but they also suggest careful linking of particular concepts: 'licht' (light or thin) and 'dicht' (dense or thick) both rhyme and are contrasted in meaning, a contrast underlined by the further contrast of 'dunkle(n) Schwinge' (dark wing, here in the dative form) and 'grelle Glut' (bright or glaring glow or blaze). This contrast between light and dark is the key to understanding both the point of the story and the link between its narrative point and its style that constitutes the poetics of the text.

The adjective 'licht' is rather unusual in German. Though the noun 'Licht' is equivalent to 'light' (rays emanating from a source) in English, as an adjective it has a somewhat different meaning, even though, like the English adjective 'light', it derives from the Latin noun 'lux', light. The German adjective suggests something thinned out, as in 'Lichtung', a clearing in a forest, and thus able to admit (but not to emit) light. In English 'light' is ambiguous: it is also the opposite of 'heavy', but this is not a possible meaning in German. It is of course metaphorical: we understand 'licht' in German to mean free of thoughts that seem, metaphorically, to darken the mind.

And yet, though 'licht' in German cannot mean 'not heavy', it seems likely that Schmidt-Sas here alludes to the use of 'lightness' in Tolstoy's 1869 novel *War and Peace* (Edmonds 1957: 162), where it also refers to freedom from burdensome thoughts as death approaches. The Russian word *legkost* means lacking in weight (and not 'light' in the sense of admitting or emitting illumination), and the phrase in which it is used appears in several English translations as 'strange lightness of being' (e.g. Edmonds 1957: 162). Milan Kundera's much later Czech novel, first published in 1984 in English translation, as *The Unbearable Lightness of Being* (Heim 1984), also uses 'lightness' (lehkost) in this sense.

In both these cases 'lightness' suggests an absence of heaviness, rather than an absence of darkness, though in the English translations the word automatically acquires both meanings. However, though there is no etymological connection between 'light' meaning 'not dark' (from Latin 'lux') and 'light' meaning 'not heavy' (from Latin 'levis'), there does appear to be a semantic one: to make less dense so light can enter can also be to make less heavy. The latter meaning, though not usually a connotation of 'licht' in German, can be seen in an almost obscure verb: 'lichten' means to remove the cargo of a boat in order to make it less heavy.

The connection between the two senses of 'licht' is rather opaque – or is absent – for most German speakers. We have no way of knowing whether it is coincidental that Schmidt-Sas chose a somewhat obscure word for 'not dark' that would acquire, in English translation, exactly the additional meaning of 'not heavy'.

For the translator, the lucky chance that 'levitas' and 'lux' both resulted in 'light' in English means that translations of Tolstoy's *War and Peace* and Kundera's *Unbearable Lightness of Being* gave the words of both authors both connotations. A translation of 'licht' as 'light' in Schmidt-Sas's poem cannot help but pick up the allusion to Tolstoy and Kundera. Kundera's novel, though written after Schmidt-Sas's poem, will form part of the context in which its translation will be read in 2019, in *Poetry of the Holocaust: An Anthology* (Boase-Beier and de Vooght 2019).

In the German poem, the sense of 'licht' as 'thinned-out, admitting light', further underlined by its contrast with 'dicht' in the title, is picked up by 'weißgetüncht' (whitewashed) in line 2, and by 'grelle Glut' (bright or glaring glow or heat) in line 9, as well as in the final line. In German as in English 'whitewashed' suggests a disguise or attempt to hide uncomfortable facts, a connotation that was possibly stronger in German in 1954, since 'getüncht' (related to Latin 'tunica', an undergarment) is literally 'dressed' and to disguise is to 'mis-dress' (*verkleiden*). The contrast between the whitewash of the cell walls and the lightness which death brings only becomes clear to the reader as the poem progresses.

'Der große Schlaf', the big sleep, in line 7, is the title of Raymond Chandler's 1939 book (Chandler 2011), which was not translated into German until 1950, seven years after Schmidt-Sas was writing, and it was given the title *Der tiefe Schlaf* (the deep sleep). Sleep as a euphemistic metaphor for death is common to many languages, but the specificity of the phrase suggests an allusion to the English book and that therefore both Schmidt-Sas and Marga Dietrich knew it. This allusion would not have been very recognizable to the 1954 German reader but becomes so again today in the English translation.

Possibly the most strikingly deviant line in the poem is line 10: 'Er sänftigt die längsten, allerbängsten'. It is foregrounded not just because of the repeated sounds, which include the final word of the previous line (Ängsten // sänftigt – längsten – allerbängsten) but also because 'allerbängst' is not a lexicalized adjective. The prefix 'aller-' forms adjectives such as 'allererst' (first of all), 'allerhöchst' (highest of all), so the adjective 'allerbängst' means 'the most frightening of all' and provides a clue to the conflict in the speaker's mind between fear and calm. Line 10 marks the point at which that conflict is resolved. Because it is both stylistically foregrounded, and also comes as a surprise to the reader since it marks a change in the narrator's inner state from fear to calm (and consequently encourages rereading of lines 8 and 9 to see death's dark wing as something to be welcomed) it constitutes what we might call 'the eye of the poem' (Boase-Beier 2009; Freeman 2005: 40). According to Labov (1972: 366–75), stylistic devices can in themselves be 'evaluation devices' that indirectly serve to give weight to the point of the story.

It is at this point that the contrast between the whiteness of the walls and the lightness of life as death approaches becomes clear to the reader: death's approaching darkness is a mental thinning-out that allows real light in, rather than the light of whitewash.

8.3 Translation as retelling

When considering translation, it is important to look both at what happens and also at how an understanding of the style and narrative structure of the original text might influence what a translator does. When this poem is translated, many changes happen both to the style of the poem in a narrower sense – for the language changes – and to the framework of its narrative. The audience, already in 1954 not only Marga Dietrich but potentially all readers of German, now changes again, for the new readers are likely to be English-speaking. The original narrator would have been identified by Dietrich in 1943 with her fiancé and in 1954 by German readers either with all resisters executed in the Nazi years or with the poet Schmidt-Sas, depending on their background. But in translation it becomes more difficult to identify the narrator, who is now speaking English, with the poet, though contextual aids in the form of prefaces and notes can be given.

My English translation (Boase-Beier and de Vooght 2019: 92) follows:

Strange Lightness of Life so Close to Death

1	Nearly nine paces long
2	is my final whitewashed world
3	perhaps nine days left
4	then off,
5	my head
6	that now still thinks and speaks and sees and hears.

7   So near me now the big sleep waits
8   with its dark wing casting into shade
9   the luminous blaze of hopes or fears,
10 to lighten the longest, the blackest,
11 the bitterest moments of human despair.
12 Strange lightness of life so close to death.

Gutt (2000: 105–7) saw translation as on a par with indirect speech, where the translator is telling us what someone else said. While the original poem imposes constraints, in that the new poem must be acceptable to its readers as a translation of it, the translator has the freedom to make stylistic choices.

The anthology in which the English version appears is explicitly a collection of poems from and about the Holocaust and thus contextualizes this poem for today's reader as a Holocaust poem by one of the many victims of the Nazis. But though the immediate context is thus similar to that in which the German reader of 1954 would have read the original, we read now with hindsight, since we are likely to be aware (or can read in the introduction to the English anthology) of some facts about the Holocaust that were unknown in 1954: for example, that 6 million Jews and many thousands of others were murdered, including those who were physically and mentally ill or disabled, or belonged to Sinti or Roma communities, or were gay, or Communist, or Christian, or merely failed to conform. Where the German reader of 1954 had the letter to Marga Dietrich as context, today's English reader will know little about Schmidt-Sas and is more likely to read the poem as a meditation on what it is like to face death, with no specific addressee.

In other words, history, knowledge of history and our interpretation today of the history of the Holocaust will all affect our reading. That reading might prompt us to undertake research so that we discover nearly 3,000 people were executed in the Plötzensee prison, most by beheading, which was done by axe in the courtyard until 1936, thereafter by guillotine in a small shed. But many readers of the English translation will not know this and will not discover it. Thus the first event of the poem, the speaker's execution by guillotine, which, at the time the narrator is speaking, is to happen soon, is likely to have a much greater impact on the new readers. This is in part because of our likely knowledge schema of beheadings. Even if we do not know they ceased in England in 1747, to be replaced by the apparently bloodless method of hanging, we feel confident they disappeared centuries ago. Especially in the last forty years, since it was finally abandoned by France, beheading has come to be associated with particularly violent groups, such as Isis. Yet beheadings (originally seen by Joseph Guillotin as a humane method of killing criminals) were carried out in West Germany until 1949 and in the GDR until 1966. This means that the German readers of the original anthology would have had a different schema: beheading might have been rejected as capital punishment, and Nazi beheadings seen as particularly repugnant because they were undertaken without proper trials, but as an event it is likely to have been far less shocking.

The effect of the new context on the translated poem is thus to make the beheading a more tellable event than it would have been to the 1950s German reader, though it would of course have had a greater impact on its first reader, Schmidt-Sas's fiancée, even though she knew of his death sentence. In narratology, the point of the text in Labov's sense (1972: 366; see also Hühn 2013b) can be either physical or mental. In the narrative time of the German poem the imagined future change in the narrator's physical state that will be caused by his decapitation (which after all is just the normal outcome of a death sentence) is overshadowed in unexpectedness by the present change in his mental state. It is this second change, introduced in the second stanza, which marks the greater event in the German poem, as the 'dark wing' of death not only overshadows the turmoil of thoughts but calms it, bringing a lightness that contrasts with the superficial whiteness of the walls.

Because the imagined but certain death of the prisoner is far more shocking to the English reader, the cognitive effects of the narrative are somewhat different: it is difficult to make the unexpected calming effect of execution more of an event than the execution itself in the translation, because the reader's mind inevitably gets caught by the image of head separated from body, pushing the main turning point further back in the poem and threatening to lose the very point – that now, in this moment, he can welcome the loss of his head – that the condemned prisoner as poetic narrator wanted to make.

One way of avoiding this shift in a translation would be to change decapitation to hanging, thus decreasing the shock effect of his execution and increasing the salience of the emotional change from agitation to calm. But though this would work for the narrative and the poetics (since its effect on the victim is very similar), it is not possible in a poem that relates directly to historical circumstances.

Another way is to ensure that the main turning point of the poem is stylistically marked, as it is in German, and in such a way that it draws the English reader's attention to the real point. But it is important to ensure that the style remains ethically appropriate and thus not to draw attention by introducing a too regular rhyme or rhythm or too much sound repetition, because that would risk sounding at best like mere embellishment and at worst frivolous.

To try and mark the turning point, I have used expressions that make more obvious the change in perspective from seeing death as obscuring light to death as the bringer of light: 'luminous' for 'grell' (bright, glaring), 'blaze' for 'Glut' (glow, fire, heat), to give assonance (and thus mark the contrast) with 'shade', and 'lighten' for 'sänftigen' (to calm, to assuage), so that it can take on connotations of both 'not dark' and 'not heavy' and anticipate the 'lightness' of the final line. By thus making sure that line 10 remains the stylistic eye of the poem in English, it can be hoped that it will also be seen as the narrative turning point, when the mental change the speaker experiences in the poem's present is greater than the physical change he anticipates.

When we translate someone else's poem we indicate both empathy and approval. If translators, as Gutt (2000: 105–7) suggests, are indeed telling their audience what someone else says, then translation results in narrative embedding, such as is described by Herman (2006), even if the reader of the translation does not specifically identify the translator as a narrator.

Schmidt-Sas's first-person narrator is giving us an insight into how it feels to know you are going to be executed. By translating, and therefore retelling a story about telling someone how it feels (to adapt Herman's point; 2006: 372), the translator demonstrates that it is both possible to enter the mind of someone distant in culture and time from the reader's present, and in a situation most of us are unlikely, fortunately, to experience, and that it is worth doing.

What I have been arguing is that insights from narratology and stylistics taken together not only help us to see how the original poem works, and what changes when it is translated, but they also make it possible for the translator to direct the reader's attention to the real point of the story. The point of this story, which the reader must expend considerable mental effort to grasp, is not the execution, but that it is possible to face devastating events with calm.

References

Adorno, T. (2003), *Kulturkritik und Gesellschaft*, Vol. 1. Frankfurt am Main: Suhrkamp.

Bal, M. (2009), *Narratology: Introduction to the Theory of Narrative*, 3rd edition, Toronto: University of Toronto Press.

Baroni, R. (2014), 'Tellability', in P. Hühn, J. Pier, W. Schmid and J. Schönert (eds), *The Living Handbook of Narratology*, Hamburg: Hamburg University. http://www.lhn.uni-hamburg.de/.

Boase-Beier, J. (2009), 'Translating the Eye of the Poem', *CTIS Occasional Papers*, 4: 1–15.

Boase-Beier, J. (2011), *A Critical Introduction to Translation Studies*, London: Continuum.
Boase-Beier, J. (2015), *Translating the Poetry of the Holocaust: Translation, Style and the Reader*, London: Bloomsbury.
Boase-Beier, J. (2017), 'Holocaust Poetry and Translation', in J. Boase-Beier, P. Davies and A. Hammel (eds), *Translating Holocaust Lives*, 149–66, London: Bloomsbury.
Boase-Beier, J., and de Vooght, M. (eds) (2019), *Poetry of the Holocaust: An Anthology*, Todmorden: Arc Publications.
Caruth, C. (2013), *Literature in the Ashes of History*, Baltimore, MD: Johns Hopkins University Press.
Chandler, R. (2011), *The Big Sleep*, London: Penguin.
Edmonds, R. (trans.) (1957), *Leo Tolstoy: War and Peace*, Harmondsworth: Penguin.
Frank, A. (2007), *The Diary of a Young Girl*, trans. S. Massotty, London: Penguin.
Freeman, M. (2005), 'The Poem as a Complex Blend: Conceptual Mapping of Metaphor in Silvia Plath's "The Applicant"', *Language and Literature*, 14 (1): 25–44.
Furniss, T., and Bath, M. (2007), *Reading Poetry: An Introduction*, 2nd edition, Harlow: Pearson.
Gollwitzer, H., Kuhn, K., and Schneider, R. (eds) (1954), *Du hast mich heimgesucht bei Nacht*, Hamburg: Siebenstern Taschenbuch Verlag.
Greenspan, H. (2010), *On Listening to Holocaust Survivors: Beyond Testimony*, 2nd edition, St. Paul, MN: Paragon House.
Gubar, S. (2003), *Poetry after Auschwitz: Remembering What One Never Knew*, Bloomington, IN: Indiana University Press.
Gutt, E.-A. (2000), *Translation and Relevance*, Manchester: St Jerome Publishing.
Heaney, S. (1995), *The Redress of Poetry: Oxford Lectures*, London: Faber and Faber.
Heim, M. H. (trans.) (1984), *Milan Kundera: The Unbearable Lightness of Being*, New York, NY: Harper and Row.
Herman, D. (2006), 'Genette Meets Vygotsky: Narrative Embedding and Distributional Intelligence', *Language and Literature*, 15 (4): 357–80.
Hühn, P. (2013a), 'Narration in Poetry and Drama', in P. Hühn, J. Pier, W. Schmid and J. Schönert (eds), *The Living Handbook of Narratology*, Hamburg: Hamburg University. http://www.lhn.uni-hamburg.de/.
Hühn, P. (2013b), 'Event and Eventfulness', in P. Hühn, J. Pier, W. Schmid and J. Schönert (eds), *The Living Handbook of Narratology*, Hamburg: Hamburg University. http://www.lhn.uni-hamburg.de/.
Hühn, P., and J. Schönert (2002), 'Zur narratologischen Analyse von Lyrik', *Poetica*, 34 (3/4): 287–305.
Hühn, P., and J. Schönert (2005), 'Introduction: The Theory and Methodology of the Narratological Analysis of Lyric Poetry', in P. Hühn and J. Kiefer (eds), *The Narratological Analysis of Lyric Poetry: Studies in English Poetry from the 16th to the 20th Century*, 1–14, Berlin: De Gruyter.
Kafalenos, E. (2006), *Narrative Causalities*, Columbus, OH: Ohio Stata University Press.

Klimek, S. (2013), 'Functions of Figurativity for the Narrative in Lyric Poetry – With a Study of English and German Poetic Epitaphs from the 17th Century', *Language and Literature*, 22 (3): 219–31.

Labov, W. (1972), *Language in the Inner City: Studies in the Black English Vernacular*, Philadelphia, PA: University of Pennsylvania Press.

Labov, W. (2013), *The Language of Life and Death: The Transformation of Experience in Oral Narrative*, Cambridge: Cambridge University Press.

Lambrou, M. (2014), 'Narratives of Trauma Re-lived: The Ethnographer's Paradox and Other Tales', in B. Thomas and J. Round (eds), *Real Lives, Celebrity Stories: Narratives of Ordinary and Extraordinary People across Media*, 111–28, London: Bloomsbury.

McHale, B. (2009), 'Beginning to Think about Narrative in Poetry', *Narrative*, 17 (1): 11–30.

Miall, D. (2007), *Literary Reading: Empirical and Theoretical Studies*, New York, NY: Peter Lang.

Nader, A. (2007), *Traumatic Verses: On Poetry in German from the Concentration Camps, 1933–1945*, New York, NY: Camden House.

Phelan, P. (2004), 'Rhetorical Literary Ethics and Lyric Narrative: Robert Frost's "Home Burial"', *Poetics Today*, 25 (4): 627–51.

Phelan, J. (2014), 'Voice, Tone and the Rhetoric of Narrative', *Language and Literature*, 23 (1): 49–60.

Reiter, A. (2000), *Narrating the Holocaust*, trans. P. Camiller, London: Continuum.

Rothberg, M. (2000), *Traumatic Realism: The Demands of Holocaust Representation*, Minneapolis, MN: University of Minnesota Press.

Toolan, M. (2014), 'Afterword', *Language and Literature*, 23 (1): 89–98.

9

Retelling Hillsborough: A critical stylistic analysis of witness statements

Patricia Canning

9.1 Introduction

This chapter considers retellings of the Hillsborough Football Stadium Disaster through analyses of witness statements taken for the investigative process. It examines linguistic strategies, namely negation and 'disnarration' (Prince 1988) in statements scripted by the presiding police forces that led the initial investigation. Ultimately, it argues that 'retelling' is an institutional practice in most UK and European statement-taking contexts. That is not to say such practice is sinister or even intentional. Rather, it is often so because the production of a witness statement involves both what has been variously called 'entextualisation' (Bauman and Briggs 1990) and 'recontextualisation' (Linell 1998), which is the recapitulation of an oral narrative (in this case spoken by a witness) into a textual product for use in a different discourse context. Although Ministry of Justice (MOJ) guidelines advise law enforcement that '[t]he witness statement must, **if practicable**, be in the intended witness's own words' (2011: 18.1, my emphasis), this is rarely the case in practice. Typically, a witness statement is a dialogic, co-constructed story (Bakhtin 1981, 1984) between the witness and the statement-taking police officer reproduced 'on-line' (face to face) and in writing. Police often interrupt or ask questions to 'steer' the process, which controls the flow of information to some extent (Shepherd and Milne 1999). The process is often 'managed' by the presiding officer(s) to achieve best evidence (Jönsson and Linell 1991, MOJ). The resulting textual account is typically ordered in a formulaic, chronological sequence to reflect events as they unfolded.

Current UK police training guidance on taking witness statements is vague (compared to the taking of suspect statements). However, general practice in the UK requires that 'vulnerable' (Youth Justice and Criminal Evidence Act 1999) and 'significant' witnesses are routinely audio-recorded (Ministry of Justice 2011). Therefore, aside from any notes made during the statement-taking process, the final statement is the only extant record of the witness's oral account. When considering other forensic evidence, such as blood samples, DNA or fingerprints, protocols maintain evidential integrity, guarding against potential contamination, loss or corruption. There are, however, few safeguards in place to preserve the integrity of the witness's account (Clarke and Milne 2001; Shepherd 1995). A lack of scholarly research into the production and reception of statements by *witnesses* as opposed to *suspects* (Malsch et al. 2018)[1] compounds the issue. Indeed, much research tends to focus on the investigative interview (Poyser and Griffiths 2013).[2] Findings show that while there have been improvements in practice, the interview quality remains poor (Clarke and Milne 2001) not least because corresponding handwritten accounts are 'full of inaccuracies' (Smith and Milne 2018). Additionally, witness statements are negotiated so sources of information contained therein are 'systematically blurred' (Jönsson and Linell 1991: 434). Research in the Netherlands has shown how this is problematic for the witness, as the intended reader, often a judge, can treat it as a verbatim account by the witness when it is not (Komter 2012). Moreover, according to an ex-police chief, the '**witness** is the most vulnerable interviewee' (my emphasis) as they tend towards cooperation and validation of the interviewer's suggestions (McLean 1995: 117).

A witness is defined in Black's law dictionary (Garner 2019) as 'a person who has knowledge of an event' and judicially as a 'central lead' in investigations (Milne and Shaw 1999: 128).[3] The primary purpose of a witness statement is to capture this knowledge. The statement often operates metonymically, 'standing in' for the witness in court as 'evidence-in-chief' (Milne and Shaw 1999: 128). But a statement may also *construct* knowledge, 'standing in' for the institution that helped create it and whose voice is embedded within it. As a result of this dialogicity a witness statement may inadvertently tell more than one (version of a) story. Using data from statements given within days of the disaster by seventeen residents from around Hillsborough stadium I develop previous research in the UK (Coulthard 1994, 2004; Haworth 2017; Rock 2001) and in Europe (Jönsson and Linell 1991; Komter 2012 and Malsch et al. 2018) arguing that dialogicity can function to steer the witness's narrative along institutionally sanctioned lines with powerful ideological consequences. In so doing I will make a case for the utility of stylistic analyses for understanding how institutional discursive practices may inadvertently or otherwise recast witnesses' stories. Such recastings can compromise the evidential value of a witness's testimony and the very institution whose responsibility it is to preserve and protect it.

9.2 Background

On 15 April 1989, Liverpool Football Club played Nottingham Forest in a semi-final at Hillsborough Stadium, in Sheffield, UK. Over twenty-three thousand fans queued at the Leppings Lane end of the ground to enter via a restricted bottleneck long identified as a serious hazard. Before the 3.00 pm kick-off the arrival of fans outside the stadium led to congestion and crushing as the turnstiles could not process their entry. The police match commander, David Duckenfield, ordered the opening of an egress gate directly opposite a tunnel leading to the central enclosed spectator 'pens', thus relieving the crush. However, these 'pens' were already full to capacity. Over two thousand fans, unfamiliar with the stadium's layout, but visible to police on CCTV (and from the elevated control room), descended the tunnel unpoliced and unstewarded into the backs of the fans on the terrace into a deadly crush. By the time the match kicked off at 3.00 pm, men, women and children were being crushed to death. At 3.06 pm the match was abandoned. Within minutes, Chief Superintendent Duckenfield falsely instructed the Football Association chief executive that Liverpool fans had forced entry and caused the crush. This precipitated a retelling of Hillsborough that was to become institutionally cemented through the media (Scraton, Jemphrey and Coleman 1995; Scraton 1999a, 1999b, 2004; *The Sun* 1989).

In the following police investigation, over 3,350 witness statements were collected, initially by South Yorkshire Police (SYP) and subsequently West Midlands Police (WMP). A judicial inquiry in 1991 returned a verdict of 'accidental death', and a criminal investigation followed. In the thirty years since, independent research reports (Hillsborough Independent Panel Report (*HIP*) 2012), a drama-documentary (McGovern 1996) and academic analysis (Scraton 1999a) have challenged official accounts of the disaster and have revealed that police statements had been systemically reviewed and altered. In 2016 a new inquest formally exonerated fans and returned a new verdict of 'unlawful killing'. The disaster, one of the worst football stadium disasters of our time, claimed the lives of ninety-six men, women and children.[4]

9.3 (Co-)Constructing witness narratives

Labov (1972) and others[5] have shown that oral and written narratives are constituted by identifiable linguistic properties and structural elements.[6] Witness statements serve an evidential function and so it is perhaps not surprising that 'orientational' elements (Labov 1972) such as time adverbials (Fox 1993: 187–8) often assume greater significance than in other discourse situations (Rock 2001; Komter 2012). By way of example, Rock (2001) cites an interview extract that was reconstructed by police in which it took eight conversational turns to establish the timing of a suspect-witness's arrival at a friend's house, agreed upon as being 'probably after 3[pm]' (2001: 55). This dialogic exchange was reconstructed in the written statement as follows: 'On the 5th [month name] 2000 **at about 3pm** I was a [sic] friends [sic] house called Jerry' (2001: 55). The officer's determination of timing in the written record is more specific than in the witness's oral description. Additionally, temporality is considered more salient by the officer than by the witness as the former not only introduces it but revisits it later in the interview (2001: 56). While the officer may have collapsed the heavily modalized dialogic exchange into a simple assertion for economic purposes (i.e. to be informative or be seen to have produced a 'good statement') (Jönsson and Linell 1991; Shepherd 1995), the interactional exchange that resulted in negotiating this orientational detail is completely lost in the written report (Komter 2012; Malsch et al. 2018).

Labov and Waletzky (1967) argue that evaluation is a fundamental element of experiential narratives as it justifies their 'reportability' (Labov 1972: 366). Additionally, evaluation encodes the speaker's stance (Martin and White 2005), for example, through pejorative, honorific, formal or informal lexis; compare, for example, the use of 'vomit' versus 'sick deposit' (WMP 1990: 1396).[7] Comparatives also evaluate, for instance, '[t]he **only difference** from last year's semi-final was the sheer volume of fans coming at such a late stage in the proceedings' (WMP: 1376, my emphasis here and throughout the chapter). Additionally, research shows that police personnel have an identifiable institutional register known as 'policespeak' (Coulthard and Johnson 2007; Fox 1993; Hall 2008), a particular variety of language use that incorporates, among other things, formal lexis, formulaic phrases (Larner 2011) and over-explicitness. Some of these features can be discerned in two examples taken from the Hillsborough corpus which describe the deadly crush – one is from a football fan and the other is from a police officer:

(a) 'I found that I was having great difficulty in breathing, not being able to expand my chest so I ended up sucking in air to breath [sic]. By this time there was a lot of moaning, the screams had died out. I saw several people, I don't know who they are, had passed out. These were all blokes about my own age.' (Survivor, pen 3, statement SYP000000020001)[8]

(b) 'The crowding was very tight and it was becoming difficult to raise my arms from my sides. To be closely compact [sic] was becoming clostrophobic [sic] and because we were so close, the smell of stale ale on the breath of the supporters was strong.' (South Yorkshire Police Constable, statement SYP000082950001)

While (a) foregrounds material action (Halliday 1985) through informal lexis and syntax, 'so I ended up sucking in air' and refers colloquially to 'blokes' (males),[9] (b) displays greater lexical formality and backgrounds the 'doing' through nominalizations '[t]he crowding' and grammatical complements, 'closely compact'. The latter also includes an incongruous reference to alcohol, which is foregrounded (van Peer 1986). The 'smell' of 'stale' alcohol during a deadly crush (when bodily fluids were being excreted by the dead and dying) seems disproportionately 'newsworthy', so its 'telling' may be directed towards a 'super-addressee' (Bakhtin 1986: 126–7) not immediately present during the discourse situation. Ultimately, this could be a jury, who in turn may infer causality between alcohol and the crush to make sense of what is arguably a co-textually anomalous inclusion (see, for example, Sanford and Emmott 2012).

As a starting point then, *that* a witness chooses (if indeed it is they who choose) to report is itself an act of evaluation. Furthermore, *how* their oral reports are recapitulated or 'recontextualized' (Linell 1998) for use outside the contemporaneous discourse context may be influenced by the institutional stance of the statement-taking officer. Indeed, it raises the question: whose narrative (and by extension, stance) is recorded and preserved in the written record? Is all content attributable to the witness? If not, are embedded (institutional) voices discernible? What are the implications of such 'blurring of source distinctions'? (Jönsson and Linell 1991: 434). Who decides what is reportable? The following sections address these questions.

9.4 Retelling witnesses' stories

In its report, the Hillsborough Independent Panel (2012, chapter 12) exposed the presence of 'other' voices in witness statements through deletions and amendments. However, there are more subtle linguistic cues that give rise to embedded voices that, to date, have received little attention (but see Canning 2018). One such indicator is negation, typically understood as the denial or refutation of an expressed or implicit proposition or expectation. In English, negation is marked (Horn 1989) and 'all things being equal' deemed to be 'less informative than their positive counterparts' (Leech 1983: 100). This view is rooted in Aristotelian logic, which *a priori* posits the affirmative as a preferred and necessary antecedent for its denial ('affirmation explains denial just as being is prior to not-being' (*Metaphysics* 996b 14–16)). Its occurrence points to what Karttunen calls a '*sensus communis*', 'inform[ing] people of the beliefs they are supposed to hold and the expectations they are supposed to have of particular events and of particular kinds of people' (2008: 426). Karttunen's study also holds that negation 'only' makes sense 'if an explicit (co-textual) or implicit (contextual) expectation or claim is being refuted' (2008: 423). However, the adverb here is misplaced; making sense of negation is not predicated 'only' on explicit or implicit expectations or claims, but rather needs only to satisfy the precondition of *plausibility*. In this way, negation can help steer us to the very expectations it refutes and the addressee (whether a jury, judge, layperson) need not have held or been aware of the expectation prior to encountering the negation in order to make it make sense.[10]

Negation-led sense-making can have great evidential impact in a high-stakes discourse setting like a police investigation. Given the infinite number of things that do not happen, when one of them is reported it is afforded special significance ('newsworthiness'). In this way, negation can be more informative than affirmation (Jordan 1998; Leech 1983). By way of example, imagine being told a story about an accident that required the attendance of the emergency services in which the ambulance driver '**did not know** the way to the hospital'. This negated information is considered newsworthy as being an ambulance driver carries with it a schematic expectation that one would know the route. Thus, the negated clause is tellable; as Jordan puts it, 'in general, writers indicate what is *not* there only when there is a reasonable expectation that it *is* there and also when it is important for readers to know of its absence or its invalidity' (1998: 717, italics in original; see also Werth 1999: 120). As this story is part of a police investigation into Hillsborough, the not knowing has higher stakes given its potential impact on a possible prosecution case. Consider the relative redundancy or uninformativeness of the affirmative in the same scenario: 'the ambulance driver knew the way to the hospital'. Without a specific context the affirmative could hardly be deemed newsworthy. Telling what did *not* happen or what was *not* the case, then, invokes the very state of affairs it denies – the *sensus communis* (that the ambulance driver *did* or *should* know how to get to hospital). Additionally, it is likely to motivate us to negatively evaluate the competency of the ambulance driver.

9.5 Negotiating narratives: Telling it like it wasn't

Following the first inquiry led by Chief Justice Taylor, the West Midlands Police (WMP) compiled a report for the Director of Public Prosecutions (DPP) (1990). It included seventeen residents' statements, which comprise my corpus,[11] in which residents establish their ethos as proximate authorities, either by reporting their locations in relation to their proximity to the ground, 'Our house is situated off Leppings Lane' (WMP: 1350), or by explicitly narrating their ethos as credible witnesses: 'On cup semi final day **I am used to** the large numbers of supporters who attend our locality for the event ... **as is usual on these occasions** I saw 200 or 300 football supporters' (WMP: 1395); 'I am **quite used to** Football fans on [*sic*] visiting ... to seeing them stop off at [redacted] Pub' (WMP: 1398). Having established credibility, these witnesses secure valid 'speaking rights' (Heffer 2005). This and the forensic discourse situation itself (i.e. giving a statement to police) confer 'tellability' (Sacks 1995) or newsworthiness on what is subsequently reported.

There are a total of 143 occurrences of overt negation across the seventeen statements included in the WMP report and they are categorized in Table 9.1:

Table 9.1 Types of negation in residents' statements

Type of negation	Frequency (n)	Explanation
Informative	31	'Informative' refers to their co-textual or contextual relatedness in the narrative. These negations can be reasonably expected to occur in the course of the 'telling'.
Epistemic (bound)	13	This refers to witnesses' ability to 'know' or 'see' goings-on. By 'bound' (Emmott 1997) I mean that their relevance and relatedness are supported pragmatically, either contextually or co-textually, earlier in the narrative.
Epistemic (unbound)	24	As above, but for which there is no anaphor and, as such, are more marked than the previous type.
Tautological	25	These negations restate affirmative clauses (or vice versa).
Paraliptic	20	*Paralipsis* is a rhetorical term that means saying what you cannot or will not say. These negations are explicit statements of what the witness cannot report.
Infelicitous	19	This type concerns denials of actions, states or events (as opposed to denials of what the witness has seen (epistemic) or can say (paraliptic)) but which has low or no contextual/co-textual relevance or relatedness.
Metanoic	11	Another rhetorical term *metanoia* concerns the correction of a proposition or claim during a speech. It refers here to negations that correct or mitigate the extent or force of actions, events or states.

Of these 143 negations, thirty-one are reasonably 'informative' such as 'They [fans] **do not** normally like to park in our road' (i: 1345).[12] A further thirty-seven relate to epistemic distance; thirteen of these are 'bound in' (Emmott 1997: 123) satisfying what Wason calls a 'context of plausible denial' (1965: 7): 'I **don't know** the specific place she told me' (iii: 1358). The remaining twenty-four are unbound and thus appear to be prompted: 'I **don't think** there was one who was not holding a can of alcohol' (i: 1348), '**I did not see any loitering** with the exception of several fans who were openly urinating in the road' (xii: 1396, said of fans 'rushing' to the match). Expressions of epistemic commitment would not be unusual in witness statements as the discursive practice of evidence-gathering often incorporates the pursuit of clarity. This manifests linguistically in over-explicitness or over-specificity (Fox 1993: 188), which often indicates questioning or 'probing' by the officer (PEACE guidelines)[13] (College of Policing). However, these twenty-four epistemic negations overwhelmingly concern pejorative behaviours; in fact, all but one of them indicates probing of Liverpool fans drinking or carrying alcohol, urinating or arriving late:

(c) '**I saw no damage** caused to the bus or **no person** threatened **at all** as we negotiated the crowd in Leppings Lane. **I saw no people** selling tickets close to the ground.' (iii: 1357)
(d) '**I did not see** any of the supporters drinking beer at this time.' (iv: 1360)

Up to this point in (c) there is no mention of damage, threatening behaviour or ticket-selling so inclusion of these disnarrated events is odd. Indeed, narrative cohesion is attempted a few sentences later with: 'I feel that the trouble was caused on the day by the late arrival of supporters to the ground' (1357). Similarly in (d), the reference to 'not see[ing] supporters drinking beer' has not been bound in and its co-textual position (it follows orientational material) carries no expectation for encountering 'drinking' or 'beer'. Therefore, it indicates undocumented questioning. The adjunct 'at this time' binds in the expectation of beer-drinking at a later time and indeed we are told: 'I saw that the cans they were drinking from were beer cans ... They were still just talking to each other **and not misbehaving**' (1360).

Eleven negations are examples of 'metanoia' that either correct earlier affirmative statements, 'when I said the gates were being pushed, **I didn't see** the fans pushing it' (x: 1390), or mitigate propositions with scalar concessives, 'they were boisterous **but not** unruley [sic]' (ii: 1351). All of these eleven instances establish 'positive-assessment' relations (Jordan 1998: 717), in that they deny (through correction or mitigation) the occurrence or extent of pejorative behaviours: 'they were drinking from beer cans but **weren't** causing any problems' (vi: 1369); 'I say "selling tickets" **I didn't** actually see him pass the goods over' (ii: 1350). All of the instances of metanoia invoke pejorative actions before denying their extent or occurrence.

A further function of negation in the statements seems to be for emphasizing pejorative behaviours or the expectation of pejorative behaviours, making them more prominent than they may otherwise have been originally reported. I classify these as 'tautological' negations as they exhibit re-statement through a structural pattern of 'affirmative ≈ negative' where the first clause or sentence is affirmative, followed by a negative clause or sentence that conveys more or less the same semantic content as its antecedent. Consequently, the negation could be considered semantically redundant. There are twenty-five tautological negations and seventeen (68 per cent) of them establish 'negative-assessment relations' (Jordan 1998: 718), presenting Liverpool fans unfavourably. The following four examples are illustrative:

(e) 'The supporters were **all** holding their tickets which **had not been handed in**. During the following hours I was shown literally dozens of complete tickets which **had not been handed in** at the gates.' (i: 1347)
(f) 'I could see small groups of supporters who **all** had cans of beer in their hands … They all seemed to be in good spirits but there were very few who **had not got** a can of beer with him.' (i: 1346)
(g) 'there were hundreds of Liverpool supporters making their way down Halifax Road. **They were not restricted** to the footpaths and were walking in the road holding up the traffic.' (iii: 1355)
(h) 'The lad was on his own, **there was nobody else** with him, or in the area.' (iii: 1358)

All of these examples affirmatively present information that is then stated negatively with the exception of (g) which reverses the structure so the negative is stated first. In (e) the *context* (Jordan 1998; Pagano 1994) renders the negation informative (at such matches tickets are surrendered upon entry). Notably, the witness is referring throughout this example to fans outside the ground after the disaster occurred and so the tickets that are claimed as seen should have been surrendered. The inference then can be drawn that fans 'forced' their way in (in keeping with the dominant police and media narrative). All of these examples (e–h) function to foreground explicit or implicit negative-assessment relations when referring to Liverpool fans. Example (h) appears neutral enough; however, the 'lad' is preceded by 'The lad was urinating against the garages … he continued urinating for approximately three minutes. I formed the opinion that the lad must have been drinking for a long time prior to him needing to urinate.'

Of the twenty-five tautological negations, there are six (24 per cent) that establish positive-assessment relations of which the following are examples:

(i) 'The atmosphere [between police and Nottingham Forest supporters] was one of good humour. **There appeared to be no ill feeling** between the [Forest] supporters and the police.' (iii: 1354)
(j) 'I saw groups of supporters standing around on pavements talking. **They were not misbehaving** at all.' (iv: 1360)

Example (i) here is referring to the opposing team's fans, Nottingham Forest. As Labov has argued, comparative statements often signal evaluation – here the Nottingham Forest supporters' positive behaviour (and hence positive-assessment) is foregrounded as being in contrast to the reported behaviour of Liverpool fans, thus implicitly negatively evaluating the latter. Example (j) is interesting for the additional emphasis supplied by the adverbial adjunct 'at all' as there is no mention of 'misbehaving' up to this point – it has not been 'bound in'. The negation itself could encourage the expectation that fans would 'misbehave'. In Werth's words, the 'very act of denying it brings it into focus' (1999: 251). The negation, therefore, may indicate that it is an answer to an undocumented question in which case the topic of 'misbehaving fans' has likely been introduced as part of the 'probing' protocol and thus formed part of an off-record discussion. The probing of topics is part of police interviewing and of the statement-taking process both for suspects and witnesses. Therefore, it is not necessarily unusual to find what appears to be a focus on pejorative behaviours in a witness statement through negation of undocumented questions. However, what is significant in the Hillsborough corpus is that the attention paid to Liverpool fans' behaviours, from arrival time, to drinking alcohol, to urinating, is not given to Nottingham Forest fans' behaviour, nor is there any focus on the actions of the police in spite of Lord Justice Taylor's finding that the primary cause of the disaster was a 'failure of police control' (Taylor 1989).

Many of the examples discussed thus far are what Prince (1988) calls 'disnarration' (stating something that did not happen). Disnarration is important in the elicitation and production of witness narratives as it confers 'tellability' which, according to Prince (1988: 1), is 'assessed' differently depending on the discourse situation ('one narrator's unnarratable can very well be another's narratable' (1988: 2)). In forensic contexts it may be reasonable to clarify what did not happen and so some disnarrations may fall within the 'threshold of narratability' (Prince 1988: 1). However, many of the disnarrated occurrences in the seventeen residents' statements do not; instead they 'contribute' to borrow Prince's phrase, 'to the development of a theme' (5), namely the hooliganization of Liverpool fans. There are nineteen specific instances of disnarration that are especially marked because they deny propositions or expectations for which 'reasonableness' is not so easily attributed. I have classified this type as 'infelicitous', although in three of them their 'reasonableness' is explicitly expressed or explained:

(k) 'As we travelled along the road I saw that **there were no supporters** walking down to the Halifax Road, even though this is the route the supporters have to take to ensure segregation of their correct end of the ground, Leppings Lane.' (iii: 1355)

(l) 'I also noted that in view of the situation at Leppings Lane the [Liverpool] supporters at the two pubs I had seen **would not make** the start of the game.' (iii: 1357)

(m) 'I have lived here for three years and whenever there is a big match I have a walk up to the ground to see the supporters but I have **never** seen anything like the crowd outside the turnstiles. **I am not a football supporter** and **do not attend** any matches.' (iv: 1364)

These examples 'show why the narrative is tellable' (Prince 1988: 5). Both (l) and (m) share the structure of 'basis for denial'>denial (Jordan 1998: 722) while (k) reverses the structure. The embedded sentence in (k) beginning 'even though' provides justification or basis for the denial by explicitly stating the presupposition. In examples (l) and (m) the basis for denial is foregrounded perhaps to build the witnesses' ethos as providing a credible deduction in (l) and comparative (and thus, evaluative) evidence of fans' behaviour in (m). Either way, the over-explicitness is foregrounded, particularly as (l) is hypothetical. The two negated clauses in (m) are co-textually incongruous – perhaps they too are functioning ethically to confirm a lack of allegiance to either team and thus imply neutrality. Thematically, these extracts all relate to the dominant 'late arrival' narrative promulgated by the police and media (*HIP* 2012, *The Sun* 1989). In the remaining fourteen (74 per cent) of the nineteen examples[14] there is no co-textual explanation or basis for the denial (like the previous three, they have no anaphor and are unbound) and so their appearance is marked. The following is an example:

(n) 'On Saturday (150489) most of the supporters I spoke to left and **didn't cause** any trouble.' (vii: 1371)

Again, here, as in (j), the topic of pejorative behaviour ('misbehaving', 'trouble') is disnarrated; it has been introduced only in order to negate it (Werth's 'negative accommodation', 1999: 254; Martin and White 2003:118). A similar deduction can be made from (o) below:

(o) 'I had on more than one occasion, to go outside and tell some of the supporters to go elsewhere when they wanted to use our [redacted] as a toilet. **There was no responsive aggravation** to this and they turned and walked away.' (xvii: 1413)

Incidentally, of these nineteen infelicitous negations, over half (n = 10) establish positive-assessment relations by denying what appears to be an unstated proposition or allegation that if agreed with would reflect badly on Liverpool fans.[15] Given that all nineteen of them deny pejorative actions relating to alcohol, late arrival of fans or misbehaviour, these negations do not foreground fans' negative actions – but rather the *expectation* of negative actions. To quote Werth again, 'the negation introduces not only the denial of the expectation, but also the expectation itself' (1999: 255). Therefore, such infelicitous negations may well point to an institutional preoccupation with eliciting evidence (through probing topics) that accords with its own ideological expectations.

Finally, in 23 of the 143 cases of negation across the statements, the negated element relates to the witness's (in)ability to commit to an unstated proposition. All are mediated through meta-narration in which the witness explicitly disclaims for the record: 'I saw at least ten of them [fans] come over the small wire fence and urinate against the walls of the garages. **I can't say for sure** what fans they were **but** I could hear the odd "scouser" accent' (vi: 1369). The meta-narration 'I can't say for sure' explicitly expresses the witness's lack of epistemic commitment yet is followed by a concession ('but … ') that unequivocally reverses the negation by encouraging the inference that the urinating men were Liverpool fans. I classify these as 'paraliptic' negations (from the rhetorical term 'paralipsis'). Some indicate officers' attempts to elicit as much orientational material as possible: 'I **don't feel that I can say** much more' (x: 1390) and 'I **could not describe** a particular person who did this **but** there were a lot of fans who were doing it' (viii: 1375); 'he appeared to have an Irish accent, **I can't really describe** him other than a white male in his forties wearing dark clothes' (x: 1389). However, in all instances the negated component appears to be the result of questioning along a key theme of pejorative behaviour. The following six examples are illustrative:

(p) '**I can say there no** [*sic*] **supporters** in the area of the large blue solid gate which is marked as "C" on the plan. **I cannot say** whether the gate was open, or closed.' (iii: 1356–7)

(q) '**I am not in a position to say** whether the people in Leppings Lane had tickets to get in.' (iii: 1357)

(r) 'Due to the amount of people at the gate **I cannot say** whether any cans of beer were being carried or drunk.' (iii: 1357)

(s) 'I saw seven to eight youths standing on the forecourt drinking from pint glass [*sic*], the youths were shouting full of high spirits for the game **but I wouldn't describe** them as drunk.' (x: 1382)

(t) '**I could not say** how long these [Liverpool] fans had been in the Pub but I would estimate a group of twenty left, all in high spirits.' (xiii: 1399)

(u) '**I can't say** which team they supported but at that time, so close to the kick off and that location being the part of the ground reserved for the Liverpool supporters, I presumed that they were supporters of Liverpool.' (xvi: 1409)

Effectively, witnesses are emphasizing (through meta-narration) that which is being disclaimed as well as the act of disclamation thus further distancing themselves from the implicit expectations. Therefore, it would be reasonable to assume that such themes or 'topics' (and their corresponding expectations) have been introduced and thus rendered newsworthy by the interviewing officer rather than the witness. Put another way, the negations (manifested through negative accommodation) suggest topic control, with the result that expectations of fans behaving badly are introduced in a backgrounded way by the police interviewer.

9.6 Summary

Topics are often introduced in forensic statement-taking contexts through questioning or conversational turns (Sacks 1995; Sacks, Schegloff and Jefferson 1974; Shuy 1982) and the power asymmetry between police scribe and lay-witness places the latter under 'obligation' to respond (Frankel 1984). Whoever controls topics, usually the more powerful discourse participant (in the forensic context here, the police officer) determines what gets discussed and what does not (van Dijk 1996: 86). In the corpus under analysis, topic control suggests that witnesses have been probed to elicit negative appraisals of Liverpool fans. Given that the police response to the disaster was also under scrutiny, it seems odd that the topics probed in these 'representative' residents' statements are disproportionately oriented to Liverpool fans' behaviour yet do not include references to the behaviour of the police. Moreover, many of the negations give rise to pejorative behaviours through denying or mitigating their occurrence, indicating that the expectation of such behaviours has been introduced into the discourse situation by someone other than the witness. This potentially reframes the witness's testimony that is then (re)presented as a single, monologic story, both before the court and in the community. Once that occurs, these institutionally controlled and ideologically loaded stories are in danger of being recapitulated and remembered as historical fact. Therefore, it is vital to preserve the integrity and transparency of telling and recording witnesses' testimonies to ensure the integrity and transparency of history.

Notes

1   Additionally, see Griffiths, Milne and Cherryman (2011); Jönsson and Linell (1991); McLean (1995); Poyser and Milne (2015); Lamb et al. (2000).
2   The following studies are instrumental: Shepherd and Griffiths (2013); Westera, Kebbell and Milne (2011); Aldridge-Waddon (2010); Aldridge-Waddon and Luchjenbroers (2007); Heaton-Armstrong, Shepherd and Wolchover (1999).
3   Kebbell and Milne (1998); Sanders (1986); Zander and Henderson (1993).
4   At the time of going to press, David Duckenfield was found not guilty of gross negligence manslaughter in 2019: Sheffield Wednesday's health and safety executive at the time, Graham Mackrell. The SYP match commander, David Duckenfield, stood trial for ninety-five counts of manslaughter, but the jury could not agree a verdict. The ninety-sixth person to die following the disaster, Tony Bland, suffered severe brain damage and remained in a persistent vegetative state for almost four years after Hillsborough. His life support was withdrawn to allow him to die with dignity on 3 March 1993.
5   Bell (1991); Galtung and Ruge (1965); Labov and Waletzky (1967); Propp (1968); Todorov (1977).
6   Witness statements also exhibit patterns and as they originate as oral narratives the model proposed in Labov (1972) and Labov and Waletzky (1967) is particularly serviceable, specifically the structural components of 'orientation' (the 'who', 'what', 'when' and 'where') and 'evaluation' (the 'so what?').
7   The references here and throughout refer to the West Midlands Police report, Part IV, to the Director of Public Prosecutions (1989), followed by witness statement number (where applicable) and the page number within the report.

8   These references relate to the unique code given to documents disclosed to the Hillsborough Independent Report and which constitute the corpora shared on the www.hillsborough.gov.uk website (which has been temporarily withdrawn pending the current prosecution cases).
9   The negation 'I don't know who they are' indicates an embedded institutional voice which I will discuss later.
10 I agree with Tottie (1982) here, who claims that the negation itself can create the belief it seeks to deny. Jordan is more cautious when he says that a 'pragmatic understanding of negation must not be restricted to an assumption that the readers' presupposition has been created earlier in the text' either implicitly or explicitly (Jordan 1998: 711). He refers here to the contextual knowledge of the reader as instrumental rather than explicitly stated presuppositions. My point about plausibility is similar to Givón's (1993) claim that addressees are 'at least familiar' with the expectation implied or explicit in the negation.
11 There were hundreds of statements taken from residents. The WMP report offers no explanation for selecting the seventeen analysed here.
12 The roman numerals relate to the numbered statements (i–xvii).
13 The framework adopted for investigative interviewing and for eliciting a statement is called the 'PEACE' model, an acronym that translates as 'Plan and Prepare, Engage and Explain, Account Clarification and Challenge, Closure, Evaluation'. 'Probe' comes under the 'A' section, 'account clarification and challenge'. Hillsborough predates the framework; however, 'probing' has always been part of the investigative interview.
14 Two instances are neutral.
15 Seven establish negative-assessment relations.

References

Aldridge-Waddon, M. (2010), 'Vulnerable Witnesses in the Criminal Justice System', in M. Coulthard and A. Johnson (eds), *The Routledge Handbook of Forensic Linguistics*, 296–314, Abingdon: Routledge.

Aldridge-Waddon, M., and Luchjenbroers, J. (2007), 'Linguistic Manipulations in Legal Discourse: Framing Questions and "Smuggling" Information', *International Journal of Speech, Language and the Law*, 14 (1): 85–107.

Aristotle (1966), *Metaphysics*, H. Apostle (ed.), Bloomington: Indiana University Press.

Arnold, H. (1989), *The Sun*, ed. Kelvin Mackenzie, 19 April 1989, London: News Group Newspapers, UK..

Bakhtin, M. M. (1981), *The Dialogic Imagination. Four Essays*, M. Holquist (ed.), trans. C. Emerson, Austin: University of Texas Press.

Bakhtin, M. M. (1984), *Problems of Dostoevsky's Poetics*, trans. C. Emerson, Minneapolis and London: University of Minnesota Press.

Bakhtin, M. M. (1986), *Speech Genres and other Late Essays*, Austin: University of Texas Press.

Bauman, R., and Briggs, C. L. (1990), 'Poetics and Performance as Critical Perspectives on Language and Social Life', *Annual Review of Anthropology*, 19: 59–88.

Bell, A. (1991), *The Language of News Media*, Oxford: Blackwell.

Canning, P. (2018), 'No Ordinary Crowd': Foregrounding a "Hooligan Schema" in the Construction of Witness Narratives Following the Hillsborough Football Stadium Disaster', *Discourse and Society*, 29 (3): 237–55.

Clarke, C., and Milne, R. (2001), *National Evaluation of the PEACE Investigative Interviewing Course*, Police Research Award Scheme, Report No: PRAS/149.

College of Policing: Guidance on Witness Statements. Available online: https://www.app.college.police.uk/app-content/investigations/investigative-interviewing/#witness-statements (accessed 28 September 2019).

Coulthard, R. M. (1994), 'Powerful Evidence for the Defence: An Exercise in Forensic Discourse Analysis', in J. Gibbons (ed.), *Language and the Law*, 414–42, London: Longman.

Coulthard, R. M. (2004), 'Author Identification, Ideolect, and Linguistic Uniqueness', *Applied Linguistics*, 24 (4): 431–47.

Coulthard, R. M., and Johnson, A. (2007), *An Introduction to Forensic Linguistics: Language in Evidence*, London and New York: Routledge.

Emmott, C. (1997), *Narrative Comprehension: A Discourse Perspective*, Oxford: Clarendon Press.

Fox, G. (1993), 'A Comparison of "Policespeak" and "Normalspeak": A Preliminary Study', in J. M. Sinclair, M. Hoey and G. Fox (eds), *Techniques of Description: Spoken and Written Discourse*, 183–95, London: Routledge.

Frankel, R. M. (1984), 'From Sentence to Sequence: Understanding the Medical Encounter through Microinteractional Analysis', *Discourse Processes*, 7 (2): 135–70.

Galtung, J., and Ruge, M. H. (1965), 'The Structure of Foreign News: The Presentation of the Congo, Cuba and Cyprus in Four Norwegian Newspapers', *Journal of Peace Research*, 2 (1): 64–90.

Garner, Bryan A. (2019), *Black's Law Dictionary*, 11th edition. The Lawbook Exchange, Limited.

Givón, T. (1993), *English Grammar: A Function-Based Approach*, Amsterdam: John Benjamins.

Griffiths, A., Milne, R., and Cherryman, J. (2011), 'A Question of Control? The Formulation of Suspect and Witness Interview Question Strategies by Advanced Interviewers', *International Journal of Police Science and Management*, 13 (3): 1–13.

Guidance on Investigative Interviewing. Available online: www.app.college.police.uk (accessed 1 May 2019).

Hall, P. (2008), 'Policespeak', in J. Gibbons and T. Turell (eds), *Dimensions in Forensic Linguistics*, 67–94, Amsterdam: John Benjamins.

Halliday, M. A. K. (1985), *An Introduction to Functional Grammar*, London: Arnold.
Haworth, K. (2017), 'The Discursive Construction of Evidence in Police Interviews: A Case Study of a Rape Suspect', *Applied Linguistics*, 38 (2): 194–214.
Heaton-Armstrong, A., Shepherd, E., and Wolchover, D. (eds) (1999), *Analysing Witness Testimony*, London: Blackstone Press.
Heffer, C. (2005), *The Language of Jury Trial: A Corpus-Aided Analysis of Legal-Lay Discourse*, Basingstoke: Palgrave Macmillan.
Hillsborough Independent Panel. (2012), *Hillsborough: The Report of the Hillsborough Independent Panel*, London: The Stationery Office. http://hillsborough.independent.gov.uk
Home Office. (1999), *Youth Justice and Criminal Evidence Act*, London. Available online: www.legislation.gov.uk (accessed 16 March 2019).
Home Office. (2014), *Police and Criminal Evidence Act (1984) Code A – Revised Code of Practice for the Exercise by Police Officers and Police Staff of Requirements to Record Public Encounters*, Norwich: TSO.
Horn, L. (1989), *A Natural History of Negation*, London: The University of Chicago Press.
Jönsson, L., and Linell, P. (1991), 'Story Generations: From Dialogical Interviews to Written Reports in Police Interrogations', *Text*, 11 (3): 419–40.
Jordan, M. P. (1998), 'The Power of Negation in English: Text, Context and Relevance', *Journal of Pragmatics*, 29: 705–52.
Karttunen, L. (2008), 'A Sociostylistic Perspective on Negatives and the Disnarrated: Lahiri, Roy, Rushdie', *Partial Answers; Journal of Literature and the History of Ideas*, 6 (2): 419–41.
Kebbell, M., and Milne, R. (1998), 'Police Officers' Perceptions of Eyewitness Performance in Forensic Investigations', *The Journal of Social Psychology*, 138 (3): 323–30. DOI: 10.1080/00224549809600384.
Komter, M. (2012), 'The Career of a Suspect's Statement: Talk, Text, Context', *Discourse Studies*, 14 (6): 731–52.
Labov, W. (1972), *Language in the Inner City: Studies in the Black English Vernacular*, Philadelphia: University of Pennsylvania Press.
Labov, W., and Waletzky, J. (1967), 'Narrative Analysis', in J. Helm (ed.), *Essays on the Verbal and Visual Arts*, 12–44, Seattle, WA: University of Washington Press (reprinted in 1997, *Journal of Narrative and Life History* 7: 3–38).
Lamb, M. E., Orbach, Y., Sternberg, K. J. Hershkowitz, I., and Horowitz, D. (2000), 'Accuracy of Investigators' Verbatim Notes of Their Forensic Interviews with Alleged Child Abuse Victims', *Law and Human Behaviour*, 24 (6): 699–708.
Larner, S. (2011), 'A Preliminary Investigation into the Use of Fixed Formulaic Sequences as a Marker of Authorship', *The International Journal of Speech, Language and the Law*, 21 (1): 1–22.
Leech, G. (1983), *Principles of Pragmatics*, London: Longman.
Linell, P. (1998), 'Discourse across Boundaries: On Recontextualisations and the Blending of Voices in Professional Discourse', *Text*, 18 (2): 143–57.

Lord Justice Taylor. (1989), *Interim Report of the Inquiry into the Hillsborough Football Stadium Disaster*, London: Her Majesty's Stationery Office.

Malsch, M., Kranendonk, P. R., De Keijser, J. W., Komter, M. L., and Elffers, H. (2018), 'Reporting on Police Interrogations: Selection Effects and Bias Related to the Use of Text, Video and Audiotape', *Investigative Interviewing Research and Practice*, 9 (1): 61–76.

Martin, J. R., and White, R. (2003), *The Language of Evaluation*, London: Palgrave Macmillan.

Martin, J. R., and White, P. R. R. (2005), *The Language of Evaluation: Appraisal in English*, Hampshire and New York: Palgrave Macmillan.

McGovern, J. (1996), *Hillsborough*, Drama Documentary, Independent Television (ITV), Manchester: Granada Studios.

McLean, M. (1995), 'Quality Investigation: Police Interviewing of Witnesses', *Medical Science and Law*, 35 (2): 116–22.

Milne, R., and Shaw, G. (1999), 'Obtaining Witness Statements: The Psychology, Best Practice and Proposals for Innovation', *Medicine, Science and Law*, 39 (2): 127–38.

Ministry of Justice. (2011), *Achieving Best Evidence in Criminal Proceedings: Guidance on Interviewing Victims and Witnesses, and Using Special Measures*. Crown Prosecution Service.

Pagano, A. (1994), 'Negatives in Written Text', in R. M. Coulthard (ed.), *Advances in Written Text Analysis*, 250–65, London and New York: Routledge.

van Peer, W. (1986), *Stylistics and Psychology: Investigations of Foregrounding*, London: Croom Helm.

Poyser, S., and Griffiths, A. (2013), *Investigative Interviewing: The Conversation Management Approach*, 2nd edition, Oxford: Oxford University Press.

Poyser, S., and Milne, R. (2015), 'No Grounds for Complacency and Plenty for Continued Vigilance: Miscarriages of Justice as Drivers for Research on Reforming the Investigative Interviewing Process', *The Police Journal: Theory, Practice and Principles*, 88 (4): 265–80.

Prince, G. (1988), 'The Disnarrated', *Style*, 22 (1): 1–8.

Propp, V. I. A. (1968), *Morphology of the folktale*, Austin: University of Texas Press.

Rock, F. (2001), 'The Genesis of a Witness Statement', *Forensic Linguistics*, 8 (2): 44–72.

Sacks, H. (1995), *Lectures on Conversation*, New Jersey: Blackwell Publishing.

Sacks, H., Schegloff, E. A., and Jefferson, G. (1974), 'A Simplest Systematics for the Organization of Turn-Taking for Conversation', *Language*, 50: 696–735.

Sanders, G. S. (1986), 'On Increasing the Usefulness of Eyewitness Research', *Law and Human Behavior*, 10: 333–6.

Sanford, A. J., and Emmott, C. (2012), *Mind, Brain, and Narrative*, Cambridge: Cambridge University Press.

Scraton, P. (1999a), *Hillsborough: The Truth*, 1st edition. Edinburgh: Mainstream Publishing (updated in 2016).

Scraton, P. (1999b), 'Policing with Contempt: The Degrading of Truth and Denial of Justice in the Aftermath of the Hillsborough Disaster', *Journal of Law and Society*, 26 (3): 273–97.

Scraton, P. (2004), 'Death on the Terraces: The Contexts and Injustices of the 1989 Hillsborough Disaster', *Soccer and Society*, 5 (2): 183–200.

Scraton, P., Jemphrey, A., and Coleman, S. (1995), *No Last Rights: The Denial of Justice and the Promotion of Myth in the Aftermath of the Hillsborough Disaster*, Liverpool: CSCSJ and Liverpool City Council.

Shepherd, E. (1995), 'Representing and Analysing the Interviewee's Account', *Medical Science and Law*, 35 (2): 122–35.

Shepherd, E., and Griffiths, A. (2013), *Investigative Interviewing: The Conversation Management Approach*, 2nd edition. Oxford: Oxford University Press.

Shepherd, E., and Milne, R. (1999), 'Full and Faithful: Ensuring Quality Practice and Integrity of Outcomes in Witness Interviews', in A. Heaton-Armstrong, E. Shepherd, D. Wolchover (eds), *Analysing Witness Testimony: A Guide for Legal Practitioners and Other Professionals*, 124–45, London: Blackstone Press Limited.

Shuy, R. (1982), 'Topic as the Unit of Analysis in a Criminal Law Case', in D. Tannen (ed.), *Analyzing Discourse: Text and Talk*, 189–202, Washington, DC: Georgetown University Press.

Smith, K., and Milne, R. (2018), 'Witness Interview Strategy for Critical Incidents (WISCI)', *Journal of Forensic Practice*, 20 (4): 268–78. https://doi.org/10.1108/JFP-03-2018-0007

Todorov, T. (1977), *The Poetics of Prose*, Oxford: Blackwell.

Tottie, G. (1982), 'Where Do Negative Sentences Come From?', *Studia Linguistica*, 36 (1): 88–105.

van Dijk, T. (1996), 'Discourse, Power and Access', in C. R. Caldas-Coulthard and M. Coulthard (eds) *Texts and Practices*, pp. 84–104. London and New York: Routledge.

Wason, P. C. (1965), 'The Contexts of Plausible Denial', *Journal of Verbal Learning and Verbal Behaviour*, 4: 7–11.

Werth, P. (1999), *Text Worlds: Representing Conceptual Space in Discourse*, London: Longman.

West Midlands Police. (1990), *Report to the Director of Public Prosecutions into the Hillsborough Stadium Disaster*, Part IV: 1145–520.

Westera, N. J., Kebbell, M., and Milne, R. (2011), 'Interviewing Witnesses: Do Investigative and Evidential Requirements Concur?', *The British Journal of Forensic Practice*, 13 (2): 103–13.

Zander, M., and Henderson, P. (1993), *The Royal Commission on Criminal Justice: Crown Court Study*, London: HMSO.

10

'This is a sponsored post, but all opinions are my own': Advertising (re)tellings on social media

Helen Ringrow

10.1 Introduction: Cosmetics advertising discourse

Critical linguistic studies of cosmetics advertising discourse have previously tended to focus primarily on print advertising (cf. Coupland 2007; Lazar 2011; Ringrow 2016). Key themes which emerge from this literature examining cosmetics advertising texts include the connections made between a certain kind of femininity and a youthful, unblemished appearance; women's bodies being conceptualized as problematic and always requiring 'work' in the form of cosmetics products; and the use of seemingly self-empowering or liberating discourses to describe and sell beauty products (Ringrow 2016). Feminist linguists and scholars from various disciplines analyse cosmetics advertising discourse with the aim of exploring commonplace texts that are intrinsically connected to gender and identity. With increasing change in the media landscape and the move to newer forms[1] of (often social) media, advertisements, especially for cosmetics products, increasingly appear on Instagram celebrities' social media platforms in the format of an advertorial: '[...] a highly personalized, narrative advertising format that resembles an opinion-editorial' (Abidin 2018: 76). These advertorials are generally a retelling of a brief which has been given to the Influencer by a representative on behalf of the brand (often via their management agency and in discussion with the brand, who may have final editorial approval). This chapter explores the finished product of the retelling, that is, the advertorial itself. The chapter analyses in particular the construction of 'problems' in these texts, disclosure language (in which the text draws attention to itself as a form of promotional material), and personalization of text and image (whereby the person promoting this product will explain how it suits their particular wants or needs). These advertorials will be explored in light of the complex intersections between gender, identity and newer forms of advertising discourse, considering the ways in which social media celebrities tell stories of how these products fit into their daily lives and routines. The next section provides contextual information on the authors of these advertorials, referred to interchangeably in this chapter as *Influencers* or *microcelebrities*. The focus in this chapter is on two popular UK-based Influencers.

10.2 Influencers and social media

Social media figures such as bloggers, vloggers and other content creators are often described using the terms *microcelebrity* or *Influencer*.[2] Microcelebrities are 'internet famous' (Tanz 2008) to a particular group of people (Jerslev 2016; Marwick 2013; Marwick and Boyd 2011) and share content relating to their daily lives and lived experiences with their followers or fans. Influencers are, in essence, a kind of microcelebrity; they can be defined as 'vocational, sustained, and highly branded social media stars' (Abidin 2018: 71). Crucially for brands, Influencers can command a sizeable audience (over 1 million in some cases) and online following on their (often multiple) social media platforms through 'engaging and personalized content production, which can be used as conduits of information to amplify messages' (Abidin 2018: 71). Of all the social media sites, Instagram, a social media app in which users can produce and edit images accompanied by a caption, seems in many ways extremely suitable for advertorial content. Although the original photo and caption format still tends to dominate, there are now additional features of Instagram, including the ability to produce Instagram stories: short snippets of video content. Instagram users with more than ten thousand followers currently have access to an increased range of functions, such as a 'swipe up' feature where the audience can click on affiliate links and purchase the product the Influencer is recommending. Instagram does not require advanced technical knowledge to use and, perhaps more importantly, it had no specialized advertising tools until 2014. As a result, 'in the absence of such devices, brands have developed uses of the platform that engage with the productive ability of cultural intermediaries and consumers to create and circulate images of their bodies, everyday lives, and cultural practices' (Carah and Shaul 2016: 69).

One of the key benefits for brands using Instagram Influencer advertorials is that Influencers have (or at least appear to have) personal, lived experience of using the brand and can promote it to their followers in a way that 'native' advertising coming directly from the brand cannot (Abidin 2016a: 7).[3] Through advertorials, microcelebrities share with their followers products they (apparently) use in their daily lives. This sharing can be aspirational or inspirational for some of the audience (Abidin 2016b: 87) who may grow to trust and value their favourite Influencer's endorsement of a certain brand or company (Abidin 2018: 33). In this way, the Influencer industry

> has stimulated innovative forms of digital labor on the internet, encouraged an increasing uptake of young people in entrepreneurship, generated new models of work life, fostered cross-cultural literacies, raised the value of digital estates, demonstrated the potential of networked social movements, and seen the spread of vernacular practices on a global scale.
>
> (Abidin 2018: 87)

This digital labour is, however, often overlooked or not made very visible.

10.3 Instagram advertorials as invisible retellings

It is quite difficult for the wider public to know the exact details behind creating Instagram advertorial texts. In general, a brand may approach an Influencer (if they are a well-established microcelebrity, this contact will be via their management agency) to inquire about paid-for content. Influencer and brand (again, possibly via a management agency) must agree on the type of content (multi-platform, time frame and so on) and a payment.[4] The Influencer is then sent a text or brief to personalize; this may go back and forth between brand and Influencer, but this text is then presented as a finished product with the retelling element not visible. What I argue in this chapter is that Influencers do *retelling work* by personalization of the text. The level and degree of personalization may vary. When brands approach several Influencers to produce advertorials for them within the same time frame, comparing and contrasting advertorials for the same product but from different Influencers can often show traces of the original brief (e.g. keywords, key hashtags and so on; see also Abidin 2016a: 9–10). Influencers may have one preferred or dominant platform, but it is often likely they are maintaining more than one social media profile and 'multitasking' their advertising content across platforms to cross-traffic and reach a bigger audience (Abidin 2018: 92–3). As such, they must successfully present a coherent and consistent story of themselves across different media. As noted earlier, the process of social media advertorial creation is not always very evident for outsiders, but often Influencers are approached by brands who think they might be a good conduit for their product, in terms of their demographic and their audience. Instagram advertorials from Influencers can therefore be viewed as a form of retelling with the retelling element backgrounded. The briefs given to Influencers are in their very essence texts made for retelling.

Occasionally, and very much accidentally, the retelling element (or at least part of it) may be made visible to the audience. One Singaporean Influencer, @xiaxue, once mistakenly copied and pasted the instructions from her manager instead of just the edited content for her advertorial:

> Hello Wendy! Here's your EDITED caption for skinny mint 2nd IG: Loving my SkinnyMint tea! The morning boost is supposed to make you less bloated, increase alertness, lessen cravings and snackings, and have anti anxiety properties!
>
> (Abidin 2016a: 13–15)

Perhaps unsurprisingly, this caption was hastily deleted and the correct one uploaded, much to the amusement of many of her followers (Abidin 2016a: 14). In most cases, however, the audience is not privy to any of the textual changes from the brief to the finished product.

As social media advertising continues to increase, advertising watchdogs and regulatory bodies (in the UK and elsewhere) are increasingly concerned that it may not always be easy for the consumer to identify an advertisement as such. An Influencer's Guide[5] was launched in 2018 in the UK from the Committee of Advertising Practice (CAP) and the Advertising Standards Authority (ASA), in conjunction with the Competition & Markets Authority (CMA). A main objective of the guide is to advise Influencers on how to comply with relevant legislation and make clear to the audience the product is an advertorial, which can be seen in the following extract:

> Most influencer marketing appears alongside independent/editorial content in a very similar style, so it often isn't immediately obvious when something is or isn't an ad from the content alone […] There are potentially loads of ways you could make advertising content 'stick out' as being advertising, but by far the easiest is to include a prominent label that makes this clear.[6]

The advertorials selected for analysis in this chapter are discussed in the next section ('Methods').

10.4 Methods

10.4.1 Data analysed

This chapter explores data from two popular UK-based Influencers, Anna Newton (The Anna Edit @theannaedit) and Lily Pebbles (@lilypebbles).[7] Both broadly fit into the category of 'lifestyle Influencer'; both are represented by Gleam Futures (a high-profile UK-based Influencer talent management agency); and both frequently discuss cosmetics on their social media channels (mainly Instagram, YouTube and their blogs; both also have books). As of 11 June 2019, Anna has 444k Instagram followers and Lily 430k. All content labelled with disclosure language was selected from the beginning of their Instagram accounts to 31 January 2019 (when this research project began). This resulted in a total of fifty advertorials (thirteen from Anna, twenty-seven from Lily), of which thirty (six from Anna, twenty-four from Lily) displayed evidence of Problem-Solution patterning in which the advertorial aims to respond to a problem faced by the consumer (cf. Hoey 1983, 2001; Ringrow 2016). These thirty advertorials were therefore selected for further investigation in this chapter. Since this dataset is relatively small, the discussion will be qualitative.[8] The data follows standard Instagram formatting; the majority of the post is an image with an accompanying caption.[9]

10.4.2 Approaches to the data

On a macro-level the approach to the data in this chapter is Multimodal Critical Discourse Analysis (MCDA) (see, for example, Ledin and Machin 2018; Machin 2013) in that it explores how both visual and textual modes combine to create certain kinds of meaning. For the purposes of my analysis, images of the Influencer and/or of the product add to the narrative of how this product is used by them and fits into their routine. The image and text both help to create the story of the advertorial. On a micro-level, the language of the advertorials was analysed in relation to Problem-Solution patterning (Hoey 1983, 2001; Ringrow 2016), disclosure language (Evans et al. 2017) and the personalization of the text (drawing on Abidin 2016a, 2016b, 2018). The personalization of images was analysed using Zappavigna (2016)'s framework (see also Zhao and Zappavigna 2015) for exploring the producer-audience relationship in social media images.

10.5 Findings and discussion

10.5.1 Problem-Solution patterns

The presence of Problem-Solution patterns in these advertorials was a common theme. The analysis applied Hoey's (1983, 2001) Problem-Solution model, as adapted for specific application to cosmetics advertising discourse by Ringrow (2016). This pattern in beauty advertising 'both creates and affirms a notion of femininity that can be continually improved by use and purchase of beauty products' (Ringrow 2016: 33). The model begins with the **(Optional) Situation** (e.g. 'summer is here') and then the **Aspect of Situation Requiring a Response (Problem)** (e.g. 'your hair is not summer-ready – it's flat and dry'). This problem is not, in many cases, an obvious one (Ringrow 2016: 37). The problem can take multiple forms: **Problem 1: Fragmented Aspect of Appearance** (e.g. 'flat hair'), **Problem 2: Existing Product** (e.g. 'is your current conditioner weighing down your hair and leaving it lifeless?'), and/or **Problem 3: Lifestyle or Environment** (e.g. 'you don't have time to go to the hair salon'). The **Response (Solution)** element often combines both **Positive Evaluation** and **Positive Result** (e.g. 'this conditioner improves hair's texture without weighing it down. Your hair is so shiny – it has never looked better!'). An **(Optional) Basis for the Response (Solution)** may be provided (e.g. 'we've been testing this product for years with hundreds of women with different hair types'). All **Response (Solution)** elements can include **Surface Appearance discourse** (e.g. 'your hair *appears* healthier'), **Transformation discourse** (e.g. '*transforms* your hair') and/or **Fragmentation** of body parts (e.g. 'leaves your *hair* shinier and more hydrated'). An overview of the model can be seen in Figure 10.1.

The focus in these Instagram advertorials draws particularly on Problem 2: Existing Product (Ringrow 2016: 37–40), which suggests that existing products or earlier formulas of this product are somehow lacking or can be improved upon, in terms of aspects such as product texture, longevity or packaging (Ringrow 2016: 38). There are some key elements at play here: firstly, this 'problem' may not be entirely apparent to the potential consumer before they encounter the advertisement or advertorial, reinforcing the idea of continual 'newness' built into capitalist systems; an updated version is always imminent

Advertising (Re)tellings on Social Media

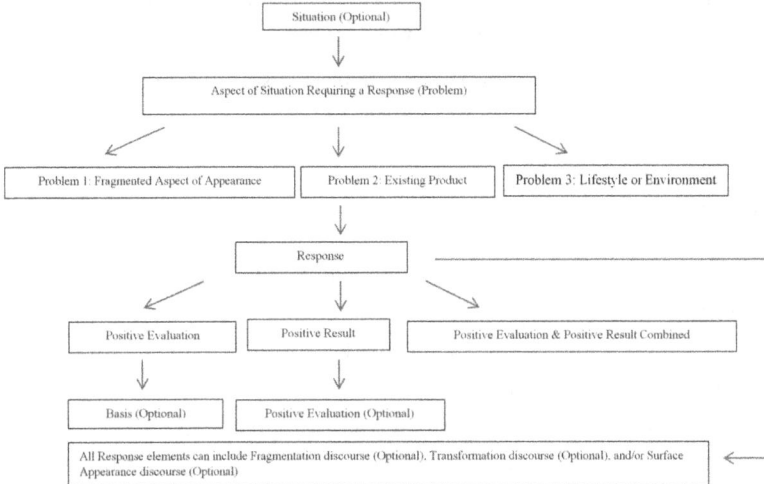

Figure 10.1 A Problem-Solution pattern for cosmetics advertising discourse (Ringrow 2016: 37)

(Benwell and Stokoe 2006: 176; Ringrow 2016: 38). Examples from this data set of Problem 2 include the following examples (with relevant Problem 2 features highlighted):

> I'm also showing you how to use the new @Batiste_hair **invisible 2in1 shampoo & conditioner – yep, you heard right, it does both**! [@lilypebbles, Batiste dry shampoo Instagram advertorial, 20/04/17]

> Throwback to my trip to Paris with @bourjois_uk. There's a new vlog on my channel if you want to see what I got up & hear about their exciting launches including the **newly reformulated** Healthy Mix foundation [@lilypebbles, Bourjois foundation Instagram advertising post, 15/02/17]

> Today's blog post is a review of the new Origins Original Skin Renewal serum that I've been testing for a couple of months. **Finally something aimed at us twenty-somethings with stressed out skin!** [@lilypebbles, Origins skin serum Instagram advertising post, 11/03/15]

> I'm currently testing out the Grow Gorgeous Cleansing Conditioner. **It cleanses whilst conditioning but doesn't strip the hair at all.** [@lilypebbles, Grow Gorgeous cleansing conditioner Instagram advertising post, 06/06/14]

These posts may present the product as answering some kind of problem faced by the Influencer (which is not adequately solved by existing products) and, by extension, their followers. Through the Problem-Solution narrative,

Influencers can tell a story of their own experiences using this product. However, it may not always be entirely clear at first glance that these posts are paid-for content. The following section discusses the presence of language attempting to highlight just that.

10.5.2 Disclosure language

Disclosure language has become a key feature of social media advertorials, predominantly due to stricter new advertising regulations in the UK, as noted earlier in this chapter (see also Evans et al. 2017). Advertorials may resemble editorial content and therefore the paid nature of advertorials is not always very apparent; adding disclosure language draws attention to this genre of text as an advertisement (Evans et al. 2017: 140). The presence of disclosure language is also an indication that this text has gone through a retelling and that the original content or impetus came from or on behalf of the brand. The data analysed for this chapter displayed a range of different kinds of disclosure language, with what can arguably be seen as a slight shift in labelling practices in response to recent guidelines. Older posts used #spon or #sponsored, often at the end of their posts to indicate that this is not their usual editorial content:

> **#sponsored** [(@lilypebbles, Revlon makeup Instagram post, 05/09/14]
> **#sponsored** [@lilypebbles, Max Factor Gel Shine Lacquer nail polish Instagram post, 28/07/14]
> **#spon** [@lilypebbles, Grow Gorgeous Cleansing Conditioner Instagram post, 06/06/14]
> **#spon** [@lilypebbles, L'Oréal Mythic Oil hair oil Instagram post, 16/02/13]

Arguably, #sponsored, #spon or the ambiguous #sp may not be as transparent as other terms. In their 2018 guidelines,[10] the ASA explain their preferred disclosure labels are *ad, advert, advertising, advertisement* or *ad/advert/advertising/ advertising feature*. These types of labels were common in my dataset, especially with many of more recent advertorials:

> **#AD** [@theannaedit, Caudalie Beauty Elixir Instagram advertising post, 04/09/17]
> **#AD** [@theannaedit, Sally Hansen Miracle Gel nail polish Instagram advertising post, 15/11/16]
> **#ad** [@lilypebbles, Sally Hansen Color Therapy nail polish Instagram advertising post, 12/04/17]

#ad [@lilypebbles, Armani Beauty lip magnet Instagram advertising post, 22/11/16]

#ad [@lilypebbles, Rimmel London Lip Library lipstick Instagram advertising post, 31/10/16]

#ad [@lilypebbles, Olay 2-in-1 moisturising range Instagram advertising post, 23/09/15]

Stating **paid partnership with [brand]** is becoming increasingly common to emphasize the nature of the text; this is an in-built feature of business Instagram accounts to label posts as such. This label comes before the text proper, so the audience should know that this is an advertorial before engaging with the rest of the text. Some examples from my data include:

Paid partnership with bourjois_uk [@theannaedit, Bourjois Deliciously Nude lipstick collection Instagram advertising post, 21/02/18]
Paid partnership with kiehlsuk [@theannedit, Kiehls Powerful-Strength Line-Reducing Concentrate Instagram advertising post, 07/02/18]
Paid partnership with thewhitecompany [@lilypebbles, The White Company sleep-remedy collection Instagram advertising post, 13/09/18]
Paid partnership with elizabetharden [@lilypebbles, Elizabeth Arden Eight Hour Cream Instagram advertising post, 28/03/18]
Paid partnership with esteelauderuk [@lilypebbles, Bumble and Bumble and Aveda hair products Instagram advertising post, 05/09/17]

There are huge ongoing debates surrounding this imperative to now include disclosure language, and many Influencers are quick to reassure their followers that just because it is paid for does not mean this is *not* their honest opinion (*this is a sponsored post but all opinions are my own; I only work with brands I really trust and want to share with you;* and similar sentiments). Evans et al.'s (2017) study on Instagram influencer advertising found disclosure language in the form of 'paid aid' had a positive influence on brand recall; this response may partially relate to the transparency shown. Followers can be understandably irritated if adverts are not clearly marked as such, but too much labelled paid-for content may create negative reactions as the ratio of sponsored to unsponsored content can seem unbalanced. These debates tie into broader cultural and socio-economic discussions about the labour of social media Influencers. These Influencers are arguably engaging in a new form of work which is not always recognized as such (cf: Abidin 2016b). This work may involve photography skills, post-photography editing of images, and writing. Some of the writing involves the personalization of the brief they have been given.

10.6 Personalization of advertorials

10.6.1 Personalization of text

For many advertorials, Influencers have some degree of flexibility to renarrativize the advertorial in their own voice. The Influencer has to tell a story about the product in a format which will be understood by their audience. There may be specific aspects of the product that are highlighted in the brief, for example *soothes dry skin and tames flyaway hair,* but the Influencer will explain why this aspect is so useful to them. This renarrativizing tends to involve an emphasis on how these products fit into their daily lives and routines. Indeed, a key part of lifestyle Influencer content constitutes microcelebrities promoting their own lifestyles, including products, to their followers (Abidin 2018: 95; Evans et al. 2017: 139). Influencers also promote *themselves*, often using paid-for content as a way to increase their credibility and status as celebrities, and sometimes later in their careers they launch their own brands (Abidin 2018: 78). Their many followers are therefore also target consumers and may be (not always) more likely to buy something recommended by one of their favourite Influencers. This can be viewed as part of the Halo Effect Theory whereby followers may have a positive association with a brand because it is promoted by an Influencer they like and trust; in this way microcelebrities have the potential to build brand credibility (cf. Djafarova and Rushworth 2017). Although followers may express displeasure at sponsorship deals and the increased monetization of microcelebrities, Djafarova and Rushworth's (2017) study found that participants seemed to trust Influencers' reviews as genuine and, on the whole, believe that Influencers do not want to harm their reputation by lying to their audience in product reviews. In the examples below, textual elements of personalization have been highlighted:

> Can you believe that the @Caudalie Beauty Elixir is celebrating it's [*sic*] 20th anniversary? **I've loved this stuff for years** and **find it handy** to keep on my bedside table as a pre-sleep pillow spritz, or on my desk for a hydrating complexion top-up. **I still think** it's the best smelling beauty product out there. FACT! [@theannaedit, Caudalie Beauty Elixir (facial spray] Instagram advertising post, 04/09/17]

> September always feels like a new year **to me** and with a new year comes some **new personal goals. Mine?** Getting in an earlier bedtime and getting better at falling asleep quicker. It really is essential for **my wellbeing and productivity**. The sleep experts at @thewhitecompany have launched a sleep-remedy collection, with

six peace-inducing essential oils to help you drift off with ease and **it's totally transformed my wind-down routine. My favourites are** the diffuser for my bedside table and the calming bath soak. [@lilypebbles The White Company Sleep-remedy Collection Instagram advertising post, 13/10/18]

There are so many different ways to use the @elizabethardenuk Eight Hour Cream. **One of my faves** is to rub into my cuticles and knuckles, where my hands get the most dry throughout the day. **At night I** apply it extra thick so it works like an overnight hand mask. [@lilypebbles Elizabeth Arden Eight Hour Cream Instagram advertising post, 20/03/18]

The highlight of my current winter morning routine (aside from my cashmere socks!) is this face, body & hair oil. It's really hydrating & smells incredible ☺ You can now pick up your free deluxe sample from @ElizabethArdenUK counters [@lilypebbles Elizabeth Arden Eight Hour Oil Instagram advertising post, 03/02/16]

In these examples, Influencers highlight how much this product fits into their needs, their routine and indeed their life narrative, often through personal pronouns or possessive determiners (*I've loved this stuff for years; my favourites are [...]; the highlight of my current winter morning routine [...]*). The suggestion here (framed more explicitly on some occasions than others) is that the audience can benefit from these products too and trust these products to address their specific needs. In effect, Influencers weave these products into their life stories, suggesting that these products form part of their daily routines and daily lives.

10.6.2 Personalization of images

The images also do some of the personalization work as they show how Influencers incorporate these brands and products into their lives (cf. Abidin 2018). The availability and accessibility of social media technologies have a 'you could be here with me' style of photography, in which 'photographers include part of themselves in the image and invite the viewer to imagine themselves into the frame' (Zappavigna 2016: 272). Zappavigna (2016) and Zhao and Zappavigna (2015) outline a range of subjectification strategies which can be used on Instagram to create or maintain some kind of relationship between addresser and addressee. The photographer (in the case of my data, this tends to be the Influencer) can choose between an *as photographer* or *with photographer* viewing position. For the *as photographer* viewing position, the photographer can be represented clearly in the image, such as via what is known as a selfie [*as photographer – represent*]; represented to a more limited degree, such as a photo of their legs on the beach which seem to belong to the photographer [*as photographer – infer*]; or implicated through the composition of the photo; for example, if there is a baby in the pram in the image, we presume the photographer is the one who will be pushing it [*as photographer – imply*]. If there are no real clues indicating the subjective presence of the photographer, Zappavigna (2016) labels this *with photographer,* suggesting we might presume the Influencer took the photo through other clues such as the accompanying caption. Crucially, there are various degrees of subjectification afforded through these different kinds of photography, but

> [t]he close-to-real time pace at which images can be posted by the photographer and viewed by the ambient audience invokes the possibility that the ambient viewer 'could be there', that they are sharing in the experience at the time that it is happening.
>
> (Zappavigna 2016: 279)

All of the different subjectification strategies identified by Zappavigna (2016) were found in the data analysed in this chapter, but predominantly *as photographer – represent*, *as photographer – infer*, and *with photographer.* For the *as photographer – represent* category, examples include selfies of the Influencer, either presumably wearing/using the product and/or holding the product itself (e.g. @theannaedit Bourjois Deliciously Nude lipstick Instagram advertising post, 21/02/18; @lilypebbles Wella Ecaille hair care Instagram advertising post, 03/03/16; @lilypebbles Revlon make-up Instagram advertising post, 05/09/14). Selfies are a key component of most Influencers' social media accounts, used to foster a sense of community between themselves and their followers (Abidin 2016a: 3). Just as the retelling element of advertorials is not made visible, the work behind selfies is often overlooked. Abidin (2016a: 10) argues that the staging, taking and editing of selfies can be viewed as a form of 'tacit labor', which she describes as 'a collective practice of work that is understated and under-visibilized from being so thoroughly rehearsed that it appears as effortless and subconscious'.

For *as photographer – infer* examples, these photographs tended to be shot from the Influencers' point of view; notably, the Influencer looking down at her hand and/or product while painting her nails (e.g. @lilypebbles Sally Hansen Color Therapy nail polish Instagram advertising post, 12/04/17; @lilypebbles Essie nail polish Instagram advertising post, 04/04/16; @lilypebbles Max Factor Gel Shine nail polish Instagram advertising post, 28/07/14). These show the product in action, as used by the Influencer, in an attempt to appeal to their audience.

For the *with photographer* examples in this dataset, there was a proliferation of images which showed the product in a typically aesthetically pleasing environment (possibly that particular Influencer's home). For example, the body products may be carefully arranged on a bath caddy tray in a bath, with candles, magazines and a cosy bubble bath (@lilypebbles, The White Company Sleep-remedy Collection Instagram advertising post, 13/09/18); flat lays of the skincare product on a dressing table with other items such as notebooks, pens and a jewellery box (@lilypebbles Olay Hydration 2-in-1 skincare range Instagram advertising post, 23/09/15); product (skin serum) on a bathroom shelf with other objects such as a candle, earrings, a plant and cotton buds (@theannaedit Kiehl's Powerful-Strength Line-Reducing Concentrate Instagram advertising post, 07/02/18). The use of these subjectification techniques in Instagram photography functions to invite viewers into the (very much curated) world of the Influencer: to share in their daily lives and social activities. This sharing fosters a sense of social connection, feeding into the increasing place of social media in many people's lives (Zappavigna 2016: 289). This sense of connection may work to increase the likelihood of positive feelings towards both the Influencer and the associated brands they are promoting.

10.7 Concluding remarks

The analysis of Influencer advertising in this chapter has intended to demonstrate the personalization of advertorials through the multimodal affordances Instagram has to offer. Problem-Solution patterning (Hoey 1983; Ringrow 2016), previously identified in more traditional print advertising, was key here, along with disclosure language as an increasingly common element of social media advertising discourse (Evans et al. 2017). In this way, Influencers tell a story about how much they like and use this product. This story, however, is also a retelling of the brief that they have been given that they then personalize (both textually and visually) in their own voice (Abidin 2018). Further research on advertorials of a broader range of Instagram Influencers would indicate how prevalent these patterns are across this genre.

The personalization of products in order to demonstrate how they fit into Influencers' arguably aesthetically pleasing lifestyles reinforces the idea that the personal brand of the Influencer is paramount. In this way, Influencers often advertise one brand and, after a brand-mandated embargo period, take on another sponsorship deal with a competitor, provided that they can make their sponsorships fit into the overall narrative of their social media presence. Abidin (2018: 94) argues that this leads to a shift for Influencers 'from the traditional but transient attention economy to the contemporary but more longstanding affection economy'. The smaller, multiple brand deals Influencers can secure are also a way in which microcelebrities can differ from more traditional celebrities, who may have one or two very lucrative sponsorship deals over a long period (Abidin 2018: 94). How Instagram advertising works is often not very visible and attracts mixed media coverage, as Abidin (2018: 82) argues:

> [N]ews reports seem to be stuck in a backdated time loop as they continually express surprise at the fact that Influencers can command a sizeable earning and that brands want to work with them, while asserting that the workings of the Influencer industry is still mysterious and a secret weapon.

Whether in conjunction with their assistant and/or under the guidance of their management team, Influencers work to write the text, choose suitable hashtags, and take and edit appealing photographs. In other words, these retellings from the brief involve labour from the Influencers which might not be easily recognized as traditional work. In producing advertorials, Influencers must 'flexibly demonstrate gradients of self-conspicuousness in digital or physical spaces depending on intention or circumstance for favourable ends' (Abidin 2016b: 87). The rendered invisibility of these kinds of retellings supports Abidin's arguments about the lack of recognition of Influencer labour (2016b). This lack of recognition is even more cause for concern when we consider that the majority of social media beauty and lifestyle Influencers creating sponsored posts are women: a Klear report found that 83.9 per cent of 1.5 million #ad posts in 2017 were posted by women.[11] Instagram personalized advertorials can therefore be seen as a form of 'feminized digital media' (cf. Wilson and Yochim 2015: 233) which might be overlooked due to a devaluing of work produced by women online (and elsewhere). Future research into Instagram advertising should further consider these complex intersections between gender, capitalism and social media.

Notes

1 There are debates over what constitutes 'new' in so-called new media; see Neary and Ringrow (2018) for more on exploring these blurred boundaries between older and newer media texts.
2 The literature tends to capitalize *Influencer* (cf: Abidin (2018) and elsewhere); I have followed this practice here.

3   A 2018 report by Business Insider suggested that Influencer adverts doubled the engagement compared with adverts posted on Instagram by the brands themselves. See https://www.businessinsider.com/the-influencer-marketing-report-2018-1?r=US&IR=T for the full report.
4   Some Influencers, especially those at the beginning of their career or those with small followings, may receive the product in exchange for a review, but no monetary payment. Established, high-profile Influencers can earn substantial amounts; the UK Bloggers Survey 2019 surveyed 534 bloggers and found that 19 per cent charge an average of £250 per post, with 4 per cent charging £1000 or more (the full report is available here: https://www.vuelio.com/uk/resources/white-papers/bloggers-survey-2019/)
5   See https://www.asa.org.uk/resource/influencers-guide.html
6   Please see pages 9 and 10 in particular of the guide for more detail here: https://www.asa.org.uk/uploads/assets/uploaded/3af39c72-76e1-4a59-b2b47e81a034cd1d.pdf
7   Their Instagram accounts can be accessed here: https://www.instagram.com/theannaedit/ and https://www.instagram.com/lilypebbles/
8   It was hoped initially to be able to access and compare the briefing notes with the finished product, but all attempts to engage in dialogue with these Influencers were unfortunately unsuccessful. It is for this reason that I have also been unable to reproduce the Instagram content in this chapter.
9   On the Instagram website, you can see an example of a typical Instagram post layout: https://www.instagram.com/
10 The full guide is available here: https://www.asa.org.uk/resource/influencers-guide.html
11 The report can be found here: https://klear.com/TheStateofInfluencerMarketingKlear.pdf

References

Abidin, C. (2016a), '"Aren't These Just Young, Rich Women Doing Vain Things Online?": Influencer Selfies as Subversive Frivolity', *Social Media + Society*, 2 (2): 1–17.

Abidin, C. (2016b), 'Visibility Labour: Engaging with Influencers' Fashion Brands and #OOTD Advertorial Campaigns on Instagram', *Media International Australia*, 161(1), 86–100.

Abidin, C. (2018), *Internet Celebrity: Understanding Fame Online*, Bingley: Emerald Publishing.

Benwell, B., and Stokoe, E. (2006), *Discourse and Identity*, Edinburgh: Edinburgh University Press.

Carah, N., and Shaul, M. (2016), 'Brands and Instagram: Point, Tap, Swipe, Glance', *Mobile Media & Communication*, 14 (1): 69–84.

Coupland, J. (2007), 'Gendered Discourses on the 'Problem' of Ageing: Consumerized Solutions', *Discourse & Communication*, 1 (1): 37–61.

Djafarova, E., and Rushworth, C. (2017), 'Exploring the Credibility of Online Celebrities' Instagram Profiles in Influencing the Purchase Decisions of Young Female Users', *Computers in Human Behavior*, 68: 1–7.

Evans, N., Phua, J., Lim, J., and Jun, H. (2017), 'Disclosing Instagram Influencer Advertising: The Effects of Disclosure Language on Advertising Recognition, Attitudes, and Behavioral Intent', *Journal of Interactive Advertising*, 17 (2): 138–49.

Hoey, M. (1983), *On the Surface of Discourse*, London: Allen and Unwin.

Hoey, M. (2001), *Textual Interaction: An Introduction to Written Discourse Analysis*, London: Routledge.

Jerslev, A. (2016), 'In the Time of the Microcelebrity: Celebrification and the YouTuber Zoella', *International Journal of Communication*, 10: 5233–51.

Lazar, M. (2011), 'The Right to Be Beautiful: Postfeminist Identity and Consumer Beauty Advertising', in R. Gill and C. Scharff (eds), *New Femininities: Postfeminism, Neoliberalism and Subjectivity*, 37–51, London: Palgrave Macmillan.

Ledin, P., and Machin, D. (2018), *Doing Visual Analysis: From Theory to Practice*, London: Sage.

Machin, D. (2013), 'What Is Multimodal Critical Discourse Studies?', *Critical Discourse Studies*, 10 (4): 347–55.

Marwick, A. (2013), *Status Update: Celebrity, Publicity and Branding in the Social Media Age*, New Haven, CT: Yale University Press.

Marwick, A., and Boyd, D. (2011), 'I Tweet Honestly, I Tweet Passionately: Twitter Users, Context Collapse, and the Imagined Audience', *New Media and Society*, 13 (1): 114–33.

Neary, C., and Ringrow, H. (2018), 'Media, Power and Representation', in A. Hewings, P. Seargeant, and S. Pihlaja (eds), *The Routledge Handbook of English Language Studies*, 294–309, London: Routledge.

Ringrow, H. (2016), *The Language of Cosmetics Advertising*, London: Palgrave Macmillan.

Tanz, J. (2008), 'Internet Famous: Julia Allison and the Secrets of Self-Promotion', *Wired*. Available online: http://www.wired.com/2008/07/howto-allison/

Wilson, J., and Yochim, E. C. (2015), 'Pinning Happiness: Affect, Social Media, and the Work of Mothers', in E. Levine (ed.), *Cupcakes, Pinterest, and Ladyporn: Feminized Popular Culture in the Early Twenty-First Century*, 232–48, Illinois: University of Illinois Press.

Zappavigna, M. (2016), 'Social Media Photography: Constructing Subjectivity in Instagram Images', *Visual Communication*, 15 (3): 271–92.

Zhao, S. and Zappavigna, M. (2015), 'The Recontextualisation of Subjective Images in Three (Social) Media Platforms: A Methodological Exploration', *Paper Presented at MODE Conference – Multimodality: Methodological Explorations*, London: 15–16 January.

Part Three

Pedagogical applications of retellings

11

Intervening in text-worlds: Retelling, Text World Theory and pedagogy

Ian Cushing

11.1 Introduction

This chapter uses and applies the cognitive stylistic framework of Text World Theory (Gavins 2007; Werth 1999) as a *critical-creative* pedagogy to secondary school English teaching in England in order to facilitate narrative retelling. Text World Theory is a cognitive discourse grammar used to describe the way in which people build fictional worlds in their minds, prototypically used in the analysis of literary texts, but increasingly used as a pedagogy in schools (e.g. Cushing 2018a, 2019a; Giovanelli 2010, 2016, 2017). Critical-creative pedagogies – especially those grounded in stylistics – are characterized by a close attention to the 'mechanics' of the writing process (Scott 2016), with activities involving the narrative retelling(s) of texts by manipulating and experimenting with them in order to uncover how they work. Of particular interest to this chapter given its pedagogical power and popularity within stylistics, I draw on the notion of *textual intervention* (Pope 1995) as a critical-creative strategy for English teachers and young students. Very broadly, I argue that intervention allows and facilitates pupils to reimagine narratives through their own rewriting and retelling practices. This helps to draw their attention to the subtleties of their own and others' language choices and the various kinds of fictional worlds and reading experiences these can construct. The data of interest in this chapter then is students' retelling of narratives that arose out of their engagement with critical-creative intervention work, facilitated by their teachers who were drawing on their knowledge of a pedagogical Text World Theory. This chapter is perhaps slightly different from other work in this volume, given its more pedagogical and applied focus of narrative retelling, and the fact that data is generated from classrooms with young readers and writers.

Nevertheless, I suggest it offers an important extension of 'prototypical' work within narratology and stylistics and serves to make connections between universities and schools.

The theoretical and pedagogical frameworks introduced above are described in further detail in the sections that follow. Before this, in Section 11.2, I begin by critically examining current education policy in England, arguing that this presents students and teachers with few opportunities for creativity. I also consider some of the current debates around the place of grammar within creative pedagogies. Following this in Section 11.3, I describe the principles of a *text-world pedagogy*, designed to open up critical-creative opportunities in schools using Text World Theory as a foundation. In Sections 11.4 and 11.5, I discuss how this pedagogy was used in a research project where I worked closely with two English teachers and then recorded them with their respective classes. The data from these recordings forms the basis of this discussion, where I look at instances of students' critical-creative work in relation to the text-worlds of a contemporary poem.

11.2 Creativity, curriculum and language

Despite the fact that English teachers typically value creativity (McCallum 2012; Smith 2019), it has been marginalized within curriculum policy, fighting its corner while policymakers decide on how much of it should happen, what it should look like and how it should be assessed. In England – the setting for the research which this chapter draws on – English teachers are currently working with National Curriculum (NC) 2014, a body of policy mechanisms setting out the subject-specific contents of what should be taught in classrooms (e.g. DfE 2013). Schools in England are divided into 'key stages' (KS), stages of education defined by age and split into primary (KS1-KS2; ages 4–10) and secondary level (KS3-KS4; ages 11–16), which is the focus for this chapter. Since its initial inception in 1988, part of which was an attempt to regulate a 'climate of unchecked creativity' (Bullock 1975: 6), the NC has undergone various iterations in prescribing subject content, with an increasingly apparent focus on standardization and assessment at the expense of creativity. With greater standardization comes loss of autonomy – indeed, many criticisms of the NC and its ideologies have been directed towards the felt sense of deprofessionalization and the tightening of pedagogical choices which teachers are felt to have (e.g. Gibbons 2017). As a Conservative curriculum, NC 2014 places a narrow emphasis on analytical reading of literary texts, 'knowledge' of which is assessed in closed-book, high-stakes examinations. Writing *about* texts, not writing texts, is ascribed much more pedagogical value within policy, and so a consequence of this means that opportunities for imaginative response and creativity (in a broad sense, creative writing) are limited (see Mansworth 2016; McCallum 2016; Smith 2019 for a discussion in reference to the current curriculum and Sahlberg 2011 for a broader discussion). Indeed, the word 'creative' or any of its derivatives does not appear a single time on the current secondary English curriculum (DfE 2013), with students instead being instructed to 'apply knowledge' and 'write accurately'. This is not to say that creativity in English is outright prohibited from classrooms, but creativity has come to occupy a somewhat surreptitious place within contemporary English teachers' pedagogical repertoires and is increasingly 'vulnerable in a test-laden regime' (Smith 2019: 56). My focus in this chapter then is in how Text World Theory and cognitive stylistics can inform the teaching of writing as a genuinely critical-creative practice and as one way in which teachers might carve out spaces for creative work within an educational policy context which constrains it.

Whereas the role of language and grammar in a creative writing pedagogy has long been an area of debate and interest (see Myhill 2018), this work has typically overlooked stylistics and its potential (Cushing 2018b). Research on grammar and writing has tended to be polarized in whether or not teaching students about grammar has any positive impact on their writing quality, in terms of accuracy, expression and conforming to generic conventions. One variable in this debate has been that of 'context', in defining 'contextualized' or 'decontextualized' grammar pedagogies. Contextualized grammar pedagogies are characterized by grammatical work being situated 'within' the teaching of writing more broadly, where students might critically reflect on a piece of 'authentic' writing, consider the linguistic and generic conventions of this writing, and then apply some of these ideas in their own writing. Research in secondary schools has shown that contextualized grammar pedagogies do have a positive effect on creative writing (Myhill et al. 2012), as well as being the approach to grammar that English teachers generally 'believe in' and aspire towards (e.g. Cushing 2018b; Watson 2015). Decontextualized grammar pedagogies treat grammar as a separate entity, focusing on the teaching of structures in examples that are designed explicitly to demonstrate a particular grammatical point. In this chapter, I advocate for a contextualized grammar pedagogy, building on previous work by incorporating aspects of Text World Theory and cognitive stylistics. This – the *text-world pedagogy* – is described in full in the following section.

11.3 Text World Theory and pedagogy

In this section, I first describe the principles of Text World Theory and then the text-world pedagogy which underpinned the teaching materials used in the research. It was a *critical* pedagogy (e.g. Pennycook 2001: 130–3) in that it sought to challenge some of the problematic discourses and issues within L1 English education policy as discussed in the preceding sections, such as a lack of creative opportunities and decontextualized grammar pedagogies.

Text World Theory (Gavins 2007; Werth 1999) is a cognitive discourse grammar which accounts for and describes the way in which discourse participants construct rich, mental representations of language, known as *text-worlds* (see Gavins 2007: 35–52). The construction of text-worlds is derived from two inputs. The first, the *discourse-world* consists of the kind of contextual and experiential knowledge that a participant has (Gavins 2007: 18–34). The second consists of the grammatical content of the text itself, split into *world-builders* (deictic and referential elements which populate a text-world, typically realized as noun phrases, adjective phrases and preposition phrases; see Gavins 2007: 36–8) and *function-advancers* (constructions which result in the dynamic movement of a text-world, typically realized as verb phrases; see Gavins 2007: 56–9). Because participants have unique stores of discourse-world knowledge, text-worlds are idiosyncratic yet likely to include some mutually shared aspects, given homogeneities in cultural reference points and shared experiences. As discourse unfolds, text-worlds can undergo changes in their deictic parameters, triggered by various constructions such as changes in narrative viewpoint, modality, negation and shifts in time and location. These result in new text-worlds, defined as *world-switches* or *modal-worlds* (see Gavins 2007: 45–50).

Typically used for cognitive stylistic investigations of literary discourse, Text World Theory has increasingly been recalibrated as a pedagogical tool for young readers in schools (Cushing 2018a, 2019a; Giovanelli 2016, 2017). In this work, teachers have used the model as a 'tool for thinking with' (Giovanelli 2016: 123), using text-world metalanguage to explore how readers build and experience fictional worlds in their minds and as a pedagogy to facilitate cognitive stylistics in the classroom. As with all work within cognitive stylistics, the objective is to understand how readers' responses can be accounted for in terms of textual structure. The following sections build on this 'applied' Text World Theory in defining the principles for a text-world pedagogy and how this relates to instances of critical-creative work (see Cushing 2019a: 73–9 for a full discussion).

11.3.1 Space

Classrooms are complex social spaces with multiple readers, writers and minds. Text World Theory frames individual and mutual knowledge as part of the discourse-world, with participants' own discourse-world knowledge positioned as a filter for the interpretations and creations of texts. This is crucial in the text-world pedagogy then, in that it foregrounds all of the discourse-world conditions that arise out of reading in the classroom, including participants' background knowledge, memories and identities, as well as physical aspects of the environment itself. The pedagogical intention of this is to 'anchor' students' literary experiences in reference to their own identities as readers and writers, in an effort to legitimize students' responses as valid or 'authentic', in environments where they can often be downplayed or heavily refereed by more 'authoritative' discourse participants such as teachers (Giovanelli and Mason 2015).

11.3.2 Creativity

Creativity was central to the text-world pedagogy. Firstly, as alluded to in the previous section, readings are seen as 'creative' in that they require readers to draw on individual discourse-world knowledge in order to build text-worlds, inferentially filling in gaps with their own memories and experiences. As Rosenblatt states:

> The reader, too, is creative. The text [...] will not be the result of passivity on the reader's part; the literary experience must be phrased as a *transaction* between the reader and the text.
>
> (Rosenblatt 1976: 34–5, original emphasis)

The text-world pedagogy encourages students to reflect on their responses to literary texts, accounting for their own reported text-world constructions in terms of their own discourse-world knowledge. In perhaps more prototypically 'creative' terms, the text-world pedagogy also asked students to respond to texts by creating new texts, engaging in *textual intervention* (Pope 1995), a critical-creative strategy for engaging with and interrogating how language works. At the heart of interventionist strategies is the notion of 'recentring' (ibid. 1995: 4), whereby readers take a 'base text' and, through various linguistic means and modes, retell it in some way. These interventions have infinite possibilities: for instance, they might be at clause or discourse level, adopt new vantage points and voices, change genres and audiences, and so on. The pedagogical purpose is to lead readers to uncover linguistic meaning through their own writing choices. In discussing a text-world approach to writing, Scott argues that

> the writer can gain sophisticated and nuanced appreciation of the ways in which language can be used to create and manipulate worlds that exist at different cognitive, discoursal and rhetorical 'levels' and in different relationships to one another.
>
> (Scott 2016: 128)

While previous work has been useful in theorizing the place of textual intervention within text-world pedagogies (e.g. Giovanelli 2010; Scott 2016), these have remained theoretical, and so this chapter seeks to build on this by exploring empirical work from the classroom.

11.3.3 Text

The text-world pedagogy maintains that readings must be accountable to the text itself and so draws significantly on the principles of stylistics in the way that it theorizes the teaching of grammar. The purpose of teaching grammar here is to heighten students' sensitivities to the conceptual effects created by a range of linguistic patterns, rather than the decontextualized grammar pedagogies as discussed in Section 11.2. Grammar is conceived of as a descriptive series of patterns and choices, which students use in helping to rationalize their readings and writings. This view of grammar is in contrast with some of the more prototypical views that English teachers hold, tending (a) to be negative and (b) not to be explicitly linked to any theoretical grammatical framework (Watson 2015: 10). While many English teachers tend to construe grammar as a system of 'rules' and 'regulations' (Cushing 2019b), the text-world pedagogy sought to challenge this by framing grammar as a 'resource' or a 'construction material', highlighting the creativity and meaning potential of grammar.

11.3.4 Metalanguage

Metalinguistic concepts were used in the text-world pedagogy as a facilitative set of terms used to provide students and teachers with ways of describing the conceptual experiences that took place during reading and writing. Many of these terms are metaphorical, serving a 'pedagogic function' (Boyd 1993: 485), in that they help to explain theories or concepts. For instance, the TEXT AS WORLD metaphor underpinning Text World Theory is key to explaining how language has the capacity to trigger fictional worlds in the minds of readers.

Other metalinguistic terms such as 'world-builders' and 'world-switches' provide a metaphorical way of describing the cognitive processes at work when readers and writers engage in discourse.

11.4 Methods, participants and data

In order to investigate the efficacy and affordances of the text-world pedagogy and its approach to creativity in practical terms, I worked closely with two secondary English teachers (Rosie and Daisy, both pseudonyms) and their Year 8 (age 12–13) classes in one London school (Green Tree School, a pseudonym). Text World Theory was a new concept to Rosie and Daisy, who both held degrees in English literature and identified as 'literature specialists'. Over a fieldwork period of eighteen-months during regular visits to the school, I worked with them in exploring key aspects of the theory and co-designing the pedagogical principles as outlined above. They also experimented in their own pedagogies, working with the framework and becoming familiar with the approach and building their own confidence in it. During this time, we collaborated on the design of a fifteen-lesson, six-week intervention which actualized the text-world pedagogy in relation to the teaching of poetry. Rosie and Daisy delivered these lessons with their classes, and I filmed and then transcribed them for post-hoc analysis.

I was keen to not present the research to participants as a prototypical top-down 'intervention', where I was seen as a researcher who arrives into schools to try and assess a theoretical concept with little concern for the participants themselves and a lack of sensitivity for the sociopolitical aspects of the research context. Instead, I sought to undertake research where participants are a genuine part of the research process, drawing on design-based research (DBR) (Barab 2014) to help formulate the research plan, principles and pedagogical materials. DBR is a pragmatic approach to education research, where researchers and participants collaborate to address a particular issue, problem or question through the iterative design and development of intervention materials or strategies. The goal is then to study how these interventions work in practice and reflect on their effectiveness.

All transcriptions of the classroom recordings were analysed thematically using an inductive coding approach using NVivo. The purpose of coding was to provide a way of organizing the data for post-hoc analysis. Although I allowed the data to drive the coding labels, I made use of cognitive stylistic concepts to inform my code labels (e.g. 'discourse-world memories') and so the coding decisions were in part driven by linguistic theory. In the discussion that follows, I draw on discourse tagged under codes that are most relevant for this chapter, these being 'discourse about world-building', 'discourse about world-switching' and 'discourse reporting about writing choices'.

11.5 Intervening in text-worlds

This section explores some of the critical-creative responses to literary text-worlds, whereby students responded to a text in two ways: firstly, in critical terms by exploring its world-building structure, and secondly, in creative terms by producing a new text, employing some of the world-building strategies they had thought particularly important in the base text. Daisy and Rosie were especially keen to include critical-creative opportunities in the pedagogy because it resonated with their own professional identities and cultural knowledge of what they thought constituted meaningful English teaching, especially given the limited space for creativity within current curriculum policy as discussed in Section 11.2. Various lessons in the text-world pedagogy included opportunities for critical-creative opportunities, and creative responses took shape in various forms: poems, drawings and movement pieces.

11.5.1 Critical

Across two lessons and independent work outside of school, students explored the text-worlds of *Spinning* by Kevin Griffith (Griffith 2006). This is printed in full here (with line numbers added) and is followed by my own brief text-world analysis, before presenting some of the students' responses.

Spinning

1   I hold my two-year-old son
2   under his arms and start to twirl.
3   His feet sway away from me
4   and the day becomes a blur.
5   Everything I own is flying into space:
6   yard toys, sandbox, tools,
7   garage and house,
8   and, finally, the years of my life.

9   When we stop, my son is a grown man,
10 and I am very old. We stagger
11 back into each other's arms
12 one last time, two lost friends
13 heavy with drink,
14 remembering the good old days.

Spinning is told from an adult's perspective, who recalls memories of time spent with their son. There was fairly unanimous agreement among myself, teachers and students that themes of the poem included time, memories, nostalgia and parent-child relationships. The establishing text-world (TW1) features two enactors ('I', 'two-year old son') in an unspecified time, but with a present tense time signature, marked through simple present tense verbs such as 'hold' and 'sway'. In Cushing (2019a: 159–63) I showed how students suggested that the clause 'flying into space' triggers a *world-transition*, a kind of gradient world-switch where the contents of one text-world is perceived to gradually blur into another. As TW1 gets backgrounded and ever more remote, the contents of TW2 become fully realized in line 9 at the clause 'when we stop'. TW2 features older versions of the enactors from TW1, realized through function-advancers such as '[we] stagger back' and world-builders such as 'very old'. The poem ends with a world-switch back to 'the good old days' of TW1.

Students discussed the significance of each text-world and the way that the various world-switches and transitions prompted them as readers to move between conceptual spaces, highlighting the structural significance of the poem as a way of showing how relationships and people change over time. The final world-switch was deemed to be particularly important in contributing to the overall themes such as age and memories. In these discussions, they critically engaged with the language of the poem, retelling the events of the original narrative by adding their own thoughts and ideas. For example:

Daisy: ok so I want to hear some suggestions from some of your interesting feedback (.) so let's start at the beginning (.) what are some of the things that are foregrounded in your text-world for you and building that world? Ruksana?

Ruksana: when it says the day becomes a blur because it's always like time is passing (.) time can only go one way and it's getting really blurry (.) I think that is a really important moment

Daisy: right so it doesn't give you the chance to sort of focus on the finer detail (.) lovely (.) Sara what about you?

Sara: yeah I had something similar to Ruksana's text-world (.) I looked at the day becomes a blur as well and it's almost like they're in a giant yard filled with loads of things from the house like the nouns that are world-builders like the toys and the tools and things and he's spinning around and the day becomes a blur and the son suddenly grows older and he's still there with all of those things

Louisa: in my text-world it's filled with things from my own house and like bits from my garden

Initial, critical and exploratory discussions such as these were an important part of the pedagogy, serving to legitimize student responses as 'authentic' (Giovanelli and Mason 2015) and create a space where readings were valid and accountable to the text. In each turn, students foreground parts of the text that they deem to be particularly important – such as Ruksana's idea that line 4 is a 'really important moment' and the various world-builders that Sara offers as being significant. Louisa's turn is especially interesting in how she explicitly reports drawing on her own discourse-world knowledge in order to construct a text-world and then use this to retell this part of the text to the class. She situates the text within her own memories and life, responding to it on her own terms and in a creative way.

11.5.2 Creative

The kinds of discussions in the preceding section set the groundwork for the more prototypical creative work which followed. Rosie and Daisy set a task where students were asked to write a poem which featured a temporal/spatial world-switch, realized by any kind of linguistic trigger they deemed appropriate and used in order to show the significance of a change in time or place or to foreground the recalling of a memory. Instructions were kept broad so that students felt a sense of agency and choice in what they could write about, echoing the GRAMMAR AS RESOURCE metaphor introduced in Section 11.3. After being given lesson and independent time to complete the writing task, students shared their retelling along with a brief textual commentary on their choices and aims. The commentary was important in that it asked students to rationalize their decisions and provide a critically reflective outlook on their creative work.

There are many retelling I could choose to show and discuss here, but given space limitations, I will focus on just one: a poem from Charlotte, a student in Daisy's class. Charlotte's poem is illustrative of the kind of high-quality, thoughtful writing which students produced in this task and is a good example of how students were drawing on their knowledge of world-switches in order to retell the base text. Her untitled poem recalls a childhood memory of preparing and performing a show for her family in the living room and is printed in full here.

1   We walk downstairs, ready for the living room show.
2   We spent all of ten minutes on it.
3   That is a lot when you are six.
4   Everything goes wrong, but we don't care.
5   Seven eight nine ten eleven twelve –

6   We sit downstairs on our phones in the living room.
7   We spend hours on them, communicating,
8   but not with each other.
9   Every so often mine flicks back
10 to who we were
11 and the living room shows.

In her critical stylistic commentary, Charlotte said that she wanted to 'use a world-switch to travel back and forward in time and show the importance of memories'. There are numerous textual traces in the poem which support this sense of authorial intention, some of which I will discuss here.

Firstly, Charlotte's poem shows a sensitive understanding of the complexities of world-switches and how they can be used by writers to introduce time shifts, used here to show how a (possibly personal) memory contrasts with a current family state. As in the base text, the location of the family environment is clearly important, and she allows her discourse-world knowledge of this to drive her world-building decisions, drawing on personal memories and experiential knowledge of FAMILY and HOME schemas and the typical kinds of activities associated with these environments, such as family shows, communal living room spaces and the presence of mobile phones. Given her own discourse-world identity, she chooses to write from the narrative perspective of a child, rather than an adult as found in the base text. The domestic environment is established in an initial text-world (TW1) populated by at least two enactors, whom in line 3 we discover to be six years old. World-builders such as 'living room' and 'downstairs' activate schematic knowledge related to FAMILY and HOME, situating the poem within a domestic environment and cueing up various inferences related to this, which are likely to be different across different readers. Given this setting, we presume that other enactors, introduced into the poem in stanza two but also referred to using the same pronoun 'we', include family members such as parents and siblings. Charlotte never tells us this directly, instead relying on her readers' schematic information of FAMILY and HOME and knowing that readers work creatively to fill in gaps in building their own text-worlds. The reliance on first-person pronouns as opposed to proper names is an astute crafting of language which maintains the foregrounding of people and allows the reader to populate their own text-world with their own family members. Returning briefly to the original text, the same referencing technique is found (e.g. 'I' and 'we'), although there are more uses of nominals relating to specific enactors (e.g. 'two-year-old son' and 'grown man').

Given the significance of world-switches in *Spinning* and following the teacher's instructions, Charlotte uses the same technique to her advantage in her own poem. From the initial time and space parameters of TW1, the list of numerals in line 5 ('seven eight nine ten eleven twelve') triggers a succession of brief, fleeting new text-worlds. In each of these, our attention is drawn to each one very quickly, but given their textual brevity, they are not maintained in our attention and so fade almost immediately. In my own reading of the poem, the unfolding of this world structure happens like a flip book, flicking through pages which appear and disappear with a fleeting glance. This rapid moving across world-edges or 'edgework' (see Segal 1995) is what helps to give the writing its 'texture' (Stockwell 2009), akin to the feeling of 'riding a bicycle over cracked and fractured rocks' (ibid. 2009: 90). The rapid world-switches propel the narrative forward in time at great speed, movement which ends at the beginning of stanza two, and where the reader is projected into a text-world with a different temporal coordinate – one where the narrator is twelve years old, on the cusp of being a teenager and adolescence. There is literary significance in this choice – the speed that this world-switch happens indexes the perceived speed at which growing up happens. Indeed, of this, Charlotte suggested that she 'wanted the text-worlds to shift quickly to show how quickly time moves', in an echo of the earlier student responses to the world-switches in *Spinning* and nature of the felt *transitions* between two or more different text-worlds. This text-world is sustained for much longer, fleshed out with deictic world-building detail ('we', 'downstairs', 'living room', 'phones'), indicating how family life has changed, with the enactors choosing to 'spend hours' on their phones, rather than the more prototypical childlike activities of designing and performing a family show, as was the case in TW1. A brief negated text-world ('but not with each other') emphasizes how things have changed, by first bringing into focus the contents of the text-world, before negating them (Gavins 2007: 102). The poem ends with a similar kind of world-switch as in the base text – a recalling of a memory ('mine flicks back to who we were'), conjuring up the days when the narrator was six, and a return to the establishing world of TW1.

In Figure 11.1, I have diagrammed the world structure of Charlotte's poem, revealing the clever and intricate use of world-switches she used in order to represent ideas of time, growing up and memories. In a deviation from prototypical text-world diagramming conventions, I have placed the rapid text-worlds of the numerals from line 5 so that they are in 'contact' with each other in order to represent their conceptual proximity and temporal brevity.

In this analysis, I have highlighted two things. Firstly, I have shown how one student used the concept of world-switches in her own writing, employing this successfully to create a moving and personal poem which is motivated by discourse-world knowledge and the framing of language as a 'repertoire of possibilities' (Myhill et al. 2012: 148) for constructing meaning. This happened after an initial class discussion and critical engagement with the poem, whereby students came to understand the potentiality of world-switches as an important stylistic device for exhibiting structural changes within literary worlds, before intervening in the text-worlds of a base text in order to construct a new text. Charlotte's creative response was a product of this discussion and her own sense as a writer, where I would argue that she was 'thinking as a stylistician' in the conscious choosing and deploying of different textual features. She was not simply filling her writing with as many world-switches as possible in order to complete

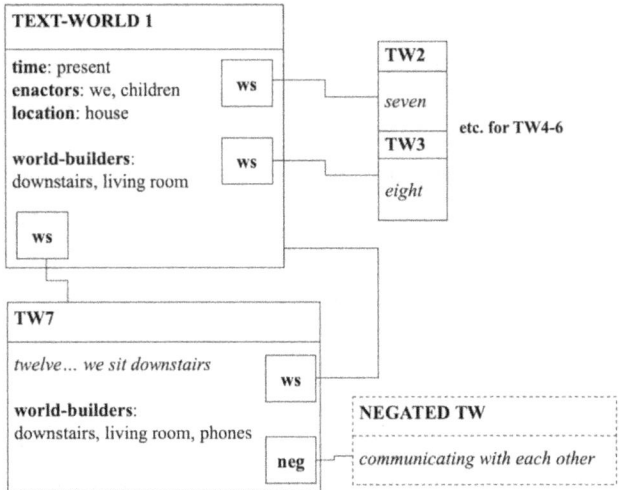

Figure 11.1 World-switches in Charlotte's poem

the assigned task but selecting them carefully in order to shape and mould meaning. This WRITING AS PLASTICINE metaphor was something explicitly used in classroom discourse during the lessons, presenting language as a malleable material for students to experiment with. Such views of writing are in stark contrast to formulaic and additive approaches, which are common pedagogies in schools whereby students are asked to simply 'insert grammatical feature X' into their writing without consideration of meaning, often to demonstrate competence in using this feature for assessment, rather than stylistic purposes (see McCallum 2016 and Myhill 2005: 83–4 for a criticism). Charlotte's 'retelling' of *Spinning* then is one grounded in her own discourse-world knowledge as a reader and a writer, employing some of the cognitive stylistic strategies present in the base text in order to reimagine a new narrative. Put simply, her writing is the result of talking about her own reading experiences.

11.6 Conclusions and implications

This chapter has explored instances of critical-creative practices within a text-world pedagogy. Set against a contextual background where opportunities for creativity within English education are often marginalized and limited, I have argued for a pedagogy informed by cognitive stylistics which serves to present creativity as a valid and legitimate activity.

I began by critiquing current conceptualizations of creativity within education policy in England, showing how these are often looked down on in favour of more 'traditional' ways of responding to literature – that is teacher-centred and assessment-driven. Within such an agenda, teachers can resist incorporating creative practices into their teaching, yet a critical-creative cognitive stylistic approach offers a balance between the two: *critical* responses to texts that are grounded in precise linguistic description and the consideration of conceptual reading experiences; and *creative* responses that exercise students' metalinguistic knowledge in meaningful ways. The concepts of textual intervention and retelling lie at the heart of this. Charlotte's poem was one example of how this happened in a real-life classroom situation and how teachers took their own knowledge of cognitive stylistics and used it in order to heighten students' sensitivities to textual structures and reading experiences.

While the data discussed here has been limited in scope, it is illustrative of many other instances of critical-creative work in the text-world pedagogy and the research project as a whole. Although this chapter has focused on creative *writing*, other creative opportunities in the text-world pedagogy were not limited to this, with students responding to and retelling literary texts in various different modes, including images (see Cushing 2018a; Giovanelli 2017) and movement. I argue that any broader limitations are a result of structural issues in curriculum policy and teacher training rather than the text-world pedagogy itself. Firstly, the teachers involved in this study were part of a collaborative and long-term research project, sensitive to their own professional identities and autonomies. They were trained in Text World Theory by an academic linguist, a crucial aspect in recalibrating/resituating a theoretical grammar into a pedagogical grammar, especially given that many English teachers have limited knowledge of linguistics and stylistics (see for example Watson 2015). I have argued elsewhere that teachers must have access to training if they are to develop their subject knowledge in these areas (see for example Cushing 2018b). It is my firm belief that this barrier is easily overcome if teachers are provided access to training by well-qualified experts in language who have a contextually sensitive understanding of school teaching and the current challenges faced by English teachers. This is a systemic, policy-level issue and an increasing concern amidst government cuts to school funding which has a serious impact on training opportunities.

While this chapter has argued for the place of cognitive stylistics in schools as a critical-creative pedagogy, there remains much work to be done if this is to be achieved in any large-scale form. Scholars working at the intersection of education, applied linguistics and stylistics are in a good position to engage with this challenge, given the increasing interest of stylistics in schools and cognitive stylistics. Given the value that critical-creative pedagogies can have in relation to reading, writing and grammar, it is my hope that policymakers will come to recognize this, broadening their own conceptualizations of what constitutes 'English teaching' and reassessing the place of creativity within curriculum policy and discourse. It is my firm belief that cognitive stylistics – striking a sensible balance between writer, reader, text and the mind – is an approach to English teaching which is only just beginning to show its enormous and powerful potential.

Acknowledgements

Thank you to the teachers and students at Green Tree School and to Kevin Griffith for granting permission to reproduce *Spinning* in this chapter.

References

Barab, S. (2014), 'Design-Based Research: A Methodological Toolkit for Engineering Change', in K. Sawyer (ed.), *Handbook of the Learning Sciences, Vol 2*, 233–70, Cambridge: Cambridge University Press.

Boyd, R. (1993), 'Metaphor and Theory Change: What Is 'Metaphor' For?', in A. Ortony (ed.), *Metaphor and Thought*, 481–531, Cambridge: Cambridge University Press.

Bullock, A. (1975), *A Language for Life*, London: HMSO.

Cushing, I. (2018a), '"Suddenly, I am Part of the Poem": Texts as Worlds, Reader-Response and Grammar in Teaching Poetry', *English in Education*, 52 (1): 7–19.

Cushing, I. (2018b), 'Stylistics Goes to School', *Language and Literature*, 27 (4): 271–85.

Cushing, I. (2019a), Text World Theory and the Secondary English Classroom. Unpublished PhD thesis. Aston University.

Cushing, I. (2019b), 'Resources not Rulebooks: Metaphors for Grammar in Teachers' Metalinguistic Discourse', *Metaphor and the Social World*, 9 (1): 33–54.

DfE. (2013), *English Programmes of Study: Key Stage 3*, London: DfE.

Gavins, J. (2007), *Text World Theory: An Introduction*, Edinburgh: Edinburgh University Press.

Gibbons, S. (2017), *English and Its Teachers: A History of Pedagogy, Policy and Practice*, London: Routledge.

Giovanelli, M. (2010), 'Pedagogical Stylistics: A Text World Theory Approach to the Teaching of Poetry', *English in Education*, 44 (3): 214–31.

Giovanelli, M. (2016), 'Text World Theory as Cognitive Grammatics: A Pedagogical Application in the Secondary Classroom', in J. Gavins and E. Lahey (eds), *World Building: Discourse in the Mind*, 109–26, London: Bloomsbury.

Giovanelli, M. (2017), 'Readers Building Fictional Worlds: Visual Representations, Poetry, and Cognition', *Literacy*, 51 (1): 26–35.

Giovanelli, M., and Mason, J. (2015), '"Well I Don't Feel That": Schemas, Worlds and Authentic Reading in the Classroom', *English in Education*, 49 (1): 41–55.

Griffith, K. (2006), 'Spinning', *Mid-American Review*, 26 (2): 17.

Mansworth, M. (2016), 'Creative Potential within Policy: An Analysis of the 2013 English Literature Curriculum', *English in Education*, 50 (2): 116–29.

McCallum, A. (2012), *Creativity and Learning in Secondary English: Teaching for a Creative Classroom*, London: Routledge.

McCallum, A. (2016), 'Dangerous and Uncontrollable: The Politics of Creativity in Secondary English', *English in Education*, 50 (1): 72–84.

Myhill, D. (2005), 'Ways of Knowing: Writing with Grammar in Mind', *English Teaching: Practice and Critique*, 4 (3): 77–96.

Myhill, D. (2018), 'Grammar as a Meaning-Making Resource for Improving Writing', *L1 Educational Studies in Language and Literature*, 18: 1–21.

Myhill, D., Jones, S., Lines, H., and Watson, A. (2012), 'Re-Thinking Grammar: The Impact of Embedded Grammar Teaching on Students' Writing and Students' Metalinguistic Understanding', *Research Papers in Education*, 27 (2): 139–66.

Pennycook, A. (2001), *Critical Applied Linguistics: A Critical Introduction*, London: Routledge.

Pope, R. (1995), *Textual Intervention: Creative and Critical Strategies for Literary Studies*, Oxon: Routledge.

Rosenblatt, L. (1976), *Literature as Exploration*, New York: Noble and Noble.

Sahlberg, P. (2011), 'The Role of Education in Promoting Creativity: Potential Barriers and Enabling Factors', in R. Schenkel and O. Quintin (eds), *Measuring Creativity*, 337–44, Brussels: The European Commission.

Scott, J. (2016), 'Worlds from Words: Theories of World-Building as a Creative Writing Toolbox', in J. Gavins and E. Lahey (eds), *World Building: Discourse in the Mind*, 127–45, London: Bloomsbury.

Segal, E. (1995), 'Narrative Comprehension and the Role of Deictic Shift Theory', in J. Duchan, G. Bruder and E. Hewitt (eds), *Deixis in Narrative: A Cognitive Science Perspective*, 3–17, Hillsdale: Lawrence Erlbaum.

Smith, L. (2019), '"We're Not Building Worker Bees": What Has Happened to Creative Practice in England since the Dartmouth Conference of 1966?', *Changing English*, 26 (1): 48–62.

Stockwell, P. (2009), *Texture: A Cognitive Aesthetics of Reading*, Edinburgh: Edinburgh University Press.

Watson, A. (2015), 'Conceptualisations of "Grammar Teaching": L1 English Teachers' Beliefs about Teaching Grammar for Writing', *Language Awareness*, 24 (1): 1–14.

Werth, P. (1999), *Text Worlds: Representing Conceptual Space in Discourse*. London: Longman.

12

Retelling stories across languages and cultures: Literary imagination and symbolic competence

Chantelle Warner

12.1 Introduction

Retellings have long been used as both a research method and a form of pedagogical intervention within the fields of literacy and second language acquisition in order to better understand and facilitate the comprehension processes of readers (e.g. Goodman 1982). Within interculturally-orientated applied linguistics, literary retellings have also been used in order to consider the emerging positions and identities of individuals who are learning to navigate new symbolic and cultural landscapes in a second or additional language (e.g. Kramsch and Nolden 1994; Kramsch 1996). The present study builds off of this earlier research and also draws from work in contemporary stylistics and poetics in order to consider how readers who are positioned as 'foreign language learners' borrow from others' stories in the construction of their own. This study will focus on the literary compositions of two individuals, who were enrolled in an advanced German language and culture course in the United States at the time that they wrote. Within this course, students had read a series of autobiographical openings, which served as models for a creative writing task asking them to write the first page of their autobiography. The literary texts written by these students are of particular interest because of the ways in which they borrow from the hypotexts (Genette 1997) and what that reveals about the potential role of stylistics and literary imagination in the development of an intercultural stance—understood here as a sense of self and other, which includes willingness to move beyond assumptions of similarity and explore possibilities of difference (Ware and Kramsch 2005: 203).

12.2 The role of retellings and language/culture learning

As evidenced by the range of contributions to this volume, 'retellings' encompasses a wide range of narrative activities including not only recounting but reimagining, reconfiguring and restorying. Within literacy studies and applied linguistics, approaches to retelling are shaped by the perceived educational and scholarly purposes at hand and these preferences are tethered tightly to understandings of language and culture learning. For example, research and teaching geared towards reading comprehension has tended to rely on personalized oral retellings, which can provide researchers and teachers alike access to '[w]hat happens during the act of reading itself and what occurs at the end of the reading that has impact on a reader's comprehension' (Goodman 1982: 301). However, as paradigms have shifted away from comprehension as core standard for literacy (see Warner and Dupuy 2018), there has been a trend within educational fields over the past few decades towards being both more explicit and more expansive about the range of semiotic resources involved in language and literacy development and accordingly those instantiated in acts of reading and retelling.

Educational scholars Cope and Kalantzis, whose work has been highly influential in shaping contemporary discussions of literacy and learning, have suggested that relying on retellings as a means of assessing reading leaves the connection between reading and other aspects of language use under-examined and, as a result, encourages students to produce a limited range of genres (1993: 6). This parallels an argument made by Kern in his book *Literacy and Language Teaching* (2000). Drawing upon a distinction made by Widdowson (1978) between language *usage* and *use*, Kern suggests that much of language teaching since the 1980s has emphasized the former (usage), that is the interpretation and production of accurate forms, whereas what he described as a literacy-oriented pedagogy would also embrace language use, language as communicative effect and purpose. Building upon multiliteracies frameworks proposed by education scholars such as Cope and Kalantzis (e.g. 2009) and the other members of the New London Group (1996), Kern and others (e.g. Blyth 2018; Byrnes and Kord 2002; Maxim 2006; Paesani, Allen, and Dupuy 2016; Warner and Michelson 2018) have advocated for approaches to second language teaching that emphasize meaning design, that is the ways in which individuals draw from repertoires of linguistic and other semiotic resources in order to make sense of, navigate and communicate the social worlds they inhabit. Many of these scholars adopt and in some cases adapt the model first proposed by the New London Group (1996), which envisions meaning-making as a cycle of *available designs*, the existing resources for making meaning afforded to speakers and composers, *designing*, the active process of appropriating and re-voicing available designs, and *redesigning*, the transformation of the world and self through the creation of new meanings. Accordingly, pedagogical research related to multiliteracies had tended to incorporate a greater awareness of genres and how our understanding of text and context shape retellings (e.g. Allen and Goodspeed 2018; Maxim 2009; Ryshina-Pankova 2011). A booming body of work focusing on digital literacies and education has also brought awareness to the potential of remixing and remediating practices as modes of retelling and responding to stories, for example in the form of fan fiction or multimodal compositions (see Knobel 2017), thereby expanding the range of semiotic resources considered in literacy studies.

Another interconnecting strand of research related to literacy and language learning deliberately reframes questions of reading and retelling within an intercultural perspective. For example, studies from Kramsch and Nolden (1994), Kramsch (1996) and more recently Kearney (2012) and Vinall (2012, 2016) have considered students' recounts of stories read in a second language as more importantly a form of cultural mediation, during which learners make use of the stylistic and narrative resources offered by the texts to negotiate their relationship to the narrative and narrated. These studies suggest that engaging in literary retellings in the language and culture classroom can contribute to the development of intercultural stance, 'a decentered perspective that goes beyond comprehending the surface meaning of words to discovering the logic of their interlocutors' utterances' (Ware and Kramsch 2005: 203). An intercultural stance provides a foundation for what is widely described as *intercultural competence*, the ability 'to communicate and interact across cultural boundaries' (Byram 1997: 7), and moreover for the development of *symbolic competence*, a more dynamic, locally contingent capacity to position oneself in symbolic systems and potentially reframe the context of interaction at hand (Kramsch 2006, 2011). As a potential desideratum of language and culture education, symbolic competence connects to Cope and Kalantzis's claim that literacy development is transformative, in that 'the process of designing redesigns the designer' (2009: 184). Kramsch argues that symbolic competence is 'nourished by a literary imagination' because 'it is through literature that learners can communicate not only with living others, but also with imagined others and with the other selves they might want to become' (2006: 251). She adds, 'Through literature, they can learn the full meaning making potential of language.'

In the section that follows, I draw from work in cognitive poetics in order to offer a model of the 'literary imagination' that is compatible with the frameworks for literacy development in a second language and culture, which have already been described. I will then turn to the literary hypotexts (the original texts that serve as inspirations) and the students' reimaginations of the 'meaning making potential' offered through those texts to show how the students 'construct personal meanings at the boundaries between the native speaker's meanings and their own everyday lives' (Kramsch 1993: 238).

12.3 Literary imagination and symbolic competence

The task of defining the 'literary imagination' could send a researcher tracing various disciplinary genealogies, some stretching far back into intellectual history. For the purpose of this article, I will limit my attention to one possible way of approaching the literary grounded in stylistics, a field of applied linguistic inquiry that intersects in productive ways with the discussions of literacy and symbolic competence. Writing from within a sub-field of stylistics that is commonly described as cognitive poetics, Stockwell (2009) argues that literature is defined first and foremost by its texture. The concept of *texture* originates from Halliday and Hasan (1976). In the functional model of language they propose, texture is an answer to the question 'what is a text?' – in other words, what allows us to read a string of clauses as a coherent piece of discourse. Stockwell (2009) shifts the question from textual function to textual quality. For Stockwell, texture is a cognitive aesthetic phenomenon. He writes, 'Textuality is the outcome of the workings of shared cognitive mechanics, evident in texts and readings. Texture is the experienced quality of textuality' (Stockwell 2009: 1). While this aesthetic model of texture has shaped the contours of contemporary stylistics, it has had less of an impact on discussions of literacy and language learning, which have been heavily influenced by systemic functional frameworks (e.g. Byrnes 2009; Byrnes et al. 2006). While both of these approaches share in common an applied orientation, and thus a broad interest in what language does in the world, stylistics broadly and cognitive poetics in particular more strongly emphasize experientialism, the interactions between texts and the thinking, feeling, perceiving individuals who make meaning through them (see Stockwell 2009: 2, 169; Gibbons and Whitely 2018: 149). Thus, this field of inquiry seems to provide an analytical and empirical basis for conceptualizing the literary imagination and the 'embodied experiences, moral imaginings, and emotional resonances' (Kramsch 2006: 251), which are also treated as important dimensions of second language and culture learning within Kramsch's theories of symbolic competence.

While Stockwell draws on a large body of rich work originating from not only stylistics and poetics, but related fields such as cognitive linguistics, for the purposes of this study, I will focus on two aspects of literary texture, which seem particularly relevant to foreign language and culture learning – world building and (dis)identification. World building concerns the ways in which humans construct 'rich conceptual models of their own reality and alternate realities' in the process of engaging with 'blueprints for the imagination' (see Gavins and Lahey 2016: 1) offered through language and other semiotic modalities. One of the dominant models of world building within stylistics and cognitive poetics is Text World Theory, a cognitive discourse model originally suggested by Werth (1994) and later developed and brought into mainstream stylistics by Gavins (2007). Text World Theory posits multiple layers of mental representations that come into play, when reading and making sense out of a text. These include the discourse world, *the* content and context of interactivity shared by the writer and reader (Gavins 2007: 18–34), text worlds evoked in the act of meaning-making, and sub-worlds that are embedded within the text world (e.g. in the form of flashbacks, flash-forwards, hypotheticals, wish worlds or the spaces created by direct speech) (see Gavins 2007: 52 and 53). One of the advantages of Text World Theory for research with an applied linguistic angle is that it attempts to account for the ways in which these worlds are deictically instantiated through world-building elements that the text offers, that is, linguistic markers of time, place, people and objects (78), while also recognizing that the particular effects of these world-building elements rely on aspects of background knowledge that allow the worlds to seem possible, realistic or even real.

Identification and its negative counterpart, resistance, describe the relationships between readers and perceived entities in the text that emerge as readers position themselves vis-à-vis the characters and aspects of their own perceived personalities (e.g. Herman 2004; Stockwell 2009: 134–67). Stockwell connects identification closely to world building and other effects of deixis, arguing that most (if not all) literary works—like other acts of communication—suggest a preferred response. Stockwell clearly distinguishes this from other rather contentious conceits within literary theory, authorial intention and idealized readers. Preferred response in Stockwell's sense draws from sociolinguistic models of natural conversation and the ways in which speakers indicate the intended pragmatic force of an utterance through the linguistic form of what is said in context, and interlocutors negotiate and display recognition of these meanings across the flow of talk. Weaving together elements that encode point of view related to perceptual, temporal and spatial deixis with those related to the positioning of social relations and of the compositional and textual mediation of the text world (a process Stockwell describes as *deictic braiding*), readers develop a dynamic sense of how the imagined world of the text relates to them. Stockwell notes that 'preferred responses are not always acquiesced responses' (269). In conversation and in reading, individuals can recognize and resist a preferred response. Identification likewise entails an ethical dimension; while world building relies on what is perceived as possible, identification also involves a sense of what is desirable, understandable and relatable. This aspect of reading is often particularly salient in the case of foreign language readers, because comparative modes of reading are already triggered by the assumed sense of alterity (see Gramling and Warner 2012; Warner and Gramling 2013, 2014).

12.4 Context of the study

This study focuses on two short autobiographical texts. At the time they wrote, both authors were enrolled in a German as an advanced literature and culture course titled 'Constructions of Identity: German Multilingualism', intended for students of German as a foreign language at a large public university in the United States. The author of this chapter was also the curriculum developer and instructor for this course. Assigned readings included a range of genres, but autobiographical essays and literary prose pieces dominated, and the focal assignment in this study – an imagined first page of their own autobiographies – followed the reading and discussion of three autobiographical excerpts.

A note about the term *foreign* in the context of this article: within US educational discourses, *foreign* is often used to broadly refer to modern languages and cultures. Although this term has been rightfully critiqued under the argument that it others languages and cultures that are not English, I will use it in this chapter to deliberately contrast the position of the two German learners, for examples, that of heritage language learners or learners of languages that are socially salient in the space in which they are being taught. This is particularly important in the context of this study, an institute of higher education in Arizona, a state in the American Southwest where 40 per cent of residents self-identify as Hispanic/Latinx and 20 per cent speak Spanish at home. While heritage learners are those who have familial connections to the language and culture being learned, the two individuals featured in this study began learning German in adolescence or adulthood and did not have any close family relationship to the German language or German-speaking cultures. Thus, *foreign* here is used cautiously to index a relationship of distance between the student-authors and the language they are learning/writing in.

Students' positionalities vis-à-vis German were deliberately thematized in the course. In various writing assignments and during in-class discussions during the Multilingual Germany course, students were encouraged to reflect on their relationship with German and their identities as (emergent) multilinguals. The two case studies chosen for this chapter are of interest because of the ways in which the student/authors used the narrative tasks as an opportunity to construct personal meanings using the narrative resources offered by the texts that they had read, while also resisting some of the assumptions set up by the texts and the assigned task. The student compositions featured in this study evidence the movement between available design, designing and redesigning conceptualized by multiliteracies pedagogies.

12.5 Reconfiguring lives: The cases of Callie and Zeng

In the set of texts that prefaced the autobiographical assignment for the Multilingual Germany course, students first read the opening of Johann Wolfgang von Goethe's (2013 [1811–1812]) *Aus meinem Leben: Dichtung und Wahrheit* (*From My Life: Poetry and Truth*), which within literary histories is often noted for its contributions to the genre of autobiography and in particular the ways in which Goethe attempts to represent his life story as both unique and historically representative, by playing with the tension indicated in the title between literary imagination and facts. Goethe's life story begins by locating the exact time of his birth with reference not only to a proximal human-made timekeeping device – the clock tower in Frankfurt, the city of his birth – but also to the astrological calendar. In the second paragraph, he suggests that the planetary positioning of his birth was indeed significant and perhaps even the cause of his 'Erhaltung' ('preservation'), given that he managed to survive in spite of the fact that he 'came into the world as dead', through the unskillfulness of the midwife, before beginning to contextualize his life within the more local social constellations of eighteenth-century Frankfurt. Goethe's autobiography was paired with the opening pages of Turkish-born German author Feridun Zaimoğlu's 'Kanak Attack: Rebellion der Minderheiten' (*'Kanak Attack: Rebellion of the Minorities'*) from the collection

Kopf und Kragen (2001). Zaimoğlu's literary essay begins not with the birth, but with the author arriving with his mother at the main train station in Munich. Zaimoğlu's inclusion of the phrase 'eher tot als lebendig' (p.8; *more dead than alive*) to describe his mother's arrival echoes Goethe's entry into the world. After describing some of the initial hardships his mother, with a seven-month-old infant in tow, encountered during this 'Deutschlandabenteuer' (9; *Germany-Adventure*), Zaimoğlu comments, 'Es ist besonders in unserer Zeit eine Binsenweisheit, dass kein Mensch mit einer strengern linearen Biographie aufwarten kann' (p.9; *It is a typical in our time, that no one can come up with a strictly linear biography*), his parents' biographies, their family histories that lead to their lives in Turkey and then in Germany, are offered here as an exemplary. The story of his birth, which appears a couple of pages later, is presented as a story told by his mother as she did housework. With references to the exact time of birth, the ringing of the minaret bells and a less than competent midwife, Zaimoğlu's story plays off of elements from Goethe's canonical version. In class discussion, students were asked to compare both accounts and consider how the authors use the context of their births in order to highlight particular aspects of their lives.

We then read the opening of Elias Canetti's (1979 [1977]) autobiographical work *Die gerettete Zunge: Geschichte einer Jugend* (*The Tongue Set Free: Story of a Youth*). Canetti was born in Bulgaria to a Ladino-speaking family of Sephardic Jews, where he spent the early years of his childhood before his family moved to Vienna after the death of his father. They then later lived in Zurich followed by Frankfurt, before escaping to England when the Nazis came to power. Students were asked to analyse the first scene of the work, which depicts an early childhood memory, a seemingly daily ritual in which the young author/narrator would enter into a staircase on the arm of a girl and then be approached by a smiling man with a knife who would threaten to cut out his tongue, only to shut his knife at the last moment, saying 'Heute noch nicht, morgen' (p.9; '*Not yet today. Tomorrow*'). In a subsequent passage, which students read after first discussing this excerpt, we learn that he at last asked his mother about this memory and discovered that their nanny from Bulgaria used to walk him around like that. One day they saw her with a strange man on her arm. They sent her back to Bulgaria. This was the threat that he must have given so that young Elias would not tell.

The first scene in Canneti's autobiography provided a stark contrast to the more prototypical beginnings of Goethe's and Zaimoğlu's life stories, by anchoring the story in the author's subjective memory, rather than the contextual circumstances of the birth. In class, we also worked closely with this passage to conceptualize some of the language that contributes to the aesthetic effects of the narrated memory. Students were first guided to use a version of Labov and Waletzky's (1967) framework for analysing narratives of personal experience, which helped them to identify different phases in this opening story. We then looked at the spatial and temporal expressions in the excerpt and how those shape point of view in the narrative excerpts (see also Simpson 1993). This provided the class with a metalanguage specific enough to hone learner's attention on the particular stylistic choices made by these authors, thus fostering their linguistic awareness in tandem with their interpretive capacities. For example, the students in the class noted that the use of the present historic created a sense that the action was happening right then, even with the opening sentence – 'Meine früheste Erinnerung ist in Rot getaucht.' = 'My earliest memory is dipped in red.' — clearly positioning the action in the distant past. They also noted the preponderance of motional expressions in German realized in this passage in large part through verbal complements beginning with her, which indicate a motion towards the speaker. Fludernik has described deixis as 'linguistic signals of subjectivity' (Fludernik 2009: 78) and indeed the students noted that the salience of these temporal and spatial expressions pointing back to the perceptions of the experiencing child's perception created an effect of immediacy (see also Warner 2009, 2013). Students were then prompted to consider perceptual deixis by focusing in particular on the use of the colour red in the first sentence, which many of the students read as negatively emotionally charged. Students also discussed the choice of imbuing significance into aspects of one's life story through the use of symbolic language.

While many of the students in the class drew elements from the autobiographical beginnings they had read, the two students I will focus on here – Callie and Zeng[1] – both reimagined narrative and stylistic elements of the three hypotexts. Callie, following the models offered by Goethe and Zaimoğlu, began her autobiography with the moment of her birth, 'on a cold day in February' in the middle of a 'big snow storm', but quickly cast doubt on the significance of this context, questioning 'Did this snow storm have a meaning for my life?' She then offered a subjective interpretation of what this could mean: 'When I was a child, I thought that snow looked peaceful, even in a storm.' By presenting this interpretation within both the distant past and the shade of epistemic modality, Callie allows the reader to be the arbiter of whether or not *peaceful* is the appropriate adjective to describe her birth. She then asserts that in actuality, 'The start of a life is usually dull' because a birth is the one aspect of a life story that can be taken for granted and all babies come to the world with the same needs. This is a departure from the literary models, which treat the birth as a momentous event. She ends with 'I knew nothing of the snow storm and the snow storm knew nothing of me'. The parallel structure of this sentence completes the epistemic pattern set up across the text, through which Callie repeatedly resists assigning meaning to the beginning of her life story.

12.5.1 Callie's text

My life began on a cold day in February. There was a great snow storm, as I was cut from the belly of my mother. Early in the morning my parents woke up and drove to the hospital through the snow storm. Perhaps it was important that my parents made this trip – how could they know that? Did this snow storm have a meaning for my life? When I was a child, I thought that the snow looked peaceful, even in a storm.

> The start of a life is usually dull. For someone it is the same as for another – We are all born. We all live. We cry. We eat from our mothers. We sleep. So I lived. I knew nothing of the snow storm and the snow storm knew nothing of me.
> (For the original German text, see Appendix.)

Zeng's autobiographical opening makes heavy use of the temporal and spatial deixis offered by Canetti's first scene, but instead of positioning the activity in an epistemically shaded past, Zeng emphasizes the potential concurrence of life in Tucson, where she is studying, and her family in Singapore.

12.5.2 Zeng's text

Now I am in Tucson, 15 hours from Singapore, 12.5 hours from India. It smells like fish at home; delicious fish, which my mother cooks for us. Perhaps they are eating fish now in Singapore, like the fish that I have just cooked here. I have just eaten my lunch and now I must write the first page of my autobiography.

> How should I do that? My life is as unimportant as my birth. Should I begin with my birth? No, I attend to traditional styles. I have read too much postmodern literature, and I have learned, that we are now in a postmodern epoch. Today one writes differently.
>
> I have distanced myself from me. Every day I go to class, happily write notes, happily learn new ideas. Do other people think of me, this normal woman? When I was a girl, I did the same things. I went to class, I happily wrote notes, I also learned new ideas. No important difference. What for a life is this! Would someone like to save me from my life perhaps?
> (For the original German text, see Appendix.)

This is highlighted in the opening sentences below, with temporal expressions in bold and the spatial expressions underlined (see the Appendix for the German):

> **Now** I am in Tucson, **15 hours** from Singapore., **12.5 hours** from India. It smells like fish at home; delicious fish, which my mother cooks for us. Perhaps they are eating fish **now** in Singapore, like the fish that I have **just** cooked here. I have **just** eaten my lunch and **now** I must write the first page of my autobiography.

Notably expressions like '15 hours from Singapore' indicate both temporal and spatial deixis, because they express the amount of time one would need to travel to those countries. The final line completely anchors the writing in the here and now of the task at hand, but the following paragraph questions the very assignment. 'How should I do that?' and then echoing Callie's stance, 'My life is as unimportant as my birth.' Zeng then goes on to associate autobiographies that begin this way with postmodern style, a likely reference to some of the earlier works from the course, which points to the textual and compositional mediation of what she writes and disrupts the *nowness* of the opening sentences.

Zeng's second paragraph shifts into a space of reflection initiated by the reference to the autobiographical task and the question, 'How should I do this?'. Like Callie, Zeng emphasizes the insignificance of her life, writing 'My life is as unimportant as my birth'; but unlike Callie, Zeng rejects the idea of beginning with her birth, noting that she has learned that we live in a 'postmodern epoch' and that 'today one writes differently'. These references to earlier texts from the course, before we had read the autobiographical beginnings, add another layer of *nowness* that is anchored in the shared discourse world of the course. Somewhat like Zaimoğlu, she questions the idea of a tidy, linear narrative; however, she attributes this to literary not sociological pressures.

Zeng's third paragraph continues the space of contemplation inaugurated in paragraph two. Marked by the past tense and the use of temporal expressions, the last part of Zeng's text includes a series of reflections on her current life as a student. This paragraph in some ways echoes the comparative texture of the first paragraph but here the relationship is between past and present and relationship of sameness creates a sense of monotony. She is doing the same things as a student now in America as she did as a young girl in Singapore. The final sentences – 'What for a life is this? Would someone like to save me from my life perhaps?' – portray her life story as something that needs to be not built but disrupted.

12.6 Discussion: World building and positioning in Callie's and Zeng's texts

Both Callie and Zeng make extensive use of resources they encountered in the literary models they had encountered in class. This includes linguistic resources more familiar to second language curricula, such as the verb forms and the temporal and spatial deictic expressions and textual and compositional deixis, in particular through intertextual references to the readings from the class. At the same time, both student-authors used these elements in resisting the kinds of world building called upon by the task and the expectations of the autobiographical genre that had been established through the hypotexts. Callie most closely followed the canonical autobiographical beginning, in this course represented by Goethe's text and Zaimoğlu's critical reinterpretation thereof, but she resists their literary designs by refusing to ascribe meaning to circumstances of her birth. Zeng appears to draw first from the texture of Canetti's autobiographical opening, with the heavy use of spatial and temporal deixis for an effect of immediacy and his use of textual deixis to shift from the presentness of that moment into a moment closer to the compositional present – for Canetti the act of asking his mother about this childhood memory as he begins to commit his life story to the page and for Zeng the unavoidable homework task of writing her autobiography. Additionally, both Callie and Zeng use perceptual deixis in the form of modally shaded epistemic worlds in order to comment on the task and call into question their positions as autobiographical subjects. Thus, while their ability to creatively appropriate and redesign suggests an acute awareness and understanding of the original texts and the narrative models they provide, both students seem to resist the idea that these same world building elements are wholly available to them. This is congruent with comments heard in class discussion from Callie, Zeng and other students over the course of the semester, in which they rejected their instructor's contention that they are multilingual subjects comparable to the authors and narrators encountered in the course readings.

12.7 Retelling as redesigning: Towards a pedagogy of translingual aesthetics

While those who read German will note the grammatical infelicities and less than idiomatic expressions present in both Callie's and Zeng's texts, a stylistic analysis of the kinds of world building and positioning they undertake in their autobiographical compositions enables us to take them seriously first as authors, that is, as meaning designers. In constructing their own personal meanings through practices of adopting, reconfiguring and reimagining elements of someone else's life story – that is, by borrowing from their texts and text worlds – the student-authors were able to negotiate their relationship to the hypotexts and the discursive spaces within which they participate. The student-authored texts seem to indicate a developing symbolic awareness, that included an awareness of a dimension that is all too often neglected in discussions of language learning, the aesthetic. The metalanguage of stylistics, in particular related to deixis and world building, may have contributed to this translingual aesthetic awareness, as evidenced by the stylistic congruencies between the literary hypotexts and the student texts and as indicated through the self-aware intertextual references. While further research is needed to explore what practices might contribute to this kind of 'discourse-based, historically grounded, aesthetic sensitivity' (Kramsch 2011: 366), this small study suggests that texture can be taught as part of second language literacy education.

Because of the autobiographical nature of the assignment, the student-authors were designing not only texts, but also their positions as German-speaking subjects. Within the pedagogical frame offered by symbolic competence, the use of retelling in literacy studies can be expanded to include redesigning and reimagining texts in ways that allow language learners to explore their positions vis-à-vis the literary works they read. This may be all the more important as one of the greatest struggles language users might face is in establishing a sense of themselves as legitimate speaking subjects in the new forms available to them in a second language. By telling some version of their story through the meaning designs afforded to them by others, students – perhaps reluctantly or timidly, but nevertheless creatively – can be afforded the ability to step into 'the actual, the imagined and the virtual worlds' in which others live (Kramsch 2011: 366).

Note

1   These names are pseudonyms for the two students who consented to share their work anonymously.

References

Allen, H. W., and Goodspeed, L. (2018), 'Textual Borrowing and Perspective-Taking: A Genre-Based Approach to L2 Writing', *L2 Journal*, 10 (2): 87–110.

Blyth, C. (2018), 'Designing Meaning and Identity in Multiliteracies Pedagogy: From Multilingual Subjects to Authentic Speakers'. *L2 Journal*, 10 (2): 62–86.

Byram, M. (1997) *Teaching and Assessing Intercultural Communicative Competence*, Clevedon: Multilingual Matters.

Byrnes, H. (2009). *Advanced Language Learning. The Contribution of Halliday and Vygotsky*, London: Continuum.

Byrnes, H., and Kord, K. (2002), 'Developing Literacy and Literary Competence: Challenges for Foreign Language Departments', in V. Scott and H. Tucker (eds), *SLA and the Literature Classroom: Fostering Dialogues*, 35–72, Boston: Heinle.

Byrnes, H., Crane, C., Maxim, H. H., and Sprang, K. A. (2006), 'Taking Text to Task: Issues and Choices in Curriculum Construction', *ITL – International Journal of Applied Linguistics*, 152: 85–109.

Canetti, E. (1979 [1977]), *Die gerettete Zunge. Geschichte einer Jugend*, Frankfurt am Main: Fischer.

Cope, B., and Kalantzis, M. (1993), *The Powers of Literacy: A Genre Approach to Teaching Writing*, London: Falmer.

Cope, B., and Kalantzis, M. (2009), '"Multiliteracies": New Literacies, New Learning', *Pedagogies*, 4 (3): 164–95.

Fludernik, M. (2009), *An Introduction to Narratology*, London: Routledge.

Gavins, J. (2007), *Text World Theory*, Edinburgh: Edinburgh University Press.

Gavins, J., and Lahey, E. (2016), *World Building: Discourse in the Mind*, London: Bloomsbury.

Genette, G. (1997), *Paratexts: Thresholds of Interpretation*, trans. J. Lewin, Cambridge: Cambridge University Press.

Gibbons, A., and Whiteley, S. (2018), *Contemporary Stylistics Language, Cognition, Interpretation*, Edinburgh: Edinburgh University Press.

Goethe, Johann Wolfgang von. (2013 [1811–12]), *Dichtung und Wahrheit aus meinem Leben*, Urbana, Illinois: Project Gutenberg. https://gutenberg.spiegel.de/buch/dichtung-und-wahrheit-erster-und-zweiter-teil-7130/1

Goodman, Y. (1982), 'Retellings of Literature and the Comprehension Process', *Theory into Practice*, 21 (4): 301–7.

Gramling, D., and Warner, C. (2012), 'Toward a Contact Pragmatics of Literature: Habitus, Text, and the Advanced L2 Classroom', in G. Levine and A. Phipps (eds), *Critical and Intercultural Theory and Language Pedagogy (AAUSC Issues in Language Program Direction)*, 57–75, Boston: Heinle.

Halliday, M. A. K., and Hasan, R. (1976), *Cohesion in English*, London: Longman Group Limited.

Herman, D. (2004), *Story Logic: Problems and Possibilities of Narrative*, Lincoln: University of Nebraska Press.

Kearney, E. (2012), 'Perspective-Taking and Meaning-Making through Engagement with Cultural Narratives: Bringing History to Life in a Foreign Language Classroom', *L2 Journal*, 4 (1): 58–82.

Kern (2000), *Literacy and Language Teaching*, Oxford: Oxford University Press.
Knobel, M. (2017), 'Remix, Literacy and Creativity: An Analytic Review of the Research Literature', *Eesti Haridusteaduste Ajakiri*, 5 (2): 31–53.
Kramsch, C. (1993), *Context and Culture in Language Teaching*, 105–29, Oxford: Oxford University Press.
Kramsch, C. (1996), 'Stylistic Choices and Cultural Awareness', in L. Bredella and W. Delanoy (eds), *Challenges of Literary Texts in the Foreign Language Classroom*, 162–84, Tuebingen: Gunter Narr.
Kramsch, C. (2006), 'From Communicative Competence to Symbolic Competence, *Modern Language Journal*, 90 (2): 249–52.
Kramsch, C. (2011), 'The Symbolic Dimensions of the Intercultural', *Language Teaching*, 44: 354–67.
Kramsch, C., and Nolden, T. (1994), 'Foreign Language Literacy as (Op)positional Practice', in J. Roche and T. Salumets (eds), *Germanics under Construction: Intercultural and interdisciplinary prospects*, 61–76, Munich: iudicium.
Kramsch, C., and Whiteside, A. (2008), 'Language Ecology in Multilingual Settings. Towards a Theory of Symbolic Competence', *Applied Linguistics*, 29: 645–71.
Labov, W., and Waletzky, J. (1967), 'Narrative Analysis: Oral Versions of Personal Experience', in J. Helm (ed.), *Essays on the Verbal and Visual Arts*, 12–44, Seattle: University of Washington Press.
Maxim, H. (2006), 'Integrating Textual Thinking into the Introductory College-Level Foreign Language Classroom', *The Modern Language Journal*, 90: 19–32.
Maxim, H. (2009), '"It's Made to Match": Linking L2 Reading and Writing through Textual Borrowing', In C. Brantmeier (ed.), *Crossing Languages and Research Methods. Analyses of Adult Foreign Language Reading*, 97–122, Charlotte: Information Age Publishing.
New London Group. (1996), 'A Pedagogy of Multiliteracies: Designing Social Futures', *Harvard Educational Review*, 66 (1): 60–92.
Paesani, K., Allen, H. W., and Dupuy, B. (2016), *A Multiliteracies Framework for Collegiate Foreign Language Teaching*, Upper Saddle River: Pearson Education.
Ryshina-Pankova, M. (2011), 'Developmental Changes in the Use of Interactional Resources: Persuading the Reader in FL Book Reviews', *Journal of Second Language Writing*, 20 (4): 243–56.
Simpson, P. (1993), *Language, Ideology and Point of View*, London: Routledge.
Stockwell, P. (2009), *Texture: A Cognitive Aesthetics of Reading*, Edinburgh: Edinburgh University Press.
Stockwell, P. (2013), 'The Positioned Reader', *Language and Literature*, 22 (3): 263–77.
Vinall, K. (2012), '¿Un legado histórico?: Symbolic Competence and the Construction of Multiple Histories', *L2 Journal*, 4: 102–23.
Vinall, K. (2016), '"Got Llorona?": Teaching for the Development of Symbolic Competence', *L2 Journal*, 8 (1): 1–16.

Ware, P. D., and Kramsch, C. (2005), 'Toward an Intercultural Stance: Teaching German and English through Telecollaboration', *Modern Language Journal*, 89 (2): 190–205.

Warner, C. (2009), 'Speaking from Experience: Narrative Schemas, Deixis, and Authenticity Effects in Verena Stefan's Feminist Confession *Shedding*', *Language and Literature*, 18 (1): 7–23.

Warner, C. (2013), *The Pragmatics of Literary Testimony: Authenticity Effects in German Social Autobiographies*, New York: Routledge.

Warner, C., and Dupuy, B. (2018), 'Moving towards Multiliteracies in Foreign Language Teaching: Past and Present Perspectives … and Beyond', *Foreign Language Annals*, 51: 116–28.

Warner, C., and Gramling, D. (2014), 'Kontaktpragmatik: fremdsprachliche Literatur und symbolische Beweglichkeit', *Deutsch als Fremdsprache*, 51: 67–76.

Warner, C., and Gramling, D. (2013), 'Gerade Dir hat er eine Botschaft gesendet: Contact Pragmatics and the Teaching of Foreign Language Texts', in J. Plews and B. Schmenk (eds), *Traditions and Transitions: Curricula for German Studies*, 209–26, Waterloo: Wilfrid Laurier University Press.

Warner, C., and Michelson, K. (2018), 'Living Literacies: L2 Learning, Textuality, and Social Life (Introduction to the Special Issue)', *L2 Journal*, 10 (2): 3–15.

Werth, P. (1994), 'Extended Metaphor: A Text World Account', *Language and Literature*, 3 (2): 79–103.

Widdowson, H. (1978), Language as Communication, Oxford: Oxford University Press.

Zaimoğlu, F. (2001), *Kopf und Kragen: Kanak-Kultur-Kompendium*, Frankfurt am Main: Fischer.

Appendix – Complete student texts

Callie

Mein Leben fing an einem kalten Tag in Februar an. Es gab einen großen Schneesturm, als ich von dem Bauch meiner Mutter geschnitten wurde. Morgen früh wachten meine Eltern auf und fuhren zum Krankenhaus durch den Schneesturm. Vielleicht war es wichtig, dass meine Eltern diese Reise gemacht haben – Wie konnten sie das wissen? Hat dieser Schneesturm eine Bedeutung für mein Leben? Als ich ein Kind war, dachte ich das der Schnee friedlich aussah, eben in einem Sturm.

Der Anfang des Lebens ist meistens langweilig. Für jemanden ist es gleich wie für die Anderen – Wir sind alle geboren. Wie leben alle. Wir weinen. Wir essen von unseren Müttern. Wir schlafen. So habe ich gelebt. Ich wußte nichts von dem Schneesturm und der Schneesturm wußte nichts von mir.

Zeng

Jetzt bin ich in Tucson, 15 Stunde von Singapur, 12.5 Stunde von Indien. Es riecht nach Fische zu Hause; leckere Fische, die meine Mutter für uns immer kocht. Vielleicht essen sie jetzt Fische in Singapur, wie die Fische, die ich gerade gekocht habe hier. Ich habe meinen Lunch genau gegessen und jetzt muss ich die erste Seite meine Autobiographie schreiben.

Wie soll ich das tun? Mein Leben jetzt ist so unwichtig wie meine Geburt. Soll ich mit meiner Geburt anfangen. Nein, ich achte auf traditionelle Stile. Ich habe zu viele postmodernische Literatur gelesen, und ich habe gelernt, dass wir jetzt in einer postmodernischen Epoche sind. Man schreibt heute anders.

Ich habe mich von mir distanziert. Jeder Tag gehe ich zu Klasse, schreibe ich gerne die Notizen, lerne ich gerne neue Ideen. Denken andere Leute an mich, diese normale Frau? Wenn ich ein Mädchen war, schaffte ich die gleichen Dinge. Ich habe zu Klasse gegangen, ich habe Notizen gerne geschrieben, ich habe auch neue Ideen gelernt. Kein wichtiger Unterschied. Was für ein Leben ist das! Will jemand mich von meinem Leben retten vielleicht?

13

Rereading as retelling: Re-evaluations of perspective in narrative fiction

Chloe Harrison and Louise Nuttall

13.1 Rereading as retelling

This chapter explores the idea of rereading as a process of retelling. Building on a burgeoning area of research in empirical literary studies, we aim to explore, specifically, how readers re-experience the fictional world of Margaret Atwood's (2014) short story 'The Freeze-Dried Groom' differently during a second reading and how this may, in part, be due to their re-evaluation of narrator perspective. Studies in this area tend to use rereading as an experimental protocol rather than an object of study in its own right (see, for examples, Bray 2007; Castiglione 2017; Cui 2017; Hakemulder 2007), but such projects have nevertheless begun to flag up differences in first and subsequent readings of a text. Notably, for example, Dixon et al. (1993) and Hakemulder (2004) observed that rereading can impact on readers' perceptions of literariness and aesthetic appreciation. More recently, such differences in experience have begun to be studied with more explicit acknowledgement of rereading as a process of reconceptualization or 'reconstrual' (Harrison and Nuttall 2019). This notion draws on the concept of construal defined in Cognitive Grammar as our 'ability to conceive and portray the same situation in alternate ways' (Langacker 2008: 43). The processes of *re*construal that occur during a rereading of a text can be seen, for example, in the acknowledgement of specific information that was 'buried' (Emmott and Alexander 2014) on a first reading but which gains in salience during a second (see Harrison and Nuttall 2018). This increase in salience can lead to the reattribution of attention to different domains of knowledge, which can impact on experiences of atmosphere and tone (Stockwell 2014), as well as alter the text world status of particular elements of the narrative through a 'world-repair' (Gavins 2000) (see also Harrison and Nuttall 2019).

The current study builds on these latter ideas to explore the specific impact of rereading on how readers construe narrative point of view (also referred to as perspective); whether the focalizer or narrator of a story remains fixed, or whether these roles fluctuate between and across multiple readings to create a retelling of the narrative. Bray (2007: 37) argues that '[l]ittle attention has previously been paid in cognitive science to the specifics of how point of view is identified during reading'. While the empirical cognitive stylistic studies in this area are certainly limited, there are a few notable papers. How perspective is encoded during reading is studied in Millis (1995), for example, which, along with assessing readers' emotional responses to a text during comprehension, aims to examine whether readers integrate point of view into their mental conceptualizations of the text. Millis identifies that participants take longer to read sentences that contain a change in perspective, but only during a first reading and not a second. These results lead Millis (1995: 245–6) to argue that perspective is conceptualized during a first reading and that – having been integrated into our mental representation of the text – it can be 'glossed over' on a second reading. Additionally, Bray's (2007) study examines the importance of both preceding and succeeding co-text in helping readers determine point of view. This experimental reader response study explores how participants attribute passages of free indirect discourse to particular narrator or character voices, and the results suggest that readers return to and modify their conceptualization of perspective in light of new information acquired by further reading of the text. He argues that 'any model of tracking the interpretation of psychological perspective will need to be flexible enough to accommodate the possibility of back-tracking' (Bray 2007: 46). Such an argument connects with existing cognitive stylistic approaches that argue for the dynamicity of discourse processing (e.g. Emmott 1997; Werth 1999).

For stylisticians, an important question underpinning any discussion of point of view variation concerns which particular textual features cue distinct perspectives or voices. Millis (1995) argues that readers' interpretation of point of view can be influenced by the presentation of a character's mental states; however, Bray (2007: 39) argues that 'recognizing a focalizer depends on more than the presence of "psychological" predicates since narrators can also function as experiencers'. Another stylistic factor that can impact on this recognition of the focalizer is the presence of multiple viewpoints, which can create ambiguity or complexity concerning whose voice (narrator- or character-focalizer) is being offered at a given point in the text (see Bray 2007; Cui 2017; Sotirova 2016). Empirical studies in this area demonstrate that such shifting point of view across a text can result in a slowing down of readers' textual processing (Millis 1995), in a lack of continuity in readers' interpretations of perspective (Sotirova 2016), or generally that such changes impact on textual processing by prolonging reading time or increasing readers' perception of difficulty (Cui 2017: 132). Unlike these previous studies that focus on point of view attribution in discrete sections of text, this study examines how readers' identification of, and alignment with, a focalizer/narrator alters between first and second readings of a complete text and whether this impacts on their conceptualization of the fictional world as a whole. These ideas are explored in further detail in the analyses in Sections 13.4 and 13.5 of this chapter.

13.2 Margaret Atwood's 'The Freeze-Dried Groom'

'The Freeze-Dried Groom' is one of nine 'tales' that appear in Margaret Atwood's most recent collection of Gothic short stories, *Stone Mattress* (2014). The story is a stand-alone tale that follows the unpleasant and morally dubious protagonist, Sam, throughout his day. It begins with a conversation over breakfast with his wife, Gwyneth, in which she announces that she wants a divorce. The story then follows Sam's trip to his counterfeit antiques shop (which is implied to be a cover for a drug-dealing business) and then to the storage units where he bids on and wins a number of lots. While the story pointedly mentions more than once the particular unit Sam is interested in ('He'll leave number 56 till the last; everyone else will have gone by then', p. 152), this is a red herring for the actual reveal of the story, which concerns the contents of the third unit he opens ('Third time lucky: what if it's a treasure trove?', p. 152). In this unit Sam encounters the contents of someone's wedding: bottles of champagne, a wedding dress, a cake – and most significantly, the eponymous, zombified, freeze-dried groom himself. A woman purporting to be the 'bride' shows up and she and Sam go to a motel, and the story finishes on an ominous cliffhanger, assuring readers that '[n]obody knows where he is' (p. 165).

In a previous study, we carried out a close textual analysis of this short story using the framework Cognitive Grammar (Langacker 2008) (Harrison and Nuttall 2019). We observed that the distinctive experience of (re-)reading this fictional world could be explained in terms of changes in 'atmosphere' and 'tone' (Stockwell 2014), which in turn could be traced to shifts in 'focusing' and 'specificity' in its construal (Langacker 2008). In Cognitive Grammar, lexical choices are said to create encyclopaedic networks of meaning in the form of knowledge 'domains' which can relate to any aspect of experience and which form the background for our understanding of language (Langacker 2008: 44). In 'The Freeze-Dried Groom', the domains build up a network of associated schematic knowledge structures which interconnect and clash. One notable domain in the story, for example, is description of the COLD, which pervades the collection of tales as a whole (and is given heightened prominence through the title of this story), and there is also a prominent domain of MARRIAGE/DIVORCE across the text. Both of these domains are referenced and conflated in the opening two sentences:

> The next thing is that his car won't start. It's the fault of the freak cold snap, caused by the polar vortex – a term that's already spawned a bunch of online jokes by stand-up comics about their wives' vaginas.
>
> (Atwood 2014: 135)

There are also descriptive elements relating to STORAGE, CLEANLINESS/DECAY, FOOD and SMELL elsewhere throughout the story. In our analysis (Harrison and Nuttall 2019: 143–7) we argue that how we (re-)conceptualize these domains has implications for our reading inferences and suggest that particular textual cues – evoking particular domains of knowledge – are more likely to be attributed to Sam's personal worldview, or 'tone', on a first reading of the story and conversely are likely to be attributed, more generally, to the 'atmosphere' of the fictional world (Stockwell 2014) on a rereading of the text. Consequently, a second reading moves us further away from Sam as the internal focalizer of the fictional world and closer to an external narrator – an unidentified voice which, we argue, could be that of a police detective or witness in an investigation of Sam's disappearance.

In Cognitive Grammar terms, 'subjective construal' refers to an account in which the conceptualizer (narrator or focalizer, in the context of fiction) is made more prominent through particular language choices, such as modality, conditionals or evaluative or expressive lexical choices. Conversely, a point of view or construal is said to be more objective if attention is directed towards the scene being described, which can be brought about through more neutral language choices (such as unmodalized language, categorical assertions and more literal descriptions) (Langacker 2008: 77; see also Verhagen 2007). For example, a shift from more objective to more subjective construal can be seen in the sentences: 'So back into the house he slouches. Good thing he still has a key, though *Change the locks* is no doubt top of Gwyneth's list. She is a list-making woman' (Atwood 2014: 141). Here, the first sentence is more objective, describing Sam's literal movement into the house. The second two sentences are arguably more subjective, as signalled through Sam's musings on Gwyneth's hypothetical list ('*Change the locks*'), the modalization ('no doubt') and the evaluative description of Gwyneth as a 'list-making woman'. It is helpful to think about objectivity/subjectivity in terms of degrees rather than absolutes, however, as any linguistic choice provides information about the scene being construed or the person perceiving it (see also Verhagen 2007: 65). Though the first sentence here is a literal description of Sam's movements, for example, the word 'slouch' suggests a particular negatively oriented appraisal of Sam's gait. Using these concepts, we argue that a first reading experience of the text is centred on the unlikeable character-focalizer, Sam, through a highly subjective construal, but that subsequent readings invite attention to other layered perspectives that construe the fictional world. In the earlier quotation from the beginning of the text, for instance, a first reading might attribute the reference to the 'bunch of online jokes' as a specific reflection of Sam's misogynistic worldview, when a rereading could suggest another, more ambiguous, perspective; readers might attribute this reference to a narrator who is not disposed to presenting Sam in a positive light or alternatively conceptualize the list-like opening 'The next thing is' as a more objective, police-report-style frame.

Our hypotheses about how the text might be reconstrued on a second reading based on this initial analysis can be summarized as follows:

1   That another conceptualizer, 'the third person narrator of the story [,] gains in prominence' during a second reading of the story; and, even more specifically,
2   That, at the macro-level of our reading experience, a second reading invites a retelling of the account through a more external narrator perspective; one which offers 'an increasingly objective construal of the fictional world or one in which attention is focused less on the focaliser, his attitudes and tone, and more on making sense of the situation he describes' (Harrison and Nuttall 2019: 147).

The participant experiment outlined in the next section attempts to explore and test these claims.

13.3 Methodology

The participants of the rereading study comprised sixty-six undergraduate students studying various English degrees (including combinations of English Literature, English Language and Linguistics, Creative Writing, Teaching English as a Foreign Language and Drama) across three UK universities: Aston University, the University of Huddersfield and Coventry University. Eighty-two per cent of the participants were female and 18 per cent were male, with a mean age of 21 and a median age of 20, and 21 per cent were non-native speakers.[1] All participants have been anonymized and referred to according to an assigned participant identifier (A, B or C depending on the allocated group, plus a number).

Participants were randomly assigned to one of three conditions (the total participant numbers for each group are listed in Table 13.1), and all were asked, firstly, to read 'The Freeze-Dried Groom' in its entirety at their own pace. The short story that was presented to the students was unmodified from the original publication in the hope of more closely simulating naturalized or 'real' reading experiences (see Peplow and Carter 2014). Intriguingly, though, many students at the end of the study asked if this version was the complete story, and so evidently there is something 'unfinished' about the text that 'seems to deliberately invite a second reading' (Harrison and Nuttall 2019: 141) or at least a closer consideration of 'what happens next'.

In all three groups, each student's copy of the story was collected in by the experiment supervisor after they had finished reading. Having read the story, participants in Group A were asked to complete a post-reading questionnaire about their individual responses to the text. Participants in Groups B and C, on the other hand, were asked to reread the text a second time. On completion of their first reading, both groups were given a short five- to ten-minute break and colouring activity distractor. After this, while Group B were asked to read the same story again, Group C were told in advance of the second reading that they would be reading an 'altered' version of the story (which was in fact unchanged from the original) and to make notes of any changes they observed. By asking these participants to read an 'altered' version of the text, we anticipated that the students would undertake a closer, or more attentive, second reading in this condition (a summary of the three conditions can be found in Table 13.1).

Table 13.1 Experimental conditions and (re)reading tasks

Experimental condition (with total participants)	First reading	Questionnaire	Second reading	Questionnaire
Group A (22)	X	X	–	–
Group B (23)	X	–	X	X
Group C (21)	X	–	X (*more attentive*)	X

All participants in Groups B and C were finally asked to complete a post-reading questionnaire at the end of their second reading. The study took up to approximately one hour and twenty minutes to complete.

An example of the post-reading questionnaire, comprising both short-answer and Likert scale questions, can be found in Appendix. For the purposes of this chapter, Sections 13.4 and 5 consider just those questions directly relevant to readers' conceptualization of narrative perspective. Section 13.4 explores responses to one of the short answer questions answered by all participants ('What do you think happens next in the story? Write the next paragraph of the story'). In turn, Section 13.5 of this chapter will focus on answers to Questions 7 ('Whose point of view did you share when reading?') and 8 ('Who do you think is the narrator of this story?').

13.4 What happens next?

The participants in all three groups were asked to write the next paragraph of the story. Participants' answers to these questions were tagged according to their narration (first, second, third person) and their chosen focalizer, if one was evident. We hoped that this instruction would invite participants to write a paragraph in the style of the story (without explicitly requesting this and hence causing them to do so self-consciously). However, unexpectedly over a third of the participants (36 per cent) instead provided a summative account of the narrative events that followed, where they either gave an answer in bullet points or in the form of a descriptive summary, as in the examples below:

→ Ran away with woman.
→ Sold cocaine [*sic*]
→ Moved to Cayman Islands + lived out hundred dollar bill fantasy.
→ She ultimately murders him right before wedding when he threatens to reveal her secret past. (C1)

Sam is probably in a storage unit somewhere, dead, and shares the same fate as 'Clyde'. (A7)

Though the story is told in third person, some students (10 per cent in Groups A and C; 5 per cent in Group B) adopted a first-person account in their paragraphs:

5 missed calls already. All from Gwyneth. Has she become desperate? I read the texts and listen to the voicemail from her. She is worried about the storm hitting and where I am.

(A4)

This suggests a particularly proximal alignment with the representing point of view in the text; for these students, the subjective construal of the focalizer, Sam, is strong enough for them to conceptualize an internal, first-person narrator and to adopt his voice in their own continuation of the narrative. Most students, however, aligned their paragraphs with the style of the original text and wrote a third-person account. This was broadly comparable across Groups A and B, with 47 per cent and 50 per cent of the students writing in third person, respectively, though it dipped slightly in Group C (30 per cent) (this is elaborated on later in this section). Similarly, the alignments with particular focalized points of view were roughly comparable across the groups: Sam was the most frequent choice (18 per cent of the total responses), followed by an omniscient stance (8 per cent of the total responses), Gwyneth (5 per cent), the police (5 per cent) and then finally the bride was also attributed perspective in 3 per cent of the responses. Five participants across the groups (two in Groups A and B; 1 in Group C) adopted a 'mixed' standpoint, as in the following example from participant C21, where the perspective combines focalization through Sam ('that pretty head') with the perspective of a more omniscient narrator (who confirms that the 'Bride' is a 'con woman') to make the ending more ominous, in-keeping with that of the original text: 'Little did he know there was a murderous instinct in that pretty head of hers. A con woman's head' (C21). This demonstrates that while Sam is the most identifiable candidate for focalization/point of view, some ambiguity about the story's narrative perspective prevails sufficiently to invite these reimagined perspectives (Gwyneth, the police, the bride), even if these are more peripheral interpretations.

Due to the number of summative accounts rather than those narrated through a particular perspective, however, it is difficult to make definitive claims about this data. It is unclear in the responses from Groups B and C to what degree the readers experienced a change in point of view during rereading (to explore this more directly, though, the next section considers the results from the Likert scales/identification of point of view/narrator questions). Despite this difficulty, what is noteworthy is that the summary-style responses from this question did increase for those readers who read the text twice (Groups B and C) compared to those who read the text just once (Group A). In Group A, 21 per cent of the respondents wrote in this summary style, but this increased to 40 per cent in Group B when this question was answered after a second reading, and 55 per cent in Group C, after an extra attentive second reading. It appears that the participants who had read the text twice were more likely to provide a summative account of the narrative events rather than characterize the voice of the narrator in their answers. One way of interpreting these results is that the participants in Group C had more to do in the study and therefore were more likely to be brief in their responses. On the other hand, the participants may have perceived the activity as resembling a test: they were asked to notice difference in advance of their second reading and therefore may be primed to answer more factually rather than creatively. Another way of interpreting this, however, is that adopting this framed response to the question indicates a 'distancing' from the narrative in itself. In other words, the emphasis in these responses was on the situation (the object of conception) rather than the focalizer (the conceptualizer), which tallies with our original hypotheses – just not in the way we expected. Alternatively, it may be that, as we argued previously (see Harrison and Nuttall 2019), a rereading experience of this text creates a conceptualization of the storyworld that becomes progressively problematized to the extent that it becomes difficult for readers to answer this question more comprehensively.

13.5 Whose point of view did you share?

Question 7 of the questionnaire more explicitly asked participants whose point of view they shared when reading the text. Participants in Group A answered this question after reading the text once, whereas Groups B and C answered this question after they had reread the text. In all three conditions, the protagonist Sam was the most popular response, appearing in 64 per cent, 87 per cent and 76 per cent of the participant responses, respectively. Clearly, there is an increase in the number of participants who reported sharing only Sam's point of view for the two rereading conditions (Groups B and C) compared to the first reading only (Group A), though this slightly declines in the 'closer' rereading condition (Group C). This again could imply support for the argument that readers' reconceptualization of point of view/perspective becomes progressively ambiguous during more attentive (re)reading. Overwhelmingly, though, the participants in all three groups felt that they were aligned with Sam's point of view to some extent. Generally, sharing a character's point of view during reading can impact on readers' interpretations of that character's actions or disposition (van Peer and Pander Maat 2001). However, unlikeable or ethically dubious points of view can problematize such feelings (see Nuttall 2018) and these feelings may be further influenced by awareness of an additional point of view, such as that of an external narrator, within the text. In line with this, when asked by another question in the study how sympathetic they felt towards the main character (the Likert scale ran from 1 ('not at all sympathetic') to 7 ('very sympathetic')), the mean response from participants was three across all groups which suggests a lack of sympathy towards Sam (and some ambivalence), despite alignment with his point of view, across first and second readings.

The stylistic cues which signal Sam's point of view include those associated with close focalization: spatial adverbs and other deictic markers (Kuzmičová et al. 2017: 141) ('He gets to the site early, parks the car, goes to the main office, registers. Everything just as usual. Now he'll have to hang around till the auction starts. He hates those blocks of dead space-time', p. 150), as well as modalization ('He should quit fooling around. He should take the money and run. But he's having too much fun', p. 159), rhetorical questions and evaluative language ('And like that, not a fucking thing anyone can do about it, so why even mention it?'), all of which could be said to closely present the character's mental states: his perceptions, moods and attitudes. Though, as noted, this is seen as an influential factor in readers' interpretation of point of view (Millis 1995), other stylistic choices in the text 'may force a reader to reinterpret a stretch of narrative or to hold two different interpretations simultaneously' (Emmott 1997: 164).

In our previous analysis of this text (see Section 13.2), we proposed that a police/investigation narrative account is suggested through particular textual cues, which suggest an itemized list of Sam's movements in the style of a police report or witness statement. Fludernik (1996: 52) argues that a report 'is used simply to summarize or present the facts of the case, to provide information' and that, consequently, they tend to be associated with 'objectivity, distance and the "point" of the story' (53). She further argues (1996: 53) that one of the characteristic style choices in reports is that they 'consist of a series of actions or events', which can be observed through the preponderance of temporal markers such as *then* clauses. This preoccupation with temporal ordering can be observed throughout 'The Freeze-Dried Groom': 'This is how the day begins' (p.136); 'That's the moment when the car decides not to start' (p. 141); 'One thing at a time. First, he opens up Unit 56' (p, 160); 'When he walks into the bar at the Silver Knight, she's there waiting' (p. 161). Also strongly contributing to this interpretation of a police account are shifts in the narrative to situations which Sam imagines taking place following his own demise. In the following example, we see Sam's accomplice in business, Ned, being interviewed following his disappearance:

> 'Should be back by four,' says Sam. He always tells Ned his ETA: it's part of the little plot-thread he can't help spinning. *He said he'd be back by four. No, he didn't seem upset about anything. Though maybe he was anxious. Asked me about some strange guy who'd been in the store. Leather jacket. Interested in desks.*
>
> (Atwood 2014: 149)

The shift to Sam's speculation is signposted through the use of italics, to the free representation of Ned's speech and the embodiment of Ned's deictic centre (e.g. '*Asked me about some strange guy*'). Notably, the voice of the interviewer (who we might infer to be a police officer) is absent from the dialogue and only indirectly referenced through Ned's responses ('No, he didn't seem upset about anything'). Having read the full story, the ontological status of such dialogue as Sam's imagination or real event is more ambiguous on a second reading (see Harrison and Nuttall 2019: 147–51).

The fleeting intrusion of these additional perspectives at some points in the text may be why the second most frequent response to Question 7 across all conditions was 'Sam + other'. The number of responses for this category was comparatively much fewer, with only five participants (three in Group A and one in each of both Groups B and C) noting multiple points of view. These responses specified Sam, but apart from a brief mention of another internal character in one response ('G [Gwyneth] = a few paragraphs; Sam = most of the time} [sic] omniscient', A12) the participants did not provide details of the particular identity of the other point of view ('third person and Sam', A7), ('At first, Sam', B8). Contrary to our expectations, however, the frequency and specificity with which participants identified an additional perspective alongside that of Sam did not increase with rereading (Groups B and C). It seemed that the participants were unclear on construing alternative perspective, and this uncertainty is evidenced in the range of other responses noted by only one or two of the participants. The third and fourth most popular answers to Question 8 were 'Gwyneth'[2] and 'Narrator', for example, but these each appeared in only three participant responses across the data. In summary, the participants in all three groups demonstrated awareness of other potential points of views or perspectives being offered in the narrative but were largely unsure who these belonged to exactly.

13.6 Who do you think is the narrator of this story?

Previous work has argued that the narrator plays an integral role in how readers construe perspective; they are seen as a kind of cooperative conversational participant who guides the reader and, hopefully, indicates narrative items of significance for them (see, for example, Mullins and Dixon 2007). A quirk of 'The Freeze-Dried Groom' is that, arguably, there is a somewhat uncooperative narrator who creates ambiguity.

Question 8 of the study asked the participants to identify the narrator of the story. As with the previous question regarding 'point of view', no definition of 'narrator' was given, as we sought to access these students' own understanding of these terms; however, it is worth noting that all students were studying or had previously studied these concepts. The number of answers identifying Sam (only) was similar across Groups A (27 per cent) and B (26 per cent) but increased to 39 per cent of respondents in Group C. This is noteworthy as the number of answers identifying an external narrator also increased in this group. Those counted among this latter 'external narrator' category included any identification of a third-person narrator who is not a named character in the story, which comprised more technical labels like 'omniscient narrator' (A15) and 'external narrator' (C4), as well as more general descriptions such as 'unknown person' (A13). The answers tagged as identifying an 'external narrator' in this sense varied from 23 per cent of the respondents in Group A to 13 per cent in Group B and then to 48 per cent in Group C. The distribution of answers identifying Sam (39 per cent) and an unknown narrator (48 per cent) in Group C, in particular, suggests that the participants in this condition were divided about how internal or external the narrator of the story was. The data also suggests that, after having read the text carefully a second time, the participants were more focused in their conceptualization of the narrator, with a narrower range of answers given. Responses to this question in Group C were grouped according to only four categories – external narrator, Sam only, Sam + other and Ned – compared with seven and nine categories in Groups A and B respectively. The participants in the latter groups additionally expressed that they 'didn't know' (one participant) or left the question blank (three participants); suggested other characters such as Clyde, the eponymous 'freeze-dried groom' (two participants) or the bride (two participants); or identified the author (two participants) as the narrator. Within the responses to this question, 'Sam' and an 'external narrator' are answers that are conceptually opposed: the former suggests a more subjective construal of the fictional world and the latter a more objective construal. This division in the reader responses supports a hypothesis made in our previous study of the text (Harrison and Nuttall 2019: 151–2) where we argued that

[u]nlike previous studies that have examined plot reversals (Emmott 2003) and world-repair (Gavins 2000), it seems that the reconstrual invited by this ambiguous story, and perhaps by other similar texts, involves a conceptualisation of a fictional world that is not resolved or corrected as a result of the reveal, but rather gets increasingly unclear.

However, those participants in the rereading groups (B and C) who identified an 'external narrator' were able to elaborate on their identity with a much higher degree of 'specificity' (Langacker 2008). The participants who identified an 'external narrator' in Group A, for example, referred to an 'Anonymous' (A11, A16) and 'Unknown' (A13, A18), 'omniscient' narrator (A15). In Group B, in addition to similar labels, some participants elaborated by offering answers that were more closely related to the POLICE domain prominent in the story: B8 identifies the narrator as 'voices of police testimonies', and B17 similarly labels the narrator as 'A witness' to events (B17), for example. Finally, some of the responses in Group C provided even more fully specified responses: participants suggested that the narrator is 'a female' (C15); 'Someone close to Sam; someone who knows him deep down' (C21); 'A witness to events – maybe a friend or companion or someone whom he told' (C18). Like the mention of 'witness' and 'police testimonies' in these responses, references to the POLICE domain can similarly be observed in the answers to the 'What happens next in the story?' question. Responses to this question related to this domain include references to particular roles, that is, 'officer' (A9, A20, B1) and 'police' (mentioned in nine responses); sensory details or descriptions such as the 'navy blue of the officers [*sic*] uniform' (A7) or the 'echo' of 'sirens' (B3); and activities associated with a POLICE script such as 'They are still looking for him [and] Asking questions' (B8) and 'Ned alerts the police' (B13). The fact that the largest number of responses (nearly half) in Group C indicates an external narrator could suggest that, following a close, or more attentive, rereading of the text, students are more likely to conceptualize a more objective construal of the storyworld in comparison to less attentive rereadings (Group B) or first readings alone (Group A). These results suggest that, despite Millis's (1995) claims that perspective is encoded on a first reading, during a more attentive rereading, readers do appear to allocate resources to recognizing and integrating narrative perspective as part of their mental representation of the fictional world. This may in part be due to the genre of the story in question: a Gothic, thriller 'whodunit' narrative with a cliffhanger ending may be more likely to require further encoding of perspective on a second reading than the modernist short story Millis used in his study. In other words, an unfinished narrative invites readers to imagine or search for a resolution, and if readers do regard the narrator as a cooperative participant who helps guide them towards particular clues (Mullins and Dixon 2007), then readers may be more likely to increasingly focus on the narrator and their role in the story.

Our results indicate that a close rereading of this story is experienced as a retelling of the same narrative from a more external, or more distanced, perspective. This is explicitly mentioned by some of the participants in their reflections on the second reading. B21, for example, says that '[p]ages 1–3 felt like they'd lost some of their personality […] I'm not entirely sure what's different but I feel like there is something missing that gave the text more life?' This distancing can also be seen in responses such as 'I felt less connected to Sam [and] like I was no longer part of the story' (C12) and 'the second text felt more distant' (B22). This lessening of subjectivity lends some weight to the argument that even though the rereaders can more fully characterize who the external narrator might be, this specified stance is still one which, at the macro-level of the text, offers a more objective construal of events. Such an interpretation supports the reconstrual of the narrator as a detective or witness, since a police testimony would be expected to generally contain a more objective, factual account of a victim's movements.

13.7 Conclusion

This chapter set out to investigate the effects of rereading for the interpretation of narrative perspective. We proposed that a second reading of this particular story is experienced as a reconstrual of its fictional world from an external, more distanced, perspective in what we describe as a retelling of the story. The small experimental study set out here indicates that a number of our intuitions about the differences in conceptualization when reading and rereading this text can be supported by evidence from participants' reported experiences. While, contrary to our expectations, the frequency with which readers identified the perspective of an external narrator alongside that of the internal character-focalizer, Sam, did not increase for those who reread the text a second time (Group B), we did find such an increase for the participants who were encouraged to undertake an extra attentive rereading of the text (Group C). More significantly perhaps, a qualitative analysis of the responses found that these readers tended to specify (or characterize) this external narrator in more detail following a closer, attentive rereading (Group C). In line with our own interpretations, the unidentified external narrator in the text was frequently associated with the POLICE domain, in particular, the voice of a witness in a police report following an unspecified crime. In addition, when asked to reflect upon their rereading experience, participants described the second reading as characterized by a greater sense of distance. The fact that the same text elicits these two highly contrasting construals – strongly inviting readers to share the restricted, subjective point of view of its main character, while inviting them to detect the more distanced, or objective, perspective of a witness – raises questions for research concerning our attentional processing of point of view. Certainly, this study has lent support to the view of such processing as inherently dynamic and subject to backtracking and re-evaluation during reading (cf. Bray 2007). As we hope to have shown here, this discussion needs to be extended to include multiple readings and the multiple retellings they may invite us to experience.

Notes

1. Due to random assignment of participants to each condition, there is a slight imbalance between the distribution of genders across the groups (there were 3 male participants in Group A, 5 in Group B and 4 in Group C, and 1 participant did not disclose an answer). Similarly, there were 5 non-native speakers in Group A, 5 in Group B and 4 in Group C, and 2 participants did not disclose an answer). It could be beneficial to control for these variables in future studies.
2. It is worth noting that such a question ('whose point of view did you share?') on its own needs further contextualization, as the participants may have understood 'point of view' differently; in other words, there is a separation between point of view in a spatiotemporal sense in stylistics as compared with point of view in the more general sense regarding empathetic stance.

References

Atwood, M. (2014), 'The Freeze-Dried Groom', in *Stone Mattress: Nine Wicked Tales*, 135–65, London: Virago, Bloomsbury.

Bray, J. (2007), 'The "Dual Voice" of Free Indirect Discourse: A Reading Experiment', *Language and Literature*, 16 (1): 37–52.

Castiglione, D. (2017), 'Difficult Poetry Processing: Reading Times and the Narrativity Hypothesis', *Language and Literature*, 26 (2): 99–121.

Cui, Y. (2017), 'Reader Responses to Shifts in Point of View: An Empirical Study', *Language and Literature*, 26 (2): 122–36.

Dixon, P., Bortolussi, M., Twilley, L. C., and Leung, A. (1993), 'Literary Processing and Interpretation: Towards Empirical Foundations', *Poetics*, 22: 5–33.

Emmott, C. (1997), *Narrative Comprehension: A Discourse Perspective*, Oxford: Oxford University Press.

Emmott, C. (2003), 'Reading for Pleasure: a Cognitive Poetic Analysis of "Twists in the Tale" and Other Plot Reversals in Narrative Texts', in J. Gavins and G. Steen (eds), *Cognitive Poetics in Practice*, 145–60, London: Routledge.

Emmott, C., and Alexander, M. (2014), 'Foregrounding, Burying and Plot Construction', in P. Stockwell and S. Whiteley (eds), *The Cambridge Handbook of Stylistics*, 329–44, Cambridge: Cambridge University Press.

Fludernik, M. (1996), *Towards a 'Natural' Narratology*, London: Routledge.

Gavins, J. (2000), 'Absurd Tricks with Bicycle Frames in the Text World of the Third Policeman', *Nottingham Linguistic Circular*, 15: 17–34.

Gavins, J. (2007), *Text World Theory: An Introduction*, Edinburgh: Edinburgh University Press.

Hakemulder, J. (2007), 'Tracing Foregrounding in Responses to Film', *Language and Literature*, 16 (2): 125–39.

Hakemulder, J. F. (2004), 'Foregrounding and Its Effect on Readers' Perception', *Discourse Processes*, 38 (2): 193–218.

Harrison, C., and Nuttall, L. (2018), 'Re-reading in Stylistics', *Language and Literature*, 27 (3): 176–95.

Harrison, C., and Nuttall, L. (2019), 'Cognitive Grammar and Reconstrual: Re-Experiencing Margaret Atwood's "The Freeze-Dried Groom"', in B. Neurohr and E. Stewart-Shaw (eds), *Experiencing Fictional Worlds*, 135–54, Amsterdam: John Benjamins.

Kuzmičová, A., Mangen, A., Støle, H., and Begnum, A. C. (2017), 'Literature and Readers' Empathy: A Qualitative Text Manipulation Study', *Language and Literature*, 26 (2): 137–52.

Langacker, R. (2008), *Cognitive Grammar: A Basic Introduction*, Oxford: Oxford University Press.

Millis, K. K. (1995), 'Encoding Discourse Perspective during the Reading of a Literary Text', *Poetics*, 23 (3): 235–53.

Mullins, B., and Dixon, P. (2007), 'Narratorial Implicatures: Readers Look to the Narrator to Know What Is Important', *Poetics*, 32: 262–76.

Nuttall, L. (2018), *Mind Style and Cognitive Grammar: Language and Worldview in Speculative Fiction*, London: Bloomsbury.

Peplow, D., and Carter, R. (2014), 'Stylistics and Real Readers', in M. Burke (ed.), *The Routledge Handbook of Stylistics*, 37–41, London: Routledge.

Sotirova, V. (2016), 'Empirical Stylistics as a Learning and Research Tool in the Study of Narrative Viewpoint', in M. Burke, O. Fialho and S. Zyngier (eds), *Scientific Approaches to Literature in Learning Environments*, 227–52, Amsterdam: John Benjamins.

Stockwell, P. (2014), 'Atmosphere and Tone', in P. Stockwell and S. Whiteley (eds), *The Cambridge Handbook of Stylistics*, 360–75, Cambridge: Cambridge University Press.

Van Peer, W., and Pander Maat, H. (2001), 'Narrative Perspective and the Interpretation of Characters' Motives', *Language and Literature*, 10 (3): 229–41.
Verhagen, A. (2007), 'Construal and Perspectivization', in D. Geeraerts and H. Cuyckens (eds), *The Oxford Handbook of Cognitive Linguistics*, 48–81, Oxford: Oxford University Press.
Werth, P. (1999), *Text Worlds: Representing Conceptual Space in Discourse*, London: Longman.

Appendix

What do you think happens next in the story? Write the next paragraph of the story.

Now, please answer the following questions by circling the relevant point on the scale.

    1 How sympathetic did you feel towards the main character?

1   *2*   *3*   *4*   *5*   *6*   *7*

1 = *Not at all sympathetic*   7 = *Extremely sympathetic*

    2 How clearly were you able to visualise the fictional world?

1   *2*   *3*   *4*   *5*   *6*   *7*

1 = *Not at all clearly*   7 = *Extremely clearly*

    3 How well do you think you understood the story?

1   *2*   *3*   *4*   *5*   *6*   *7*

1 = *Not at all*   7 = *Very well*

    4 To what extent did you find the ending to be ambiguous?

1   *2*   *3*   *4*   *5*   *6*   *7*

1 = *Not at all ambiguous*   7 = *Extremely ambiguous*

    5 Do you think the story is well written?

1   *2*   *3*   *4*   *5*   *6*   *7*

1 = *Not at all well written*   7 = *Extremely well written*

    6 Did you enjoy the story?

1   *2*   *3*   *4*   *5*   *6*   *7*

1 = *Definitely did not enjoy*   7 = *Definitely did enjoy*

7   Whose point of view did you share when reading?

_____

(Please indicate how confident you are.)

1   2   3   4   5   6   7
1 = *Not at all confident*   *7 = Extremely confident*

8   Who do you think is the narrator of this story?

_____

(Please indicate how confident you are.)

1   2   3   4   5   6   7
1 = *Not at all confident*   *7 = Extremely confident*

Index

adaptation 8–10, 11, 12, 16, 24, 45–57, 84
advertising 163–76
advertorials 14, 163–75
anaphora 66
applied linguistics 195, 199–200
Armitage, S. 11, 34, 37–9
artlangs 28
Atwood, M. 15, 217, 219, 220, 227
Aus meinem Leben: Dichtung und Wahrheit 205
Austen, J. 3, 12, 47, 50, 52–7, 77–90
The Austen Project 12, 78–80, 84, 86, 90
autobiography 13, 15, 118–19, 199, 204–10
autofiction 2, 13, 113–14, 118–19, 125
autonarration 119

Barker, P. 9
Beowulf 26
bloggers 14, 164, 177
Bonhoeffer, D. 130
Boroff, M. 36
Bridget Jones's Diary (book) 53, 55–6
Brothers Grimm 10
Brotherton library 95, 109
Buried 95, 97–100, 217
Byatt, A. S. 11, 31–3, 39

Canetti, E. 15, 206, 210
Catastrophe 129
Chandler, R. 136
Circe 9
Cognitive Grammar 13, 114, 118–20, 217–20
cognitive poetics 23, 202–3
cognitive stylistics 15, 183–4, 194–5
Cold 32
communicative act 3, 11, 45, 48, 53
communicative purpose 11, 45–8, 50
comprehension 199, 200
concentration camps 129
conceptualization 194–5, 120–4, 218–19, 223, 225, 228, 230
construal 114, 120–5, 231

context 5, 7, 14, 25, 37, 78, 84, 90, 114–15, 132–9, 143, 147–57, 183, 201–7
cosmetics 163, 167–9
Counter-Attack and Other Poems 116
creativity 2–3, 182–8, 194–5
crime fiction 9–10, 13, 93–6, 108–9
critical pedagogy 184
culture 26–9, 199–204
curriculum policy 182, 188, 195

Death Comes to Pemberley 45, 53
decontextualized grammar 183–4, 186
deictic (shift) 65, 70, 74
deixis 15, 85, 119–20, 203–4, 207–11
dialogic 3, 23–4, 143, 146
Die gerettete Zunge: Geschichte einer Jugend 206
direct speech 61, 69, 71, 124, 203
Director of Public Prosecutions 149, 156
disclosure language 14, 163, 167, 170–1, 175
discourse-world 184–5, 187, 190–4, 203, 209
disnarration 143, 152–3
The Djinn in the Nightingale's Eye 31
domains 15, 220
Duckenfield, D. 145, 156

Eddic Sagas 26
Elementals: Stories of Fire and Ice 31
Eligible 12, 78–9, 85
Emma 19, 80, 85
Emma: A Modern Retelling 12, 78–9, 84–5
empathy 73, 124, 130, 140
epic 2, 9, 11, 26–9
episode 62–3, 66, 79, 119
ethical 13, 130–2, 204
evaluation 134, 137, 146–7, 156

fabula 25, 31
fair play rule 95
fantasy 25, 30
Fielding, H. 53, 55

film poem 7–8
First World War 13, 113–14. *See also* war
focalizer 16, 218–25, 230
folk tales 10, 26, 30
foregrounding 3, 13, 38, 70, 104, 108, 192
foreign language 40, 199, 203–4, 222
frame repair 94
Frank, A. 129
free direct speech 124
free indirect thought 69, 80, 83–5
The Freeze-Dried Groom 15, 217, 219–22, 226, 228
function-advancers 184, 189

Gallows View 13, 95–7, 100, 103–8
German 15, 124, 132–9
Goethe, J. W. 15, 205–7, 210
Goodbye to All That 113
Goodreads 79, 84, 86
Grahame-Smith, S. 12, 45, 53–6
grammar 48, 58, 73, 82, 182–6, 190, 195
Graves, R. 113–14, 118, 125
Griffith, K. 15, 118

hashtags 165, 176
Haynes, N. 9
High Emotional Involvement or Immersion (HEI) 12, 63, 73
Hillsborough disaster 14, 143–57
Hillsborough Independent Panel 145, 147
The Hobbit 7, 25
Holocaust 129–32, 138
Holocaust poetry 9, 13, 14, 130–2, 138
Holocaust survivors 5, 13, 129, 130
hypotexts 199, 15, 202, 207, 210–11

Implicatures 45, 52
indirect speech 61, 138–9
Influencers 164–7, 170
Instagram 163–77
intercultural 15, 199, 201
intertextuality 24, 39
intervention 8, 15, 181, 185–7, 194, 199
intratextual 61–2, 65, 68

James, P. D. 12, 45, 54–5

The Kalevala 26–30, 35, 39–40
Kanak Attack: Rebellion der Minderheiten 205

Kantele 28
Kopf und Kragen 206
Kundera, M. 135–6

Labov and Waletzky 6, 14, 137, 145–6, 152, 156, 207
Lamentations 13, 114–18, 121–5
language games 12, 87, 90
Lerner, B. 119
literacy 7, 46, 199–202, 211
Lönnrot, E 26, 29
The Lord of the Rings 28
Love & Friendship 77

McCall Smith, A. 12, 78–9, 84–5
McDermid, V. 12, 78–9
McGahern, J. 12, 61–3, 65–9, 71–4
Marrying Mr Darcy 12, 45, 56
Meerbaum-Eisinger, S. 130
Memoir 113–14, 125
Memoirs of an Infantry Officer 13, 114–18, 121–2, 124–5
Memoirs of a Fox-Hunting Man 118
memory 2, 4, 7, 10, 37, 46, 64, 69–70, 74, 115, 118, 190–3, 206–7, 210
metalanguage 15, 184, 186, 207, 211
metaphor 33, 48, 121, 135–6, 186–7, 190, 194, 29
microcelebrities 14, 164–5, 172, 176
Miller, M. 9
Ministry of Justice (MOJ) 143–4
misdirection 13, 93–6, 109
modal-worlds 184
morphology of the folktale 31–2
multilingual 204–5, 210
myths 2, 23, 27–30

narrative 1–7, 10–16, 23–7, 31–4, 39–40, 45, 47, 61–2, 65–6, 70, 114, 131, 134, 147, 149, 153, 191, 209–10, 224, 229. *See also* oral narrative
narrative grammar 31
narrative perspective 191, 223–4, 229–30
narrative poetry 62, 131
narrative schema 30–1
narrator 13, 74, 83, 119, 121, 134, 137–40, 217–21, 224, 228–30; first-person 131, 140, 224
narrativization 6

narratology 13, 23–40, 56, 73, 131, 134, 182
National curriculum 182
negation 73, 143, 147–57
9/11 terror attack 6
Northanger Abbey 12, 78–9

O'Donoghue, B. 34, 36–9
O seltsam lichtes Leben dicht am Tod 132–3
Oh, deutsche Mutter 130
oral history 5–6
oral narrative 2, 10, 23, 144–6
orientation 156

Pear Story 4
pedagogy 15, 181–4, 188, 190, 194–5, 200, 210
Perrault, C. 10
personal experience 4, 6, 114, 207
Pirates of the Caribbean 51
plot 2–3, 9–10, 25, 30–3, 50–3, 84, 95, 108
plot-significant 95, 104
Poe, E. A 63
Poesis 26, 29
poetry 26, 35–7, 114, 116, 129–32
point of view 39, 83, 85, 174, 204, 218–28, 231
pre-text 11, 23–6, 29–30, 34, 39
Pride and Prejudice (novel) 12, 45, 50–5 (1940, film) 47, 49; (2005, film) 49; (1995, BBC tv series) 52
Pride and Prejudice and Zombies 12, 49, 54
Problem-Solution (patterning) 14, 167–9, 175
progression 25, 30, 62
prosopopoeia 13, 130

recall 2, 4, 46
recipient design 5, 6
recontextualizing 11, 25, 30
recycling 11, 24–5, 29, 74
re-evaluation 16, 114, 217, 231
reimagine 15, 181, 194, 200, 211
reinterpretation 11, 25, 34, 210
repetition 5, 12, 38, 61–2, 65, 69–75, 83, 85
reported speech 65
rereading 8, 15, 217, 225, 227, 229–30
restorying 3, 23–6, 29–40
rewriting 8–12, 93, 181
Robinson, P. 13, 95–6, 98–109

Sanditon 77
Sassoon, S. 5, 13, 113–19, 121–5
schema 4, 15, 25–7, 30, 33, 191
schema theory 4, 94, 97–101, 138–9
Schmidt-Sas, A. 132–40
second language 15, 46, 199–203, 210–11
Sense & Sensibility 12, 78–9, 82, 86
Sense and Sensibility 83, 88
7/7 terror attack 6
Sherston's Progress 118–19
short story 62–3, 72, 217, 229
Siegfried's Journey 119
Silence of the Girls 9
The Silmarillion 26
Sir Gawain and the Green Knight 11, 26, 34
Sittenfeld, C. 12, 78–9, 85–6
social media 14, 163–4, 166–70, 175–6
South Yorkshire Police 145, 147
Spinning 15, 188–94
Stone Mattress: Nine Wicked Tales 219
The Story of Kullervo 40
The Story of the Eldest Princess 32
storytelling 2–3, 5, 8, 16, 39
storyworld 3, 30–1, 34, 58, 225
Stride and Prejudice 12, 45, 56
Sutzkever, A. 129–30
Swallows 12, 61, 63–8, 72–4

tellability 131, 149, 152
10:04 119
Text World Theory 15, 181–7, 203
textual intervention 15, 181, 185, 194
text-world 181, 184–95
A Thousand Ships 9
Tolkien, J. R. R. 9, 7, 11, 25–30, 34–40
Tolstoy, L. 135–6
Tractatus Logico-Philosophicus 87
Tragedy 130
transmedia 8, 10, 12, 46, 51, 57
translation 5, 8, 9, 13, 29, 34, 37–40, 57, 84, 129–40
translators 130, 140
translingual 210–11
trauma 5, 6, 11, 14, 23, 129, 131
traumatic realism 131
Trojan War 9
Trollope, J. 12, 78, 83–4
Tsum kint 129

The Unbearable Lightness of Being 135–6
Undead 45

war 113–15, 119, 124–5
War and Peace 135–6
The Weald of Youth 118
West Midlands Police 145, 149, 156
Who Am I? 130
witness 14, 144–56, 220, 229–31

witness statements 143–7, 150, 152, 156, 226
Wittgenstein, L. 12, 87, 89–90
world-builders 8, 184, 187–9, 190–2
world-switches 184, 187, 189, 191–3

Zaimoğlu, F. 205–7, 209–10
Żorne, F. 130

www.ingramcontent.com/pod-product-compliance
Lightning Source LLC
Chambersburg PA
CBHW072145290426
44111CB00012B/1974